BREAKING THROUGH

BREAKING THROUGH

Creative Problem Solving Using Six Successful Strategies

TOM LOGSDON

ADDISON-WESLEY PUBLISHING COMPANY

Reading, Massachusetts • Menlo Park, California • New York • Don Mills, Ontario
Wokingham, England • Amsterdam • Bonn • Sydney • Singapore • Tokyo
Madrid • San Juan • Paris • Seoul • Milan • Mexico City • Taipei

The publisher offers discounts on this book when ordered in quantity for special sales. For more information please contact:

Corporate & Professional Publishing Group
Addison-Wesley Publishing Company
One Jacob Way
Reading, Massachusetts 01867

Library of Congress Cataloging-in-Publication Data

Logsdon, Tom, 1937–
    Breaking through: creative problem solving using six successful strategies /
    Thomas S. Logsdon.
        p.   cm.
    Includes bibliographical references and index.
    ISBN 0-201-63321-3 (alk. paper)
    1. Problem solving.   2. Creative ability in business.   I. Title.
    HD30.29.L64   1993
    658.4'09—dc20   93-15196
                                                                              CIP

Cover design by Fine Line Design

ISBN 0-201-63321-3

Text printed on acid-free paper.
2 3 4 5 6 7 8 9 10 DOC 96959493
Second Printing, October 1993

Contents

Preface

"If I had eight hours to chop down a tree, I'd spend six hours sharpening my ax."
— American President, Abraham Lincoln

If you are creative enough, you can—all by yourself—make an important difference in your company and in your country. This book is filled with the stories of individuals, some famous, some relatively obscure, whose simple, creative solutions have transformed whole industries and, in some cases, whole societies.

Did you know that a single individual with one powerful solution was largely responsible for putting America's astronauts on the moon? If he had not come up with his simple, but effective plan, NASA would have been unable to fulfill President Kennedy's dream. Did you know that a single individual, with only the most primitive equipment, developed the basic concepts that permitted his colleagues to construct accurate clocks, clocks that have been credited with spawning the industrial revolution? He did it effortlessly—while he was in church!

These two individuals and thousands of others like them have developed creative solutions by attacking their problems with just six simple strategies that are being used by the masters of creativity throughout the industrial world. This book introduces you to those six winning strategies and explains how you can use them to enhance your own creative problem-solving skills. It also tells you how to pick out your best ideas and package them so they will capture the enthusiasm of powerful business leaders and entrepreneurs.

Profit-seeking entrepreneurs scour the world looking for creative colleagues because they know that the simple creative solutions they devise are often worth millions, sometimes billions, in today's competitive arena. This book includes a rich sampling of billion-dollar solutions, each of which was developed by a single creative person. Many are tantalizingly simple—but don't be fooled by their apparent simplicity. They have stood the test of time. Some of them have been used and reused for decades and even *hundreds* of years!

The chapter-length introduction tells you how to get yourself into the proper frame of mind to become more creative, how to be more alert to the opportunities you may encounter, how to surround yourself with supportive people, and how to persuade them to help you polish and perfect your creative solutions.

Each of the first six chapters opens with a description of a billion-dollar break-through made by a single individual with one simple, creative idea. It then describes the specific thought processes ("winning strategies") that individual used and explains how you can use those same thought processes to develop simple, creative solutions to your own personal and professional problems. Practical hints and hard-hitting advice are sprinkled throughout the manuscript, which also includes detailed instructions on how you can use the six winning strategies in structured brainstorming sessions to enhance your own creative problem-solving skills.

Chapter 7 shows you how to polish and perfect your best ideas so they can be adopted for use in your professional organization. Among other things you will learn how to write effective interoffice memos describing your ideas, how to make powerful "technicolor" presentations, how to elicit the support of your friends and colleagues, how to identify, approach, and influence the power brokers who run your organization, and how to handle (or deflect) their most penetrating questions.

Creative breakthroughs are a jewel-like commodity in today's exciting market-place of ideas. By mastering and using the six winning strategies on the arc of creativity, you can lead a more stimulating life, help America's competitive posture, and enhance the value of your own career.

Tom Logsdon
Seal Beach, California
1993

Introduction

Getting into the Proper Frame of Mind to Devise Simple, Creative Solutions

"A diamond is a piece of coal that stuck to the job."
— American clergyman, Kenneth Hildebrand

In the 1980s when a bright, young executive was hired to manage a San Francisco hotel, he inherited a daunting difficulty: His office was flooded with complaints about the hotel elevators, which poked along from floor to floor at a maddeningly slow pace. His first inclination was to upgrade the elevators so they would run faster, until he learned that even the simplest upgrades would cost at least $200,000.

Soon, during every spare moment, he began to ride the elevators as a tourist would while pondering the problem from every possible point of view. Within a few days he had devised a marvelously simple solution, a solution that saved the hotel $196,000.

His imaginative solution did not require any extra labor, complicated equipment, or sophisticated computers; nevertheless, it satisfied nearly everyone. While ambling along from floor to floor, he merely realized that, when people are bored, they complain. But people are seldom bored by their own faces. So, on each floor—and on the four walls inside each elevator—he installed floor-length mirrors. And, immediately, all the complaints went away.

1

A few years earlier the manager of a nearby hotel had faced a different problem, but he, too, managed to put together a surprisingly simple solution. Large numbers of tourists and local residents alike were attracted to the observation deck at the top of his hotel. Occasionally, however, one of them would jump off into the grassy courtyard below.

Each new suicide drove away a few more paying customers and damaged the carefully cultivated image of the hotel. Security guards were considered, as were protective screens. But guards would be costly, and screens would spoil the view. So the manager decided to find out a bit more about how suicide victims behave. Soon his research revealed something quite intriguing: Those who plunged to their deaths from the Golden Gate Bridge almost never jumped onto the land on either end of the bridge. Nearly all of them preferred to jump into the water.

Either way they knew they would die. But, apparently, they did not want to hurt themselves in the process. This fresh, new insight put the hotel manager hot on the track of a simple, creative solution. The next morning he ordered his engineers to erect big, jagged rocks in the grassy courtyard below. When they did, all of the suicides immediately ceased.

Simple, creative solutions inspire action because they are easy to understand and remember, and because they are easy to adapt to new situations. They are also easy to explain, so we can sell them to others with power, influence, and money. American theatrical producer David Balasco built a thriving business based on simple, creative solutions. "If you can't write your idea on the back of your business card," he once wrote, "you don't have an idea."

According to a recent account in *The Harvard Business Review*, Dorothy Nelson, a judge at the U.S. Court of Appeals in San Francisco, learned an important lesson about how to use simple, creative solutions in the administration of justice. On a trip to Jerusalem she became a silent observer in a court hearing conducted by three Greek Orthodox priests in long black robes and long white beards. The hearing was held in a Quonset hut with paint peeling off the walls, furnished only with a plain wooden table and chairs.

An Israeli housewife was reluctantly petitioning the court for a divorce. Unlike the American courts where Dorothy Nelson practiced her craft, the three judges waved the lawyers aside and let the young woman tell her story in her own words. During her five years of marriage, she had been forced to share a house with her mother-in-law who was too feeble to climb the stairs. The older woman lived on the ground floor, while the wife and her husband lived on the floor above. Unfortunately, the house had only one entrance and, to get upstairs, the wife had to pass through her mother-in-law's living quarters where she was questioned unmercifully about her activities and forced to listen to a steady stream of unsolicited advice. She loved her husband, she insisted, but her situation was intolerable.

Her husband was then encouraged to relate his version of the story without legal formalities and without interruption by the lawyers. The husband loved his wife, he said. He also loved his mother, and he felt responsible for both of them. But he was a poor man and could not afford to support two separate households.

After listening to both stories, the three bearded priests stepped outside into the street for a quick conference, then filed back into the courtroom with their judgment. The husband was instructed to purchase a wooden ladder so that, when his wife needed to avoid her mother-in-law, she could use it to climb directly into her second-story window. A few minutes later, husband and wife walked out of that Quonset hut together hand in hand, ambling along the dusty street, headed toward home.

As we have seen, simple mirrors, rocks, and ladders have helped solve the problems of yesteryear. But this is the age of robotics and computers. Don't today's increasingly complicated problems require increasingly complicated solutions? Actually, my studies convince me that today, more than ever, simple, creative solutions are the key to a bright, shining future.

For nine years I worked on Project Apollo, one of the most complicated projects in the history of the world. More than 300,000 of us labored for nearly a decade to plant the first human footprints on the surface of the moon. The thundering rockets and the delicate space capsules we constructed to meet that demanding goal were made from two million individual parts, almost all of which had to function flawlessly if we were to fulfill President Kennedy's dream. Transporting astronauts across 240,000 miles of empty space was an amazingly complicated undertaking. Yet, over and over again, we noticed that the solutions that worked the best were almost invariably dirt simple.

Two years ago I became freshly intrigued with simple, creative solutions when I happened to sit beside a young man named Tom Kelly on an airline flight between Long Beach, California, and Dallas, Texas. Kelly is a biochemist at a research center run by the U.S. Department of Agriculture in Beltsville, Maryland. During that flight, he told me about a laboratory procedure that is so clever and productive I just can't seem to get it out of my mind.

For their agricultural research, Kelly and his colleagues needed to gather large quantities of mosquito heads. At first, they used a surgical scalpel to decapitate the mosquitoes one by one. In a sweaty afternoon, a talented technician could gather, at most, only about 500 tiny, round mosquito heads. But then, in a creative master stroke, they developed a simple, but surprisingly effective, way to gather millions of tiny, round mosquito heads in roughly the same amount of time.

By the time we touched down at Dallas, Tom Kelly had explained to me how they got the heads off and I had told him about Frederick Tudor who developed an equally simple solution, a solution that enabled him to sell millions of gallons of ordinary Massachusetts pond water—for as much as a dollar a gallon—to satisfied customers all over the globe. High above the red sands of Arizona we reinvigorated one another. Kelly could barely wait to get back to his laboratory, and my imagination was racing with fresh incentives to study the simple, creative problem-solving strategies of successful scientists and entrepreneurs. In the meantime, I have been researching this book for more than two years, during which I have learned many fascinating things about the way creative people devise simple solutions to the problems they encounter.

Actually, for more than three decades I have been deeply immersed in creative problem-solving in the aerospace industry and as an author and professional platform lecturer. My work on the Apollo moon landings, Project Skylab, and a variety of smaller, but equally challenging assignments, placed me in day-to-day contact with many of our country's most innovative scientists, entrepreneurs, and business professionals.

After years of careful observation in that stimulating environment, I have reached a rather intriguing conclusion: When creative individuals attack their problems, they consistently use the same six thought processes over and over again. Their personalities, their life-styles, and their innovations are all quite different, but the thought processes they use in creating their ideas are hauntingly similar. That is why all of us can learn how to be more creative. All we need to do is emulate the six winning strategies used so consistently by creative individuals when we seek solutions to our own personal and professional problems.

The heads of mosquitoes—but not their bodies—contain a neurohormone that controls the rate at which their eggs mature. So far, no one has been able to isolate that elusive hormone, but if they could, it might give scientists a better way to control mosquito-borne malaria, which constantly drains the strength of 100 million men, women, and children and kills 1.5 million of them each year, mostly in the tropical regions of planet earth.

A similar neurohormone in the heads of silkworms is known to control molting or metamorphosis, the process in which the silkworm sheds its skin in preparation for the silk-making phase of its life cycle. Two decades ago Japanese scientists realized that, if they could isolate that particular neurohormone, they might be able to tease out economically valuable insights into the silkworm's developmental processes. Their preliminary estimates indicated that at least a million silkworm heads would probably be required. But how could they harvest silkworm heads in such enormous numbers?

Only female silkworms spin silk. So, for 20 years, in every spare moment, the housewives of Japan painstakingly snipped off the head of every male silkworm they encountered. All together, they collected 20 million silkworm heads from which that valuable molting hormone was successfully extracted.

Fortunately, Tom Kelly and his fellow biochemists at the Department of Agriculture have developed a simple way to harvest mosquito heads that is thousands of times more efficient than decapitating them one by one. If large numbers of Americans can learn to solve their problems with comparable finesse, our economy will continue to blossom into the twenty-first century—and beyond.

From Plymouth Rock onward our labor-short land has always thrived on simple, creative solutions. You probably know that Abraham Lincoln earned his first pocket money chopping wood. But did you know that early American settlers learned how to fell trees with three times the efficiency of their counterparts on the European continent? Their solutions were amazingly simple. First they perfected heavier axe blades with improved weight distribution. Then they lengthened the wooden axe handle, built it with a gentle curve, and tailor-made each handle to suit the body proportions of the particular individual who intended to use it.

Frederick Tudor spent much of his adult life perfecting similar ways to enhance the productivity of semiskilled laborers. He got his start when he was a teenager sitting on the banks of a Massachusetts farm pond watching the dragonflies spiraling in complicated loops out over the water. Millions of young boys have tossed stones into farm ponds and watched the ripples create ever-expanding circles. But how many of them have ever managed to figure out how to sell the water? At premium rates?

Frederick Tudor could feel his enthusiasm soaring when he suddenly realized that he could let the chilly Massachusetts wind freeze the pond first. Then he could sell the water in the form of ice!

Many of his contemporaries could see no value in the frozen pond water he resolved to bring to market. But his enthusiastic customers always felt they got full value for their money. In those days, when household refrigeration was not yet available, ten or fifteen cents a pound was not an uncommon price.

Within a few years, Frederick Tudor's simple, creative solution had expanded into a multimillion dollar enterprise. Eventually his specially equipped ships were sailing to the four corners of the world carrying frozen pond water to people living in warmer climates, many of whom had never seen ice before. Once Tudor got started, fresh new ideas continued to crackle through his brain. To expand markets, he taught the street vendors of Martinique how to make and sell ice cream. To reduce costs, he helped perfect marvelously efficient horse-drawn cutting tools.

In 1846 Boston Harbor loaded 292 million pounds of ice bound for southern communities and foreign ports. In that year Frederick Tudor purchased exclusive rights to harvest the ice at Walden Pond where Henry David Thoreau made many of his most penetrating observations. When the Fitchburg rail line was routed near the author's home to carry loads of ice to distant ports, lonely whistles shattered the rural silence, prompting the young naturalist to ponder the effects of growing mechanization and to picture the distant beneficiaries of Frederick Tudor's expansive expertise. "The sweltering inhabitants of Charleston and New Orleans, of Madras and Bombay and Calcutta drink at my well," Thoreau wrote in his journal. "My Walden Pond water is mingled with the sacred waters of the Ganges."

In the hands of a creative entrepreneur, something quite ordinary can become extraordinarily valuable. With one simple, creative idea, Frederick Tudor found a way to make common ordinary pond water into a profitable international commodity. And, by discovering a similarly simple solution, Tom Kelly and his coworkers at the Department of Agriculture have perfected a practical way to harvest mosquito heads in stupendous quantities. First they dump the mosquitoes into a big glass flask and then freeze-dry them to make their slender necks brittle. Finally, they shake the flask to break off the heads.

But how can they manage to separate those little round heads from the thousands of other mosquito fragments heaped inside the flask? It's simple! They merely sift the contents of the flask through a set of laboratory sieves with openings of carefully selected sizes.

If their research team can be equally creative in isolating and duplicating the desired neurohormone, someday the frequency and severity of malaria outbreaks may be greatly reduced. In the future, victims who now suffer interminably may lead fruitful lives instead.

Creativity is not some obscure, mysterious, or magical power bestowed on the privileged few. It can be defined simply as "artistic or intellectual inventiveness." Creative individuals devise solutions that are both novel and useful. They learn to exploit hidden connections between things that are not obviously connected; they notice subtle patterns others fail to see.

With proper motivation and training, people everywhere can learn to accentuate their creative problem-solving skills. If you have doubts about your own natural creativity, consider for a moment some of the clever excuses you have conjured up to avoid distasteful work. If you can develop such simple, creative solutions to skirt undesirable assignments, it stands to reason that you can, with only minor redirection, learn to attack the assignments you prefer with equally powerful creativity.

In the chapters to follow, motivational exercises, diagrams, narrative descriptions, and even cartoons without captions will be used to highlight, reveal, and magnify your inherent skills for developing creative solutions. So will 140 inspirational examples drawn from the professional experiences of some of our most creative scientists, business leaders, and entrepreneurs.

Soon you will meet an industrial engineer who increased the productivity of one of Wisconsin's rust-bucket canneries using only 200 feet of inexpensive electrical cable and a management consultant who used her expertise to formulate a new kind of window-shade business by asking just the right questions. You will also meet a small-town auto mechanic who found a way to speed many of his repairs by several hours using only the freezer compartment of his refrigerator and a short length of ordinary kite string. He will be followed by a well-known billionaire who learned how to use American dollar bills in surprisingly small numbers to accentuate the cordiality and productivity of some of his most valued employees. Finally, you will meet a successful businessman who, many years ago, used his creativity to capture the lady of his dreams. He did it at minimum expense by baiting his trap with ten ounces of pizza dough.

Lesson 1
Accentuating Your Natural Abilities

"Even if you're on the right track, you'll get run over if you just sit there."
— American Humorist, Will Rogers

When my brother and I were growing up wild and free in the Bluegrass region of Kentucky, our sandlot buddies argued with great passion that superior athletic talent came mostly at birth. Professional athletes, we were told, were born with such superior "natural" abilities, they were almost inevitably destined for greatness. Gil Hodges and Peewee Reese handled line drives with such flashy expertise because they were lucky enough to be born with greatness already embedded in their genes.

For many years this seductive line of reasoning held me in its vice-like grip until I got an opportunity to watch Pancho Segura racing after tennis balls. Sitting out there on those green bleachers cheering until my voice squeaked dead, I suddenly realized that natural abilities could not possibly be the answer. Pancho Segura was a foot shorter, 15 pounds heavier, and 10 years older than any of his opponents; and he had another serious difficulty: His legs had been deformed and twisted by childhood rickets. He had no obvious advantages except maybe one—he was all heart. He had practiced so long and hard he hardly ever missed. No matter what it cost him, he always ran down one more ball . . . and then another! He excelled on the tennis court for one simple reason: Day after day, he tried harder than anybody else.

Dr. Michael Howe, who teaches at England's University of Exeter, has spent many years debunking the notion that human excellence and creativity arise automatically at birth. Some human beings do, indeed, excel. But generally speaking, they learn to do it the same way Pancho Segura did, through flame-like dedication and long hours of intensive practice.

Writing in a British journal, *The New Scientist*, Dr. Howe describes the impression most people have when they witness the performance of extraordinarily talented individuals:

> What strikes us most forcibly about people of genius is how different they are from everybody else. Their brilliance is dazzling; their exceptional powers of creativity make them seem like a breed apart, not only superior but inherently superior to other people.

However, Dr. Howe goes on to argue convincingly that these superficial impressions have always been dead wrong. Creative geniuses do not, in fact, start out much different from anybody else. They merely work harder over a longer period of time on a narrow area of expertise—sometimes with fanatic enthusiasm that borders on obsession. In one survey of 70 famous European composers, for instance, Dr. Howe discovered that "no composer has created a great work of art without having dedicated at least 10 years to mastering the craft."

By carefully analyzing the accomplishments of creative geniuses, he has advanced compelling arguments that dedication and single-mindedness are vital keys to peak performance. "There seems to be no limit to what people are capable of achieving if their experiences of life and their opportunities for learning are rich enough," notes Dr. Howe, "yet the view that exceptional abilities emerge only when inherent talents exist is one that lingers on." To counter this widespread, but erroneous notion, he cites a striking example that clearly illustrates what ordinary individuals can accomplish with expert guidance and hard work.

In 1703 the composer Antonio Vivaldi was assigned to teach young girls how to play the violin in a Venice orphanage called "La Pieta." Most of his young students were illegitimate and came from backgrounds of destitution and squalor. The ones he was assigned to teach were not chosen in any special way. Yet, by the time they reached early adolescence, more than one-third of them had become accomplished musicians. Often they played painfully difficult compositions, some of which were written by Vivaldi himself.

Patrons of the arts who were fortunate enough to visit Venice in the eighteenth century to hear them in concert were dazzled by their virtuosity. "If Vivaldi had ever entertained the view that excellence depends on innate talents," observes Dr. Howe, "it could hardly have survived his first days at La Pieta."

Further proof that almost anyone can excel with proper training and encouragement came shortly after computer expert Jaime Escalante landed his first teaching assignment as a math instructor at Garfield High School in the middle of a Southern California barrio. The students he inherited had never done well in mathematics, nor were they motivated to improve. On his first day, when Escalante reported to work, one of the older students bluntly told his new instructor: "I don't need no math, I got a solar calculator with my dozen donuts."

But Jaime Escalante's enthusiastic style of teaching—with its unique blend of compassion, challenges, and zestful good humor—soon began to help his students understand and master simple, creative problem-solving skills. Later he decided to teach them differential calculus to prepare them for California's difficult college advanced-placement exam.

His early efforts sparked powerful skepticism at Garfield High up to and including the department chairman who cheerlessly informed Escalante that "You can't teach logarithms to illiterates." Fortunately, Jaime Escalante wasted little time analyzing his students' chances for success; he used his energies to help them instead! In 1982, eighteen of them passed the advanced-placement calculus test, a number that was regarded as being so extraordinary, an investigation of cheating was instituted. However, to the chagrin of his most vocal critics, Escalante's students scored even higher on a retest. During the next five years, 336 additional Garfield students passed similar advanced-placement tests.

And how can you find an appropriate Jaime Escalante to help you excel in your chosen profession? Gifted mentors are not actually that hard to find if you are willing to carry out a systematic search. Their reputations precede them. So ask around among respected colleagues. Begin your search at well-known centers of excellence such as MIT or Caltech for engineering, New York City for the banking and the publishing trades, London and New York for legitimate theater, Southern California for moviemaking and aerospace technology. Write a few letters seeking help. Make phone calls. Relocate.

Clusters of excellence thrive and prosper because experts working together help one another learn to excel. Skills are passed from generation to generation. Socrates taught Plato who, in turn, taught Aristotle. Aristotle ended up tutoring Philip of Macedon's son who later became better known as Alexander the Great.

Cultivate the masters. Not all of them are great teachers, but all of them have great things to teach. Fortunately, in this age of electronics they are becoming increasingly easier to reach.

No one can deny that innate abilities exist. Some lucky individuals begin life with intrinsic advantages. But as you strive to excel, bear in mind that a dedicated tortoise with solid assistance can often overtake a much swifter rabbit that squanders his most effective talents along the way.

Lesson 2
Surrounding Yourself with Supportive People

"I don't believe in pessimism. If something doesn't come up the way you want, forge ahead. If you think it's going to rain, it will."
— Hollywood Film Actor, Clint Eastwood

Successful creative projects almost always involve a rich mixture of spontaneity and discipline. Discipline and patient attention to detail are vital in the implementation phase—when you are polishing and refining your creative ideas. But childlike spontaneity is crucial in the early phases of the creative process when your ideas are fragile and disorganized. As commentator Charles Brower pointedly observed: "A creative idea can be killed by a sneer or a yawn: it can be stabbed to death by a quip and worried to death by a frown on the right man's brow."

When you are in the early germination phase, surround yourself with supportive people to help insulate your ideas from heavy criticism and evaluation. Try to avoid heaping criticism on your own ideas, too. "If you try to get hot and cold water out of the same faucet at the same time, you will get only tepid water," said the leader of an early brainstorming session. "And, if you try to criticize *and* create at the same time, you can't turn on either *cold* enough criticism or *hot* enough ideas."

A few years ago I enrolled in two creative writing courses at the University of California where I learned some important lessons about the importance of a supportive atmosphere to the creative process. The first course was taught on the UCLA campus by a caustic executive from Technicolor Corporation. He spent most of his time harshly criticizing and evaluating everything his students tried to do.

The ordeal of one earnest young political science major is forever burned in my brain. He wanted to write an essay on President Kennedy's political contributions, but, before he was allowed to write anything—or even make a simple outline—our relentless instructor forced him to defend his partially formed ideas in the face of withering criticism. By the time he had finished that verbal fencing match, he was so frustrated and demoralized he was in no condition to write anything. Soon no one else was willing to take risks with their ideas either. In fact, none of us did much of anything but worry during that endless semester.

The second class was taught by the story editor from "The Waltons." A bright, optimistic individual with an impish grin, he spent most of his time complimenting and encouraging his students. No matter how little ability a project seemed to show, he always managed to find something worthy of supportive praise. I remember, in particular, a young newlywed who, in rather awkward phrases, described how big and lonely her house felt when her husband was away. Through sincere compliments—and a relaxed feeling of rapport—our instructor was able to draw out her hidden talents. "You have managed to capture the essence of being alone," he told her. "Now we all feel like we are reluctantly living in your big, empty house." Then, with consummate reasonableness and tact, he suggested a few specific ways she could strengthen her ideas to make her writing more powerful and dramatic. By the end of that joyful semester, the quality and the quantity of everyone's writing improved to a remarkable degree.

Educator Neil Postman once penned this fretful observation about our educational system: "Children enter school as question marks, they leave as periods." The first of those two California classes demonstrated with painful clarity how unskilled teachers so often take all the joy out of the question marks to make them go away; the second showed why a supportive classroom atmosphere is a highly desirable alternative for us to seek.

Have you ever noticed how some of your colleagues accentuate your creative abilities while other tend to dampen them? Think about the people who help you behave in creative ways. Don't they all have a positive outlook? A joyous approach to life? A good sense of humor? "The pessimist sees the difficulty in every opportunity," says an old proverb, "the optimist sees the opportunity in every difficulty." Choose your friends carefully. Seek out positive, optimistic people and you will feel your creative butterflies soaring on paper-thin wings toward the stratosphere.

How do you get those valuable optimists to cooperate? One good approach is to reciprocate: Find a way to help those who help you. Fortunately, helping others can be a fruitful learning experience. Another approach is to distribute (tactfully) small monetary rewards to some of your most helpful friends and colleagues. A reward amounting to 1% of the value of your idea would seem to be fairly reasonable. If someone helps you as you develop, polish, and perfect a $1,000 idea, find a way to give them a $10 symbolic reward, in return. A new pocket calculator or two discount movie tickets would probably be much appreciated. Any small amounts you end up distributing will, almost certainly, come back to you again and again.

If a suitably optimistic colleague offers to help you with your ideas, be responsive and show up on time, ready to work toward improved expertise. Roll up your sleeves and dig in. "The harder you work," said golf champion Gary Player, "the luckier you get." Take a few chances to get what you want. Science fiction writer Ray Bradbury has always led a risky existence that has brought him big dividends. "Living at risk is jumping off the cliff and building your wings on the way down," he once observed with a sheepish grin.

Lesson 3
Using Your Everyday Experiences to Enhance Your Creativity

"Play is what I do for a living; the work comes in evaluating the play."
— Computer Architect, "Mac" MacDonald

Creative individuals often develop solutions to their professional problems by taking advantage of the ordinary events that surround them in everyday life. Eli Whitney came up with the idea for the cotton gin while he was watching a kitten sticking its paw through a picket fence. Isaac Newton developed his universal law of gravitation after he saw an apple falling from a tree. Archimedes was sitting in his bath when he realized that the same physical law that made water rise in his tub could be used to determine if the king's crown was made of pure gold.

Innovative individuals work with the same raw material available to everyone else, but they learn to be far more intuitive and perceptive. They train themselves to notice subtle patterns and hidden connections that others tend to overlook. Keep your eyes open; valuable ideas come from everywhere. Two brothers from Ohio managed to build the world's first successful motor-powered flying machine because they used the condor, a soaring bird, as the model they were trying to emulate. Most of their predecessors had been distracted by the wildly agitated wings of the sparrow.

Broaden your experiences. Sharpen your powers of observation and your everyday world can become a stimulating classroom in which you can learn how to solve your problems in more creative ways. Try to regard life's little adventures as fresh opportunities to expand your horizons. Take a little time to play.

Many creative people report that their best solutions seem to come when they are doing something entirely unrelated to their usual occupations. "I have seldom or never had a momentous idea while sitting in my office at the university," wrote chemistry professor Royston M. Roberts in his book, *Serendipity: Accidental Discoveries in Science.* "Such ideas are more likely to come in the early hours of the morning . . . on an airplane or bus, on a pleasant or even boring walk, in the shower, or while enjoying a musical concert."

Royston M. Roberts's book is jam packed with interesting examples of serendipity at work. "What do Velcro, penicillin, x rays, Teflon, dynamite, and the Dead Sea scrolls all have in common?" he asks the reader in his opening paragraph; then he goes on to provide a one-word answer: "Serendipity!" Each of those items was discovered almost by *accident.* So were dozens of others that help make our lives more convenient, pleasant, healthy, and interesting.

Did you know that Charles Goodyear figured out how to vulcanize rubber when he accidentally dropped a chunk of it sprinkled with sulphur onto the top of his stove? Or that George de Mestral had no particular interest in making the Velcro fastener when he tried to figure out why some sticktights were clamped to his clothing?

Edward Jenner discovered the world's first vaccine, not as a result of long, hard hours in a laboratory as you might surmise. Instead, his landmark discovery came much easier than that. When he was only 19 years old, a former milkmaid told him that she could never catch smallpox because she had been infected with cowpox. Later, when he investigated her claim, he found that milkmaids almost never had smallpox, even if they later worked in nursing wards filled with carriers of the disease.

As your world becomes more expansive, soak up as much of it as time allows. "You can see a lot by observing," said Yogi Berra. To which Nobel-Prize-winning physicist Albert Szent-Györgyi added: "Discovery consists of looking at the same thing as everyone else and thinking something different."

Young boys by the millions have tossed stones into farm ponds and watched the soft ripples spread out in ever-expanding concentric circles. But how many of them figured out how to make money selling the water? Frederick Tudor did—on a particularly creative day. He made an enormous fortune marketing ordinary Massachusetts pond water to millions of satisfied customers. He became the toast of his era. And all of his fame and fortune came from one simple, creative solution.

Lesson 4
Writing Your Ideas Down on Paper

"Forget mistakes. Forget failures. Forget everything except what you're going to do now and do it. Today is your lucky day."
— William Durant, Founder of General Motors

In his book *The 100: A Ranking of the Most Influential Persons in History*, Michael H. Hart concludes that ordinary writing paper—so cheap and abundant today—is among mankind's greatest inventions. Shortly after he started researching his book, he realized that, when the people in each new region first learned how to make paper, they experienced a noticeable spurt in creativity and productivity. This process took nearly 1,000 years as papermaking technology gradually spread from China into the rest of the world.

Paper facilitates the communication of new ideas from person to person, but it does much more than that. It also allows one person, working alone, to untangle fragmentary thoughts, to record what has been learned so far, and to work on complicated concepts in piecemeal fashion. As you strive to develop creative solutions, get in the habit of using liberal amounts of paper. Use it to record your current difficulties, to summarize half-formed thoughts, to highlight partial solutions, and to organize future courses of action. Pictorial representations are a remarkably powerful way to represent partially formed ideas. Simple, but effective, sketches and diagrams can help stimulate your creative problem-solving skills and help you rework, revise, and polish your best ideas.

Paper is cheap, but if your superiors suddenly rationed you to a single sheet of paper, your best use of it would probably be to make a simple "Things To Do" list enumerating your current commitments. You should carry such a list with you at all times in pocket or purse. A "Things To Do" list allows you to partition your responsibilities and assignments into simple, bite-size chunks. It also helps you to separate planning from action, to coordinate your activities for maximum efficiency, and to stop worrying about the possibility of forgetting something truly important.

Such a list can also enhance your rate of advancement in your chosen profession. Whenever you agree to handle a new task for bosses or colleagues, whip out your list and write down the agreement while they are still there. Imagine how comforting it is to see that, when you make an agreement, you are so serious about it that you record it on your list in plain view for all to see. But what if the task is too complicated to record on a line or two? Bigger, more complicated, tasks go into your journal, which you also take out and review at frequent intervals.

Creative individuals as diverse as Leonardo da Vinci, Thomas Edison, Henry David Thoreau, Nathaniel Hawthorne, and General George Patton kept daily journals crammed with observations, notes, and ideas—especially in the early phases of their careers. Edison sketched the plans for the phonograph on a single sheet of paper, then instructed his assistant to build it. His assistant did not even know what the new mechanism was supposed to do but, nevertheless, it worked—on the first try! At Walden Pond, Thoreau "talked" to his daily journal as though it had become his closest friend. Sometimes we feel like merciless eavesdroppers when we read the intimate observations he set down on those yellow pages.

When you are recording your preliminary thoughts, be as wordy, informal, and imprecise as you like—you can always cut out the deadwood later. And don't be too critical of what you are recording. Get it down on paper first! There will be ample time to criticize and evaluate your ideas later. Carry a few sheets of paper wherever you go. You never know when the creative muse will strike. "The best time for planning a book is when you're doing the dishes," said Agatha Christie. Other popular writers, inventors, and entrepreneurs develop their best ideas when they are in the shower, cooking dinner, or driving to work.

Lesson 5
Advertising Your Creative Talents

"Do not let what you cannot do interfere with what you can do."
— John Wooden, Coach of Champions, UCLA

Have you ever wondered why the juiciest assignments always seem to go to those professionals who have learned how to be just a bit playful and audacious? They advance their careers (and have a glorious time along the way) with zany, unpredictable behavior that is actually a subtle form of advertising.

One young aerospace engineer, on a particularly playful day, wore a bright red Superman cape to work. That seemed to attract favorable attention and challenging assignments from company executives, so a few weeks later he turned his necktie around 180 degrees and let it drape down the back of his shirt. All that afternoon visitors from other departments kept bringing their friends into the area for a first-hand look. Within days, his identity as a creative individualist had been firmly established.

Years ago, when Kris Kristofferson was a struggling young songwriter trying to peddle his lyrics in the Nashville music scene, he couldn't seem to get an audition with any of the top stars. So he chartered a helicopter, flew it to the outskirts of town, and set it down on the front lawn at the Johnny Cash estate. Johnny Cash and his wife June were so impressed with Kristofferson's playful antics, they asked him in for supper and later helped him establish his career.

Cultivate a lethargic, hang-dog personality and no one will ask you to do much of anything. Develop responses that are just a bit off-center, and your chances of getting more creative assignments will definitely improve.

Latching onto a juicy assignment is, of course, only the smallest step toward building an interesting career. You will still have to show taste, competence, and integrity in your everyday dealings. And you will have to handle your creative assignments with perseverance, talent, and old-fashioned hard work. Stamp each product with your own personal individuality. "Every job is a self-portrait of the person who did it," says an old English proverb. "Autograph your work with excellence."

Lesson 6
Tickling the Corporate Funnybone in Constructive Ways

"Most people give up just when they're about to achieve success. They quit on the one yard line. They give up at the last minute of the game one foot from a winning touchdown."
— Texas Billionaire, Ross Perot

Writing gags and quips can be marvelous training for those who yearn to enhance their creative problem-solving skills. When we are striving to write funny gags, we are forced to ignore the usual constraints of everyday life and join diverse elements that normally do not belong together. This is precisely what we do when we are developing creative solutions to difficult technical problems. Like a baby butterfly zig-zagging across green meadows on her first solo flight, gagwriters inevitably view the world from a fresh perspective. Gags and quips often help us say things that are hard to say in any other way. "When a thing is funny," said George Bernard Shaw, "search it for a hidden truth."

Laughter brings us together in shared experiences, making it much easier to communicate. Concert pianist Victor Borge can bring the house down with his playful antics on the stage. "Humor is the shortest distance between two people," he once observed.

Humor can also help you sell your creative solutions in a large, complicated bureaucracy. As Michael Iapoce noted in his book *A Funny Thing Happened on the Way to the Boardroom*: "Even if you are not a chief executive, humor can help distinguish you as more creative, more human, and simply more appealing than the average person—in a number of ways."

When AT&T was broken up by the federal courts, Iapoce worked with phone company executives to create palatable story lines to be used in the many public appearances where they tried to explain the reorganization. When one of them was asked why long-distance rates were continuing to rise, Iapoce provided him with this creative response: "It's true that long-distance rates are going up—that's the bad news. The good news is . . . the continents are drifting closer together."

Michael Iapoce is convinced that playful good humor can help foster the teamwork necessary for truly creative solutions. Humorous observations can be invaluable for summing up a complicated message in a clear-cut manner: "Recession is when your neighbor loses his job," said Ronald Reagan at the end of one political rally. "Depression is when you lose your job. Recovery is when Jimmy Carter loses his job."

Abraham Lincoln also used humor to great advantage throughout his political career. To modern eyes, his face seems somehow handsome and noble, but during his early political campaigns, he was often said to resemble a wild monkey or ape. His gawky six-foot frame was also regarded as ill-proportioned in an era when five-foot soldiers were not at all uncommon. Once he took the sting out of an opponent's attack by describing his gaunt physique as being: "as thin as a homeopathic soup that was made by boiling the shadow of a pigeon that had starved to death."

On another occasion when an opponent's campaign manager implied that Lincoln's slender legs were much too long, he countered by noting they were, in fact, exactly the right length. "A man's legs," he observed, "should be just long enough to reach from his body to the ground."

Shortly after my fourteenth birthday, I made an enormous fortune (five weeks' allowance!) when I sold my first gag to the Louisville *Courier Journal* Sunday Supplement magazine. Those two one-dollar bills went straight into next summer's circus fund and, when my joke came out in print a few weeks later, young Tommy Logsdon became an instant one-day celebrity among the soda-fountain crowd at the Walgreen drugstore in Springfield, Kentucky. That first little quip involved a creative answer to an age-old question about Napoleon Bonaparte's classic pose:

Teacher: Why did Napoleon always keep his hand inside his shirt?
Student: Because he didn't have any elastic in his shorts.

Later, during my freshman year in college, I drew panel cartoons dealing with the playful antics of a campus prankster and wrote zany quips for the campus newspaper:

I'm glad my dorm bed sags in the middle. I like being shaped like a question mark. It makes me feel mysterious.

Love is a funny thing, it makes men out of boys and boys out of men.

It's not whether you win or lose that counts, unless you're on an athletic scholarship.

After graduation I moved into a little beach cottage on Ocean Avenue in Santa Monica, California, where I started writing gags for professional cartoonists. Gag writing can be a stimulating enterprise—and wonderful training for those who want to learn how to develop simple, creative solutions.

Professional gag writers have developed a number of clever techniques for producing large numbers of salable gags. Some flip through popular magazines to stimulate their creativity. Others study old mail-order catalogs or the Yellow Pages. One of the most popular techniques is called "switching." A gag writer switches a cartoon by taking one that was written by someone else and giving it a fresh twist. One easy way to make a switch is to cover the caption, then study the drawing until you come up with a new caption of your own.

Many professional gag writers are convinced that switching greatly enhances their creative problem-solving skills. In any case it is stimulating. And fun. Would you like to try your hand at switching? Two cartoons with the captions removed are presented in Figure I.1. Without criticizing or evaluating anything you write, develop a few original captions of your own. As you toy with various possibilities, try to approach your assignment with a playful, childlike attitude. Any time you see a panel cartoon in a magazine or a newspaper, cover the caption and let your imagination soar into adventuresome territory. Later, that same spontaneous spirit will help you stimulate your creative juices in other more important problem-solving situations.

In these exercises there are no correct answers; your captions are as valid as those your coworkers might devise, or as the two I wrote so many years ago, which are included in Appendix A at the end of this book.

Figure I-1   Cartoon captions. Practice your creativity by supplying new captions for these two cartoons.

Lesson 7
Devising Creative Solutions to Keep Your Customers Happy

"Do not anticipate trouble or worry what will happen. Keep in the sunlight."
— American Statesman, Benjamin Franklin

Commissioned studies conducted by Boston's Forum Corporation indicate that hanging onto an old customer costs only about one-fifth as much as acquiring a new one, and that customers tell twice as many people about their bad experiences compared to their good ones. It's a small wonder then, that today's savvy executives are scrambling to hire people who can devise simple, creative ways to please consumers and smooth ruffled feathers.

Simply listening to a customer's complaints tremendously boosts brand loyalty. But what is the best way to gather complaints from irate customers? British Airways devised a surprisingly productive approach when they installed video cameras at major London airports to allow disgruntled travelers to record their grievances as soon as they walk off their planes. Later, when customer-service representatives view the tapes, they strive to develop creative responses that indicate strong feelings of rapport.

If your job gives you the opportunity to deal with a customer complaint—even one that seems unjustified—mix humanity and a dash of showmanship in with your response. Studies show that flashy solutions impress customers much more than solutions that are wishy-washy or nondescript. Never respond to a complaint by telling your client you are conducting an industry-wide survey. They are interested in action, not mealy-mouthed explanations or corporate stalling.

When one customer service representative I know gets tangled up with an irritated customer, she asks herself how Mary Poppins would handle a similar situation. Another spends several days each year at Disney World trying to see how the highly trained employees in the park provide for the routine needs of lost children and Magic Kingdom guests. Even refreshment-stand clerks at Disney World are told that they are "part of the show." As performers, they are shown how to defuse customer complaints with genuinely friendly responses.

Recently when Pam Duley was shopping at Bullock's in Southern California she was happily surprised by the personable response and the showmanship the clerks displayed. As she was paying for two new pairs of shoes, she noticed that the old ones she was wearing looked a bit scruffy, so she asked the clerk if the mall had a shoeshine stand.

"The salesclerk couldn't come up with anything," Pam later told a reporter. "So another guy behind the desk opened a brand-new container of shoe polish and polished my old pair."

Managers at that same Bullock's outlet borrowed a service concept from the nearby South Coast Plaza Hotel: They hired a full-time concierge. Customers respond with surprise and enthusiasm when the concierge produces local bus schedules, freeway maps, contact lens solution, movie schedules, and sample menus from nearby restaurants and coffee shops.

Roy Dyment, a doorman at Toronto's elegant Four Seasons Hotel, recently came up with a simple, creative solution that won him a special award, company-wide recognition, and long-term gratitude from a hotel guest—even though Dyment himself had caused the problem he worked so diligently to alleviate. When Dyment failed to load a departing guest's briefcase aboard his taxi, he waited a few hours, then dialed the guest's home only to find a desperate man who needed to get his hands on the briefing charts inside for an important meeting the following day.

Without securing advance approval, Dyment scooped up the briefcase and boarded a plane bound for Washington, D.C. A few months later, in recognition of his imaginative solution, the hotel managers named him "Employee of the Year."

Creative staff members at the Domino's Pizza chain have developed an innovative way to help ensure customer satisfaction. Each year they give 10,000 customers $60 each to buy a dozen Domino pizzas at their local pizza parlors. After every pizza feast, the client fills out a simple questionnaire evaluating food and service. At small cost, they thus keep restaurant personnel on their toes while gaining access to customer responses in a useful, standardized format.

Early in his career Tom Monaghan—who helped mastermind Domino's highly effective questionnaire—displayed another creative facet of his personality when he met an appealing customer named Marge on his delivery route. From her vantage point, he was nothing more than a talkative pizza man until he delivered a heart-shaped pizza to her home. It arrived piping hot, and it must have made a big impression. That was 30 years ago and he and Marge have been married ever since.

Security analysts have often cited Wal-Mart as America's best run retail marketing chain, but "associates" (store clerks) and high-ranking executives are still finding simple, creative ways to impress faithful customers. Two years ago flagship stores instituted a program in which selected associates wore a dollar bill clipped to their outfits with a little sign that read: "If I don't smile and greet you, please take my dollar bill."

Customers loved it. And so did the associates. Any associate who was still sporting the dollar bill after 90 days could send it to billionaire chairman Sam Walton who would personally autograph it and mail it back.

Before he died, Sam Walton built up a carefully cultivated culture at Wal-Mart in which everybody's ideas were treated with consummate respect, and good ideas were converted into action with a minimum of the usual bureaucratic nonsense. Sam Walton felt that only by trying an idea on a small scale was he able to evaluate it properly and get the bugs out.

This bias toward action had a big impact on the chief executive officer at General Electric, Jack Welch, who often visited the Wal-Mart facilities. "Everybody there has a passion for an idea, and everybody's ideas count," he remarked at a 1991 *Fortune* magazine conference. "They get 80 people in a room and understand how to deal with each other without structure. Every time you go to that place in Arkansas, you can fly back to New York without a plane. The place actually vibrates."

Lesson 8
Using Simple Innovations to Enhance Industrial Productivity

"The ability to simplify means to eliminate the unnecessary so that the necessary may speak."
— German-born American Painter, Hans Hoffman

In 1784 when Benjamin Franklin was serving as minister to France, he calculated that an extra hour of sunlight on long, summer evenings could save Parisian shopkeepers 96 million candles. His simple suggestion for resetting the country's clocks twice each year was not immediately accepted. But, in the long run, it led to the adoption of daylight savings time, which, two hundred years later, stimulates the economies of numerous countries including France, England, and the United States.

Always be on the lookout for simple, creative solutions that can be put into place with inexpensive equipment. The simplest display or even a hand-lettered sign may have a bigger impact on productivity than a room full of complicated robots or mainframe computers costing a hundred thousand times more.

When I was a freshman in college during the days when the mighty brontosaurus was still munching on butterfly wings, a few of my classmates and I managed to get jobs at the Del Monte cannery in Markesan, Wisconsin. During those summers in that friendly little Wisconsin town, we learned how something as simple and inexpensive as two hundred feet of electrical cable can cause worker productivity to shoot through the roof.

At one factory site 16 workers inserted ears of corn one at a time into 16 chain conveyors leading into big green machines that automatically stripped the husks off each ear. With great effort and watchful diligence, each worker could place an ear of corn into nearly all of the 72 moving slots that swept by every minute while the machinery was in operation.

To monitor production, the company engineer mounted a digital counter on each chain conveyor. At first he installed the displays directly on the machines. But later he mounted all 16 of them side by side on a central display panel. What a master stroke! Every hour, during their 10-minute break, workers would rush over to the panel to see how their performance stacked up against that of their fellow workers. Supervisors were almost nonexistent in that part of the factory, but, because of that central display panel, the operation always ran at nearly maximum productive capacity.

Managers at the Milliken Textile Mill in Blacksburg, South Carolina, are using an even simpler creative solution to communicate with their employees. They have installed a big sign that tells how many days the plant has gone without a late delivery. Workers are never hassled, but few competitors can match Milliken's record for on-time delivery. Recently, that sign read: "283 days since the last late order."

A slightly more elaborate electronic display hangs inside General Electric's automated circuit-breaker factory in Salisbury, North Carolina. In bright red numerals it lets workers know how long they are taking to make each circuit-breaker box, how many they are scheduled to produce that day, and how many they have produced so far.

This information enables employees to pace themselves and make their own scheduling decisions. They're happier, too. "I like to be my own boss," said veteran employee Dottie Baringer. "We're behind right now, but no one has to tell us we have to work Saturday."

Executives at the Ford Motor Company recently developed a simple, creative solution that drastically enhanced corporate efficiency. Despite heavy investments in sleek new computers, the head-count in their accounts payable department had ballooned to 500 overworked professionals. Initial studies indicated that rationalizing procedures and installing still more computers might reduce staffing levels to as few as 400 employees. But a more focused analysis revealed a much simpler and more economical approach.

Under the existing system, when Ford's purchasing officers wrote a purchase order, they sent a copy to accounts payable. Then later, when the personnel at material control received the item, they sent accounts payable a copy of the receiving document. The main job of that harassed army of workers in accounts payable was to match the information on the purchase order, the receiving document, and the vendor's invoice to make sure they were all in agreement. If so, the department issued payment. But, if any one of 14 different data items failed to agree, the accounts payable clerk would delay payment and begin creating written reports in an attempt to resolve the discrepancies.

How did Ford Motor Company manage to reduce that growing mountain of paperwork? Their solution was amazingly simple: they merely decided to make payment when they received the *goods*, not when they received the *invoice*. In fact, under the new system, vendors and suppliers have been instructed not to send invoices at all. What has the payoff been from this simple, creative solution? Accounts payable now operates with only 125 staff members who process more purchase orders with fewer errors than the 500 once required.

"A penny saved is a penny earned," wrote Benjamin Franklin in *Poor Richard's Almanac*. Franklin always focused his attention on simple innovations including bifocal glasses, lightning rods, and daylight savings time. If he could somehow return from the grave to study a few of the surprisingly simple solutions that are helping today's workers save huge numbers of pennies—and have more productive careers—he would be extremely proud of his fellow Americans.

Lesson 9
Brainstorming Your Way toward Professional Success

"The work an unknown good man has done is like a vein of water flowing hidden underground, secretly making the ground green."
— British Author, Thomas Carlyle

Solitude sometimes helps us think more clearly, but our interactions with cooperative colleagues can also stimulate and refine our creative problem-solving skills. When you are working on a sticky problem, visit a few of your coworkers and talk with them about your partially formed ideas. Take along your fragmentary notes and a few sheets of paper to record any responses that may capture your fancy. Fresh stimulation will inevitably result from these encounters and, later, when you go back over your notes, your creative juices will start flowing again.

If possible, try an informal brainstorming session in which even the most bizarre ideas are freely shared. A half dozen or so participants is an ideal number. If you can get a half dozen creative people working on a well-defined problem, you can sometimes manage to reach a "critical mass" in which ideas follow one another so rapidly they never seem to stop—or even slow down! Said one brainstorming specialist: "When you really get going in a session, a spark from one mind will light up a lot of bang-up ideas in the others just like a string of firecrackers." If you can't recruit a half dozen people, try a brainstorming session anyway. Sometimes it works well with a smaller number.

In a successful brainstorming session, the participants become increasingly enthusiastic. They can feel the excitement crackling through the air as their imaginations lift them to heady heights. When you are being creative—alone or with others—you become childlike in your enthusiasm. It is an unmistakable feeling, a feeling of freedom, a feeling of unconstrained joy.

Most conferences and meetings, including those held in Congress, are purposely noncreative. Generally speaking, they are convened to impart, sift, evaluate, and modify ideas and to gain consensus rather than to come up with new ideas while they are in session. Noncreative meetings are in keeping with long, painful traditions. As Alex F. Osborne, the father of brainstorming, has observed, "Even at the council fires of the Mohawks and the Senecas there were few burning embers in the form of ideas and much cold water in the form of judgment."

The purpose of a brainstorming session is, by contrast, to inspire creative thinking. Specifically, it is set up to spark creative solutions to a precisely defined problem. Specialists from several different disciplines come together to synthesize their ideas into workable solutions. Their broad-ranging viewpoints and varied experiences are a big help in getting the best possible solutions.

Brainstorming techniques do not work well in all situations. They are not very productive for working out the details of a construction contract. Nor are they much help in writing sheet music or a catchy advertising jingle. But brainstorming has been used to solve a surprising variety of problems in business and industry.

In one session the participants were asked to try to develop ways to broaden the appeal of the Chiquita banana commercials. That group produced 100 suggestions in a little over 40 minutes. At another session a group of training directors brainstormed ways to give visitors to Washington, D.C., a clearer impression of how our federal government works. In just 30 minutes they produced 121 creative ideas. In still another session a Chicago lawyer formed a group called "Divorcees Anonymous" to brainstorm ways to save disintegrating marriages. According to an account published in a Chicago daily newspaper: "The clinic has been salvaging marriages at the rate of more than one per day."

A brainstorming session is run by a moderator who tries to keep the participants focused on the subject assisted by a recorder who lists the individual ideas on paper or on a blackboard. Every idea, crackpot or crackerjack, is recorded for later evaluation.

Comparative tests have shown that, the more ideas a group generates, the more *good* ideas it generates. In other words, the *quality* of the ideas does not deteriorate as larger numbers of them are proposed. The rate of production of ideas usually declines as the session progresses, but many of the most creative ideas seem to come near the end. Presumably this stems from the fact that, as the session unfolds, there are more old ideas to be combined with the ones just conceived.

The four basic rules that make brainstorming so powerful and successful can be summarized as follows:

1. *Criticism is ruled out*: Adverse judgment of ideas must be withheld until later.

2. *Free-wheeling is welcomed*: The wilder the idea, the better; it is almost always easier to "tame down" than to "think up."

3. *Quantity is wanted*: The greater the number of ideas, the greater the likelihood of winners.

4. *Combination and improvement are sought*: In addition to contributing ideas of their own, participants should suggest how the ideas of others can be turned into *better* ideas; or how two or more ideas can be joined into still another idea.

Brainstorming is a powerful stimulant to creativity that has helped produce thousands of simple, creative solutions. In the past it has been amazingly successful, but it can be further strengthened if we give it a little more structure. In a conventional brainstorming session, the participants are told to turn their attention toward a specific problem, but no particular thought processes are suggested.

Yet, if we study the major breakthroughs that have made a big difference in the modern world, we find that six winning strategies crop up—over and over again!

You can use those six winning strategies to extend a brainstorming session into the last few critical minutes when the most intricate and valuable ideas are usually produced. And, when you are working alone, you can use those six winning strategies to channel your thoughts into the most productive avenues—where so many billion dollar breakthroughs have occurred.

Some of the techniques for enhancing your creativity to be discussed in later chapters—the magic grid, color-coded flowcharts, balloon diagrams, industrial-strength similes and metaphors—are best suited for working on your problems alone or with a few supportive colleagues. But the six winning strategies work well in any kind of group, large or small.

Lesson 10
Mastering the Six Winning Strategies
on the Arc of Creativity

"Throughout the centuries there were men who took first steps down new roads armed with nothing but their own vision."
— American Author, Ayn Rand

My studies conducted during the past two years indicate that history's most innovative thinkers have produced thousands of major breakthroughs by using only six simple thought processes or winning strategies, which are arranged on the *arc of creativity*.[1] Despite their enormous power, these six winning strategies (see Figure I.2) are surprisingly simple:

1. **Breaking Your Problem Apart and Putting It Back Together Again:** In the next chapter you will learn how Fred Smith, the founder of Federal Express, managed to break an intractable problem apart and put it back together again in a better way. In the process he made sure millions of packages would reach their destinations within 24 hours after they were posted. You will also learn how, in a single hectic week 40 years ago, a charming and gregarious computer expert named John von Neumann used this same technique when he devised a revolutionary new architecture for digital computers, an architecture that is still being used today to generate big profits.

2. **Taking a Fresh Look at the Interfaces:** Innovative thinkers have concentrated on moving, modifying, changing, or deleting important interfaces to solve such varied problems as manufacturing electric toothbrushes, designing "theft-proof" coat hangers for exclusive hotels, and putting astronauts on the moon. In Chapter 2 you will learn why Henry Ford made his vendors deliver their parts and supplies in wooden packing crates constructed to his exacting specifications. Like many of his predecessors, Ford took a fresh look at the interfaces and ended up devising a devilishly clever cost-cutting technique.

3. **Reformulating the Problem:** Sometimes without knowing it, we spend large amounts of time, money, and energy attempting to solve the wrong problem. By properly reformulating your problems, however, you can open up vast new possibilities for simple, creative solutions. Applications of this winning strategy include a new way to fly the Saturn V moon rocket, new schemes for

---

[1] In compiling the background information for this book, I read more than 600 published sources and analyzed, in detail, the salient characteristics of more than 400 simple, creative solutions devised by a broad range of individualists over the past 2,000 years.

Figure I.2   The arc of creativity.

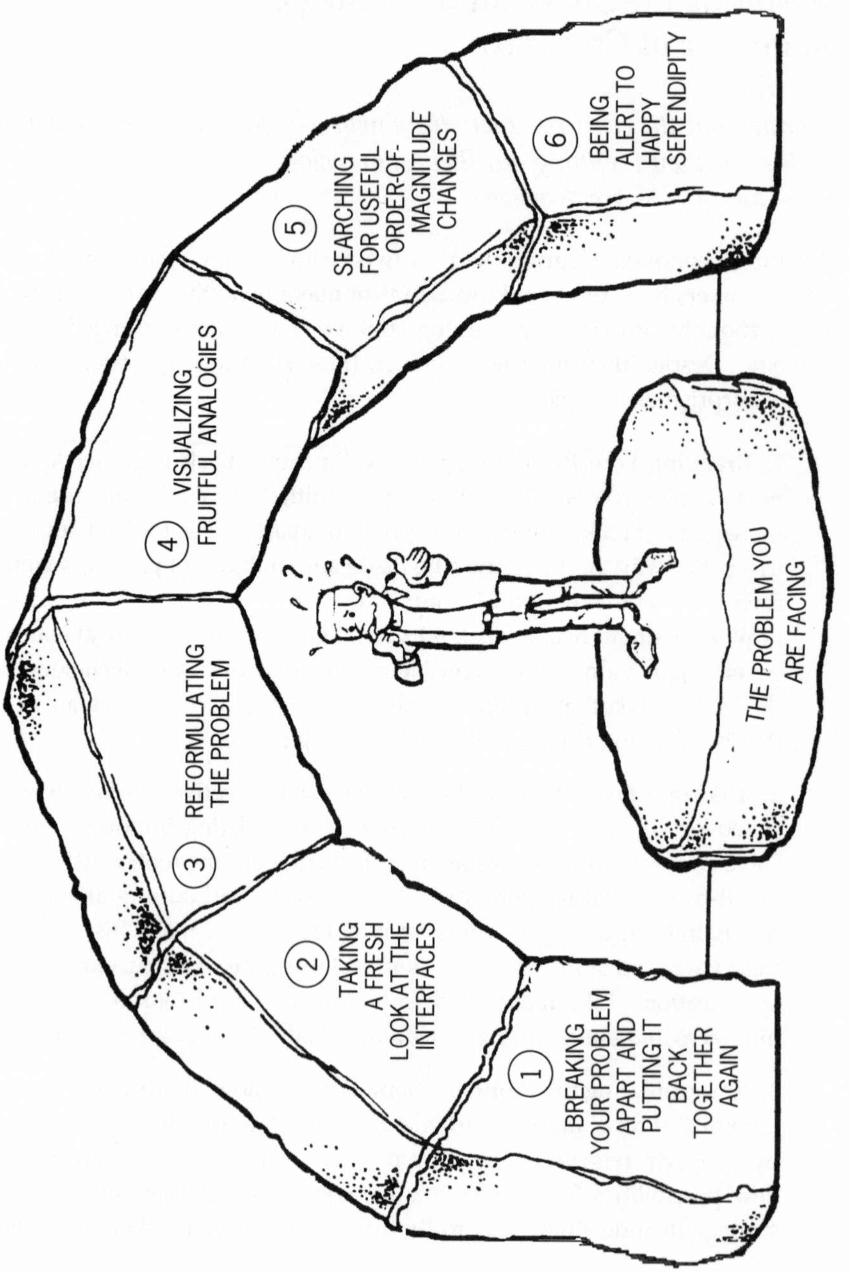

1 BREAKING YOUR PROBLEM APART AND PUTTING IT BACK TOGETHER AGAIN

2 TAKING A FRESH LOOK AT THE INTERFACES

3 REFORMULATING THE PROBLEM

4 VISUALIZING FRUITFUL ANALOGIES

5 SEARCHING FOR USEFUL ORDER-OF-MAGNITUDE CHANGES

6 BEING ALERT TO HAPPY SERENDIPITY

THE PROBLEM YOU ARE FACING

disposing of a shopping center's trash, and new techniques for helping company officials decide what business they are actually in.

4. Visualizing a Fruitful Analogy: Two brothers who quietly assembled an ungainly contraption on a windswept hill near a North Carolina beach were masters of the fruitful analogy. They saw with remarkable clarity how existing solutions could be used to solve seemingly intractable problems. Charles Babbage, a brilliant British inventor, also visualized a fruitful analogy when he masterminded a practical design for a general-purpose digital computer—in 1833!

5. Searching for Useful Order-of-Magnitude Changes: Investors and entrepreneurs feel a rush of excitement whenever they discover a new way to change an important parameter by an order of magnitude or more. Finding useful order-of-magnitude changes has led to the development of the integrated circuit, for example, the Water Pic, and an exciting new breakthrough in robotics called *nanotechnology*, which could someday help cure degenerative heart disease.

6. Being Alert to Happy Serendipity: Serendipity is responsible for a large number of important breakthroughs in business and industry. While playing, relaxing, or working on a completely unrelated problem, creative individuals have often stumbled onto some surprisingly simple solutions. Penicillin, vulcanized rubber, 3M Corporation's "Post-it" notes, and the self-starter for automobiles were all developed through the use of serendipitous problem-solving techniques. You can never be sure when serendipity will strike, but by learning to watch for it, and by skillfully exploiting it when it does occur, you can quickly expand your reputation as a "possibility thinker."

As you begin to use the arc of creativity as a practical tool for solving some of your professional problems, you may notice that the six winning strategies overlap one another in various specific ways. These overlaps are not necessarily undesirable. Depending on the infraction, the Ten Commandments may also overlap. When Lizzie Borden "gave her mother 40 whacks," she violated at least two of the Ten Commandments:

- Thou Shalt Not Kill

- Honor Thy Father and Thy Mother

Fortunately, incidents of this type do not nullify the validity of the Ten Commandments. Nor should they cause Moses to trudge back up Mount Sinai seeking deletions or revisions.

When you encounter overlap between the six winning strategies on the arc of creativity, be thankful for your stroke of good fortune. By applying any one of these strategies to your problems, you can become a creative powerhouse in your own profession. Harness two or more of them and you will be playing with creative dynamite!

Lesson 11
Formulating Your Problems So You Can Begin to Solve Them with Maximum Finesse

"If you don't place your foot on the rope, you'll never cross the chasm."
— American Author, Liz Smith

Hollywood filmmakers who put together movies about the exploits of creative personalities such as Thomas Alva Edison or Leonardo da Vinci almost always show them solving their problems by staring off into space. Talking aside, their characters never actually seem to *do* anything.

In real life, however, creative solutions come only from activity: research, observation, revision, and old-fashioned hard work. Staring into space doesn't usually help very much. In real life, symbols on paper are almost invariably the key to problem-solving success. "My books always seem to know more than I do," said Somerset Maugham. Then he went on to explain that only through writing and careful revision did his thoughts ever fully crystalize.

Of course, putting random symbols on paper will not ensure success. The ideas you record must be based on real-world observations, and they must be carefully arranged into some kind of meaningful patterns. Those who devise the best ideas lead rich, full lives. They know numerous facts; they understand a variety of concepts; and they enjoy many encounters with stimulating people. They also do what it takes to polish their ideas and sell them once they have been perfected. In other words, when they latch onto a good idea, they act!

"The vision must be followed by the venture," observed Vance Havner in *Journey from Jugtown*. "It is not enough to stare up the steps—you must step up the stairs."

Before you can attempt to devise a simple, creative solution, you must begin with a clearly defined problem. That is why this lesson ends with a one-page worksheet on which you are invited to formulate a problem you would like to solve. Your problem statement should be brief and simple, and it should involve a problem you care about solving.

State your problem in ordinary conversational English with personal pronouns included. Avoid cryptic phrases and acronyms. Your problem should be simple, self-contained, and easy to understand like this:

- "Our customers in Omaha are unhappy with our delivery services. What can we do to improve our image?"

- "Putting a satellite into orbit costs more than $3,000 per pound. How can we do it cheaper?"

- "Our copying machine jams several times each day. How can we get better service?"

In the next six chapters, you will be directed through a series of activities that will lead you toward specific solutions to your problem. At the end of this lesson all you will need to do is formulate your problem, then relax and let it percolate through your brain. Of course, your subconscious mind will also be doing a little percolating of its own. At the same time, you should be on the lookout for facts, people, articles, etc., that might help you move toward a useful solution.

Each chapter of this book ends with one or two worksheets designed to help you discover simple, creative solutions to this and any other problems you may decide to formulate. Two additional copies of the worksheets are also included in this book. The first copy, which is presented in Chapter 8, is filled out for you so you can see exactly how the process works. If you get stuck at any point, flip back to Chapter 8 to see how the worksheets were completed in connection with a specific problem. A third blank copy of the worksheets is included in Appendix C.

BREAKING THROUGH

CHOOSING THE PROPER PROBLEM

Simple, well-formulated problems lead to practical, creative solutions. Choose a simple problem that bothers or concerns you. In the box below, state your problem clearly and concisely in ordinary, everyday language. Use action words and personal pronouns in complete sentences like this:

> *Injuries costing $2 billion each year are caused by amateur baseball and softball players sliding into second, third, and home plate. How can we reduce these costly injuries?*

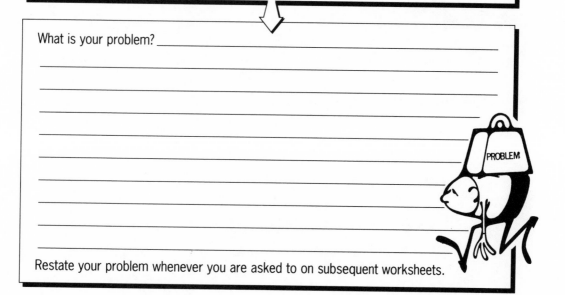

Don't try to solve the problem yet. Just state it clearly and simply.

What is your problem? _____

_____

_____

_____

_____

_____

_____

_____

_____

_____

Restate your problem whenever you are asked to on subsequent worksheets.

Chapter 1

Breaking Your Problem Apart and Putting It Back Together Again

"According to all the known laws of aerodynamics, a bumble bee can't possibly fly. The bumble bee doesn't know this, so he goes ahead and flies anyway."
— Sign displayed on the desk of CalTech engineering professor
   Dr. Theodore von Karmann

His name was Fred Smith, a gregarious, fun-loving Yale University undergraduate brimming with gusto and enthusiasm. His major was economics and political science, but his friends occasionally suggested that he must have a minor in outlandish practical jokes. As he sat on the steps at Harkness Tower watching a pair of hyperactive squirrels scampering across a thick carpet of grass, his head was swimming with dreams of greatness.

Other students hurrying by probably never had the slightest inkling that there was a billion-dollar idea percolating through his brain. The first suggestive clue came near the end of his junior year when he wrote a term paper in which he argued with great conviction that attractive business opportunities were awaiting anyone who could devise a fast and reliable package-delivery service spanning the continental United States. To win big, he believed, 24-hour package delivery would have to be guaranteed for high-value, time-sensitive goods such as medicines, contact lenses, and small electronic components.

In his spare time he conducted his own informal survey, which indicated that manufacturers and their distributors were extremely unhappy with the way their merchandise was being handled by existing package-delivery firms. Even the best of them were, by Fred Smith's cynical assessment, "erratic, often late, and, in general, unreliable."

Smith felt a chill of disgust when he first learned how packages were being routed from place to place. Generally, they were merely loaded onto any handy airplane headed in the right general direction only to be off-loaded again to await some other incoming plane that might carry them a bit closer to the intended recipient.

This mindless approach, he believed, was practically guaranteed to antagonize customers and destroy any confidence in a consistently successful result. As Fred Smith later described the techniques then in use: "Packages were hippity-hopping around the country from city to city and from airplane to airplane before reaching their final destinations." Actually, in fact, even that rather negative evaluation was a little optimistic: Sometimes they failed to arrive at all!

Of course, Fred Smith had never been instructed to shy away from worry and frustration. Instead, his business school professors instructed him to seek out exploitable possibilities that might be concealed by seemingly intractable problems. Princeton University professor Albert Einstein had often pondered the curious link between creativity and adversity. "In the middle of difficulty," he concluded, "lies opportunity."

Once Fred Smith had managed to develop a clear vision of the characteristics a successful package-delivery service should provide, he began tinkering with various possibilities for realizing that elusive dream. A half dozen messy diagrams later, he stumbled on a surprisingly simple solution that suddenly made everything else quietly fall into place.

Why not fly all of the packages radially inward to one central location in the middle of the night, sort them into different bins according to their destinations, then load them back onto the same airplanes and fly them radially outward again? Years later, when he finally got enough money together to give his exciting dream a try, he selected Memphis, Tennessee, as the central hub for his unique "hub-and-spoke" package-delivery system, which he ended up servicing with a fleet of spotless 727's trimmed with distinctive orange and purple markings.

To fashion his concept into reality, Fred Smith used the first winning strategy on the arc of creativity: *He broke his problem apart and put it back together again in a different way.* Even in his undergraduate years, he quickly realized that the piecemeal system then in use would probably never be able to provide reliable overnight delivery for the large numbers of packages he could foresee. By using dedicated airplanes all flying to the same central location, then flying them back out again, he managed to solve the overnight delivery problem in a dramatically simple way.

The end result was Federal Express, one of the fastest growing—and most admired—corporations in the United States. Business school professors often cite Fred Smith's clever hub-and-spoke architecture as a sparkling sample of entrepreneurial creativity at its best. But, like so many others who have managed to develop and exploit simple, creative solutions, his initial proposal did not elicit rave reviews. When he got back that fateful term paper in his junior year, he found that he had barely received a passing grade!

Lesson 12
Finding a Cash-Laden Customer to Fill Every Empty Seat

"A critic is someone who never actually goes to the battle, yet afterwards comes out shooting the wounded."
— American Actress, Tyne Daly

Most people are willing to spend long hours puzzling over a problem only if they are convinced that it is interesting and important. That is why you are instructed to start each exercise in this book by selecting a problem you are genuinely interested in solving. Always state your problem in simple, everyday language. Never use clipped or cryptic phrases. This will allow anyone else who might want to help you with creative solutions to understand your problem, too. Later in this chapter you will be asked to take the problem you formulated in the last chapter and begin breaking it down into smaller parts so you can start to develop simple, creative solutions.

"Nothing is particularly hard if you divide it into smaller pieces," wrote Henry Ford. Ford knew precisely what he was talking about. The big auto production plants he constructed broke the assembly operations into thousands of smaller tasks, each of which could be mastered in a relatively short time.

Modern auto production plants assemble a complete Toyota Camry or a Cutlass Supreme using only about 30 man-hours of labor. Surprisingly, that is less time than it later takes to perform some major repairs on that same machine!

"Divide and conquer" might well be the philosophical motto for this chapter. First divide. Then conquer. Then pick up the pieces and put them back together again so everything works better than it ever did before. By way of illustration, consider how the managers at a highly efficient restaurant chain broke their problem apart so they could devise a way to make sure an enthusiastic paying customer would occupy every chair at every table being served.

Even during their busiest periods, most restaurants have large numbers of empty seats scattered around their dining rooms. Customers wait impatiently while those seats are sitting empty because, when people are eating a meal, they are usually unwilling to share a table with a person they do not know. Yet, those same people will willingly sit next to strangers at a basketball game or a Broadway play.

Managers at the Benihana of Tokyo restaurant chain have figured out how to use the first strategy on the arc of creativity to fill every single empty seat. They do it by breaking the incoming crowds apart, then putting them back together again in a fresh new way.

When customers enter a Benihana restaurant, they are grouped into batches of eight, then led to a horseshoe-shaped table curving around an expert chef who chops and dices their entrees with great flourishing gestures. Because each chef puts on such an interesting display, patrons willingly sit beside strangers while they are eating their evening meal. Tight seating, in fact, helps improve the show.

By converting *restaurant* into *theater*, the managers at Benihana have devised a way to solve their seating problem with admirable simplicity. The theater-like atmosphere, which they carefully cultivate, makes it acceptable for patrons to share adjacent seats. Not coincidentally, denser seating also increases nightly gross receipts.

Boston's Legal Seafood restaurants use a vaguely similar strategy to get busy lunch-hour crowds in and out more quickly so they can serve more customers in the same amount of seating space. The serving area in most restaurants is broken into separate zones, each handled by its own dedicated team of waiters. But at Legal Seafood, any waiter can handle any table that requires service. Moreover, customers receive their check *when their order is placed*, not when the food arrives at their table. This allows busy clients to leave any time they choose without having to chase down their waiter. When the food comes out from the kitchen, any handy waiter brings it to any table, thus the meal always arrives piping hot.

Several years ago I encountered another clever way of breaking problems apart in a little restaurant with strictly limited seating space. That establishment, which was enthusiastically recommended by a local cabdriver, was in the high-rent district on the Rock of Gibraltar.[2]

When customers first arrive, they are seated in a small lobby area resembling a cozy living room furnished with three overstuffed couches surrounding a coffee table where drinks are served. As soon as customers arrive, they are immediately handed menus so they can place their orders even before they are seated at their tables. When a table opens up, a new party is escorted to the dining room where freshly prepared dishes immediately begin to arrive. Customers love the cozy atmosphere and the efficient service. Owners love the extra money that comes to them because of their clever new architectural approach.

The next time you need to devise a simple, creative solution to improve the efficiency of a complicated operation, experiment with this simple trick: Break your problem apart, then see if you can find a better way to put it back together again. Sometimes seemingly insignificant changes can bring highly profitable results.

---

[2] On the Rock of Gibraltar, space is so scarce that, when an automobile outlives its usefulness, it is literally shoved into the sea!

Lesson 13
Finding a Better Way to Manufacture an Old Army Musket

"When I was young I observed that nine out of ten things I did were failures, so I did ten times more work."
— British Dramatist, George Bernard Shaw

Some of history's biggest productivity gains have been made by breaking various manufacturing processes apart, then putting them back together again to find a better way. One noteworthy example started in 1797 when military procurement specialists ordered 40,000 muzzle-loading muskets in preparation for a possible war against France.

Twenty-five of the 26 contractors who bid for portions of the procurement planned to produce their share of the muskets in the same way they had always done—by recruiting large teams of skilled craftsmen, each assigned to fashion complete muskets by carefully forming and fitting the separate parts until a weapon was ready to fire. Every musket was thus entirely unique and, if a part of it broke in heavy use, a replacement had to be specially made, sanded, filed down, and fitted into place.

The number of muskets that could be produced in this manner was constrained by the number of skilled craftsmen who could be hired and trained. Many orders went unfilled while unskilled laborers wandered across the countryside searching for any kind of job they were talented enough to fill. Unfortunately, their lack of production skills made them useless for the exacting task of producing workable muskets in the huge numbers required.

The 26th contractor, Eli Whitney, was convinced that there must be a better way to divide the many repetitive tasks associated with musket production. Whitney understood how movable type was cast, and he intended to use printing technology as his model for making 10,000 identical muskets with fully *interchangeable* parts. "The tools which I contemplate to make," he explained, "are similar to an engraving on copper plate from which may be taken a greater number of impressions perceptibly alike."

With Whitney's clever machining tools, any unskilled workman could be trained to make innumerable copies of the same identical part. Later the parts produced were measured against a model part to make sure they had been produced with the necessary precision. The individual parts, each made by separate laborers, were then assembled to make complete muskets, hopefully in large and profitable numbers.

Eli Whitney agreed to produce 10,000 muskets for the U.S. Army within two years after the contract was signed. His imaginative concept that employed interchangeable parts made by unskilled laborers revolutionized the production of low-technology tools and machines, thus helping America become fully competitive with other countries throughout the Western world.

It would be nice to report that he profited handsomely from his courage, insight, and expertise. But, actually, he was years behind schedule and heavily in debt when, in 1801, he finally managed to conduct his triumphant demonstration for President Thomas Jefferson and a number of other officials in Washington, D.C. From random stacks of interchangeable parts, Jefferson and his colleagues were instructed to assemble several complete muskets, all of which worked as advertised!

One hundred years later Frederick Taylor and Frank Gilbreth found another way to break manufacturing down into its component parts when they conducted precise time-and-motion studies of production-line workers at work. They also found new ways to compare the performance of skilled laborers with others who were not so skilled. This approach produced big dividends for American industrialists struggling to do more with less.

In 1909, Frank Gilbreth with his wife, Lillian, studied the efficiency of the various bricklaying techniques then in use. They found that skilled bricklayers—whose motions were characterized as quick, sure, and machinelike—almost never switched hands with a brick or put it down again once they had picked it up. Soon the Gilbreths had standardized the motions of all bricklayers working in big crews—with dramatic improvements in quality and efficiency.

Their studies also showed that much motion was wasted every time a bricklayer had to reach down to pick up a brick. So they devised an adjustable scaffold that practically eliminated all stooping motions. In one widely admired test, the scaffold increased the average workman's productivity from 120 to 350 bricks per hour.

A few years ago while attending the Folkloric Ballet in Mexico City, I stumbled across another clever way to break a problem apart for improved efficiency. A young concessionaire had devised a simple way to sell far more ice-cold colas to thirsty intermission crowds. Just before the end of the first act, he hefted a wooden case with 24 colas to the top of his counter. With a hand-held bottle opener, he quickly snapped off all 24 caps, then he dropped a paper cup upside down onto the top of each open bottle. When customers came up, he took their money, then, in one quick motion, flipped the bottle over and dumped its contents into the cup!

The pages of history are alive with numerous instances in which efficiencies have skyrocketed when production tasks have been broken apart, analyzed, then skillfully put back together again. Try it with your own work; you may be surprised by the results you can achieve.

Lesson 14
Developing a Simpler Way to Build a Giant Brain

"By perseverance the snail reached the arc."
— Charles Haddon Spurgeon, 19th Century British Baptist Minister

Simple, creative solutions are often developed by dedicated individuals with slightly above-average intelligence. But a few creative blockbusters have been proposed and perfected by world-class geniuses whose intellectual brilliance sparkles and burns with star-like luminosity.

One spectacular example came about when John von Neumann broke a high-speed digital computer apart and put it back together again with extraordinarily effective results. His creative breakthrough occurred in the middle of the 1940s but, even today, many of the world's most powerful computers are still being constructed in keeping with the design philosophy he so skillfully espoused.

Born into a wealthy, cultured family in Budapest, Hungary, in 1903, "Johnny" von Neumann, as his friends called him throughout his life, was a happy, precocious youngster who loved mathematical puzzles and tricky word games. When he was only six, he and his father told each other jokes in classical Greek. Later, in the United States, Edward Teller, father of the hydrogen bomb, would pun with him in several dialects.

In 1926 at the age of 23, von Neumann left his boyhood home for a teaching post in Germany, where he began a most remarkable habit of lecturing without notes, selecting a problem that he had not yet solved and tackling the solution of it as he lectured. Unfortunately, within a short time, the sounds of the Nazi goosestep began echoing ominously through the streets of Berlin and, to escape the conflict he knew would surely come, he accepted an invitation to lecture at Princeton University.

At Princeton and later at Los Alamos he enjoyed intimate parties with robust wines and vigorous conversations. He was, according to his contemporaries, a talented host, a magnetic personality, a dedicated scientist, a gifted instructor . . . and a lousy driver! He had so many traffic accidents his students nicknamed one of the intersections near Princeton "von Neumann's Corners." Of course, he was always armed with a creative explanation for each and every accident he happened to cause. In recounting one of his more harrowing escapades, he maintained that "there was a long row of trees moving by on the side of the road at sixty miles an hour, when suddenly one of them stepped into my path."

"He had the fastest mind I ever met," stated the famous nuclear physicist Lothar Nordheim. He made a similar impression on Herman Goldstine, who helped perfect the world's first successful electronic digital computer. With blistering speed and accuracy, he could solve even the most difficult problems—in his head—problems whose solutions often took the best mathematicians hours or days of tedious pencil-and-paper calculations.

Then, as now, ingenious practical jokes were a common laboratory diversion. And, not surprisingly, "Johnny" von Neumann was nearly everyone's favorite target. When time permitted, his fellow researchers would work out a complicated problem in advance and then innocently pose it to him as though it had just arisen. As "Johnny" would race through the problem—bursting with intensity and agitation—the others would nonchalantly call out each intermediate step the instant before he could figure it out on his own. It was a fun game, but surprisingly tricky; sometimes he would discover hidden shortcuts and suddenly without warning, beat all of them to the desired solution!

In 1946, after visiting the computer facilities at the Moore School of Engineering in Philadelphia, von Neumann wrote a 40-page technical paper that provided the major thrust for the many advances in computer technology that were to occur over the next few years. Many of his most imaginative ideas had been previously advanced by other researchers, but his forceful writing style and the clarity of his presentation commanded instant attention.

When scientists describe the operating principles of an intercontinental ballistic missile or a high-performance jet plane, they do not attempt to analyze every component part as a separate entity. Instead, they break the device up into a series of interlocking *subsystems*, each of which is devoted to a particular function. Accordingly, they might focus their attention on the guidance and control system, the electrical power system, the propulsion system, and so on.

The philosophy underlying this approach is that it is often better to define a complicated device in terms of what it *does* rather than what it *is*. This was not an entirely new idea in 1946, but John von Neumann adopted it with consummate skill in his widely heralded technical paper on the operating principles of digital computers. In von Neumann's classification system, he broke the computer apart into four distinct, but interactive, components:

1. Input/output

2. Processing

3. Control

4. Storage.

Figure 1.1 shows how von Neumann then fit these four parts back together to make a functioning whole. The next four paragraphs describe the functions performed by each of the four separate pieces of equipment in a von Neumann computer.

Figure 1.1   Jon Von Neumann's breakthrough in computer achitecture.

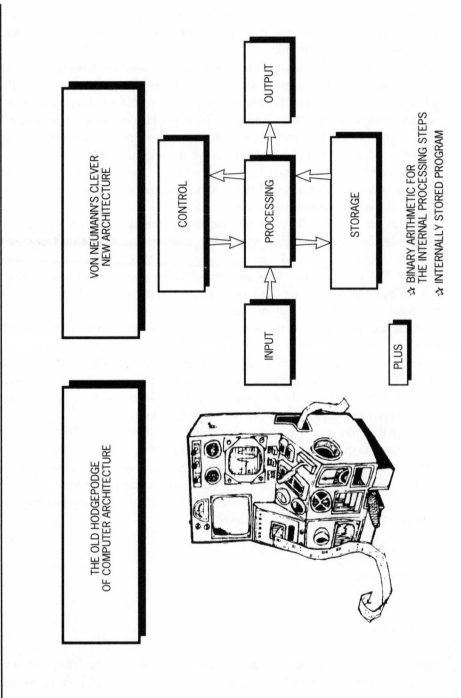

The *input/output* devices allow the computer to communicate with the outside world in a human-oriented "language." Information and program commands are fed into the computer by means of the input devices. Then, when the computations have been completed, the output devices are used to display the final results.

The *processing* mechanisms are the devices the computer uses to process the input values in accordance with its program instructions. In most modern computers, these mechanisms consist of cornflake-sized computer chips equipped with no moving parts. The only thing that moves is a series of electronic pulses, which travel through the computer at the speed of light.

The *control* mechanisms cause the computer to execute the program instructions in the proper sequence with maximum practical efficiency. The processing and control circuits operate like a railroad switching yard built on a microscopic scale. In accordance with the program instructions, electronic pulse trains (packets of electrons) are routed through a series of solid-state switches (transistors). Each time the pulse train encounters one of the switches it is automatically converted into a new set of pulses with the desired characteristics.

The *storage* devices are a kind of computer memory. They hold the data values being manipulated and the program instructions that are fed into the computer by its human operators. In modern computers solid-state switches, magnetic disks, and magnetic tapes are key components in the computer's storage.

Von Neumann realized that all of the computer's electronic switches are intrinsically bistable. Like a light bulb and many other familiar, everyday devices, a bistable switch can assume precisely two states of stability—such as "on" and "off" or their equivalents. Hence, as von Neumann pointed out in his famous paper, it is much more efficient to have the computer store and process its data values in binary, a numeration system that uses only 1's and 0's, rather than our more familiar decimal number system with its 10 decimal digits.

In such a computer, a binary 1 is represented by the presence of a pulse; its absence represents a binary 0. When a pulse train is routed through one of the computer's processing circuits, a new pulse train is automatically produced in response to the program instructions.

Von Neumann's new scheme also employed *internally stored program commands*. In such a computer system, the program instructions are stored *inside* the computer in memory slots identical to those used to store data. One advantage of this approach is that the computer need not be idle during the programming process. Of more fundamental importance, however, is the fact that the computer can be made to *alter its own commands while its computations are taking place*. As a result, the computer is able to make "decisions" and to set up loops of repeated calculations, two extremely powerful and flexible capabilities.

John von Neumann broke the high-speed digital computer apart and put it back together again to achieve vastly improved results. To accomplish this goal, he defined the computer not in terms of what it *is*, but rather in terms of what it *does*. This allowed him to break data processing machinery into four separate functions, each of which could be performed by stand-alone machines. Like a high-quality stereo system, separate *modules* could then be linked together to make a large-scale computer specifically suited to each particular user's needs. Computer design was also greatly simplified. With one simple, creative idea, John von Neumann had thus found a method for breaking all future computers apart and putting them back together again with a greatly improved results.

Lesson 15
Learning Why Writing a Book
Is Such a Simple Undertaking

"No one really knows enough to be a pessimist."
— American Writer, Norman Cousins

"I missed the first 108 annual meetings," I told them sheepishly. "But I intend to be here for the *next* 108!" Little sprinklings of laughter echoed across the lecture hall followed by appreciative applause. ". . . How many of you were here for the first 108 meetings?" This time the laughter was quite a bit louder.

Professional platform lecturers always hope for a supportive audience consisting of several hundred intelligent men and women in nearly equal numbers, keenly interested in the topic, who have just eaten a tasty meal and washed it down with moderate, but not excessive, amounts of alcohol. By that metric, the audience members at the 109th Annual Meeting of the Fargo Chamber of Commerce were perfect in every important respect. They also had come to their annual meeting to learn about simple, creative solutions and to have a good time, too.

North Dakota has more millionaires per capita than nearly any other state, mostly land-rich farmers. But, by the late 1980s, community leaders began to notice some rather worrisome economic trends. In particular, their farm-based economy was beginning to stagnate and many of their best young people were streaming out of the state. Getting them to stay had become a constant preoccupation among community leaders scattered across the state. My lecture, which was titled "Flights of Imagination: Creative Thinking for Professional Success," emphasized simple, creative solutions to some of the problems they were hoping to solve.

When you write books, people think you are doing something complicated, but, as I explained in my opening remarks, writing is surprisingly simple and easy to do: "How do I go about writing a book? It's simple, I just take the 26 letters of the alphabet and arrange them in various patterns!" Those introductory remarks helped get them into the proper frame of mind to attack their own problems in similarly simple ways. I also explained to them how I collaborate with another writer, which is remarkably simple, too. And I showed them how to break any writing assignment down into three simple tasks and how to work on each of those tasks separately, one by one.

The main body of my presentation was divided into six sections, each beginning with a billion-dollar breakthrough developed by one single individual with one simple creative solution. I then described the thought processes that person used in making the breakthrough, followed by specific suggestions on how the people of

North Dakota could use those same thought processes to help solve some of the problems facing their state.

"Our best young people are moving away. How can we get them to stay?" one of them asked me during the question-and-answer session.

"Maybe you should reformulate the *problem*," I replied. "Maybe you should concentrate on getting them to *come back* instead. When they go somewhere else, they learn new things. So, if you can get them to come back again, they may be even more valuable."

A more complete discussion of my ideas on how North Dakota's leaders can rehabilitate their state's economy is presented in Chapter 8. In this chapter we will review a few structured techniques for breaking your problems down into bite-sized chunks. Incidentally, how *do* I collaborate with another writer? It's simple, I hit the vowels, I let him hit the consonants!

Lesson 16
Using Balloon Diagrams to Break Your Problems Apart

"How far is far? How high is high?
We'll never know until we try."
— Rhyming couplet from the California Special Olympics Song

Breaking your problem apart and putting it back together again in a different way can sometimes produce amazingly fruitful results. But how can you master this strategy to enhance your inherent creative problem-solving skills? With a little training, you can employ a number of powerful methods including balloon diagrams, flowcharts, and outlines to partition your problem into smaller and more manageable pieces.

All of these methods are simple and easy to use, but many people seem to prefer the balloon diagram, a free-flowing sketch that consists of notes enclosed within ovals connected by branching lines. Simplicity is one advantage of a balloon diagram. Another is that you can start to sketch a useful balloon diagram as soon as you have the slightest inkling of what you are trying to do.

Balloon diagrams are such powerful aids to creativity that some experts call them "mind maps" to emphasize the intimate link between their free-flowing structure and the way the human mind appears to operate. You can construct such a diagram in just a few minutes and, if you do it well enough, it can display a marvelously simple summary of the component parts of the problem you are attempting to solve.

Once you have completed your balloon diagram, you will probably begin to notice that it is tied together by a number of common threads. Each time you spot one of these threads beginning to emerge, you should make a note of it in the margins, or perhaps make a separate flowchart or outline of your observations. New versions of the balloon diagram drawn with color coding or with boxes of various shades can also highlight your summary observations.

Suppose, by way of illustration, that you have been hired as a consultant to a big, downtown hotel whose new owners are hoping to attract and hold business travelers in larger numbers. To appeal to that select clientele, the owners have decided that they will probably have to find ways to reduce the number of customer complaints.

So your first step is to call a meeting of the hotel staff and ask them to list and describe the major complaints they have been hearing from hotel guests. At that meeting you can construct a balloon diagram similar to the one in Figure 1.2, which lists, in a convenient pictorial format, various representative complaints—shortages of coat hangers, insufficient lighting in the rooms, scalding showers, and the like.

By breaking the problem up into these bite-size chunks, you and your colleagues can begin to focus your attention on simple cost-effective solutions. One way to do this is to study your balloon diagram (Figure 1.2) to see if you can divide the various customer complaints into a few meaningful categories. Here is one possible categorization:

1. Problems with the staff

2. Problems with hotel engineering

3. Other types of problems.

The new balloon diagram in Figure 1.3 highlights these three categories with boxes of three different shapes. Problems with the hotel staff are enclosed in diamond-shaped boxes, hotel engineering problems are enclosed in rectangular boxes, and the various other types of problems are enclosed in ovals.

Using Figure 1.3 as a guide, your staff committee can then put together a survey questionnaire in which you ask a sampling of hotel guests to flag these and any other problems they may have encountered while they were staying in the hotel.

The results of your survey might end up looking something like Table 1.1. Notice that a few extra categories have been added because of the way the questionnaire items were broken down and because extra complaints were formulated by the guests while they were filling out the questionnaire. Some of the complaints were frequently mentioned, whereas others were hardly ever mentioned at all.

Using the questionnaire tabulations as a guide, you can now break the problem up in a slightly different manner as shown in Figure 1.4. In this new version of the balloon diagram, complaints received from more than 10 percent of your sample population are shaded with cross-hatching, complaints received from 5 to 10 percent are shaded with a dot pattern, and those received from less than 5 percent are unshaded. Another way to code them would be with colored pencils or marking pens. In fact, color-coding is a much more effective approach at every stage in the construction of a balloon diagram. Get several sets of colored marking pens and use them liberally as you perfect your creative problem-solving skills.

Figure 1.2   Problems for the business traveler (version 1).

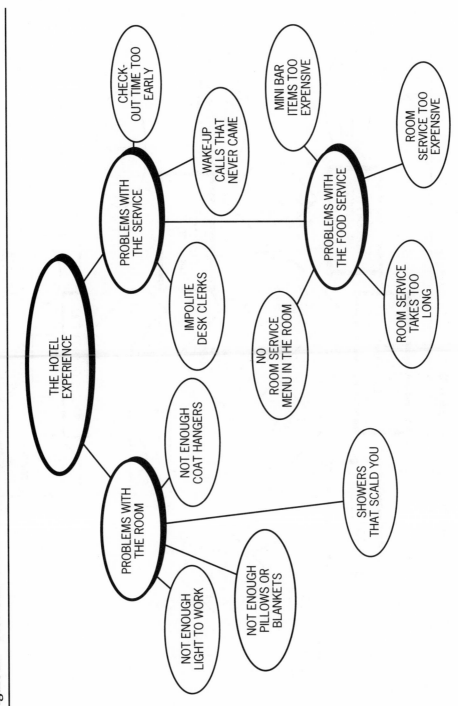

Figure 1.3   Problems for the business traveler (version 2).

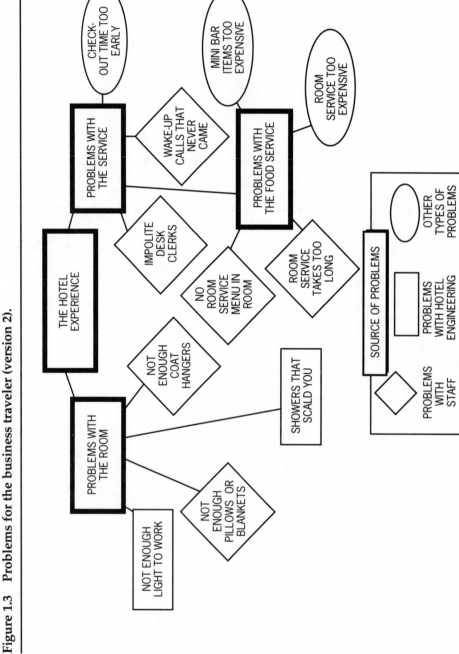

Table 1.1   Complaints from Guests of the Hotel

Complaints	Frequency of Complaints
1. Impolite desk clerks	6%
2. Room service takes too long	2%
3. Not enough coat hangers	15%
4. Mini bar too expensive	12%
5. Not enough light in the room	6%
6. Room service too expensive	7%
7. Checkout time too early	1%
8. Wakeup call never came	3%
9. Not enough pillows	1%
10. Not enough blankets	1%
11. Showers scalded me	11%
12. No room service menu in the room	2%
13. Check-in time too late	16%
14. Stamps overpriced	11%
15. Uncomfortable pillows	5%
16. TV remote doesn't work	2%
17. Luggage delivered late	3%

The third version of the balloon diagram (see Figure 1.4) is rich with useful information that almost anyone can understand and appreciate. It lists the various problems encountered by hotel guests, highlights their causes to some extent, and shows how frequently each complaint is being received. Thus far, however, no solutions to the various problems have been suggested. Fortunately, there are a number of ways in which proposed solutions can be conjured up with relative ease. Brainstorming is one effective approach.

Call together key staff members so you can hold a series of brainstorming sessions. If you write the proposed solutions directly on the balloon diagram, you can then begin to select the best ones and make plans to implement those courses of action that promise to eliminate the largest number of customer complaints in accordance with your budget.

Later, if the hotel executives want you to write up the results, you can work directly from the balloon diagram as you put the appropriate words down on

Figure 1.4   Problems for the business traveler (version 3).

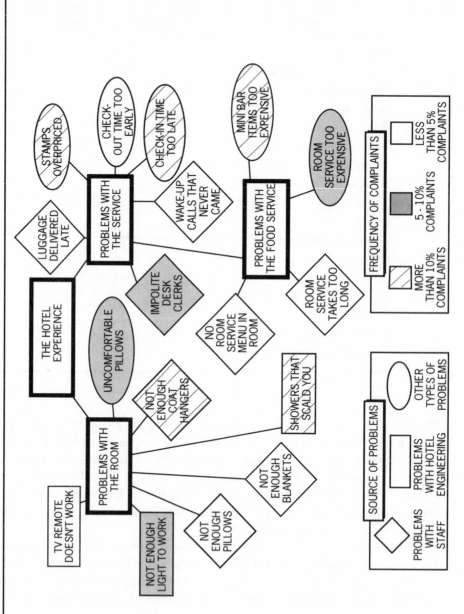

paper, or you can use the balloon diagram as a guide in making a topic outline summarizing the various complaints and their proposed solutions like this:

Attracting More Business Travelers to Our Hotel

The Hotel Experience
Customer Complaints and Proposed Solutions

1. Showers that scald you
   Proposed Solutions:
   - Extra simple shower controls
   - Showers that maintain an even temperature by means of feedback control
   - Bathtubs instead of showers

2. Not enough coat hangers
   Proposed Solutions:
   - Cheap coat hangers as a backup
   - Coat hangers that cannot be removed
   - Hooks on the walls

3. TV remote that doesn't work
   Proposed Solutions:
   - Switch to more reliable version
   - Routinely change batteries every other week

4. Not enough light in the room to work
   Proposed Solutions:
   - Overhead lights in the ceiling
   - Indirect lighting
   - More natural light from outside
   - More reflective walls

5. Not enough pillows or blankets
   Proposed Solutions:
   - Always keep extra pillows and blankets in the room
   - Warmer rooms so blankets unnecessary
   - Radiant heater panels

Notice that the partial outline presented here amplifies and expands some of the concepts presented in the balloon diagram. Minor errors in format, punctuation, etc., have also been corrected.

Once you have constructed a topic outline, writing a summary report is fairly simple. Just splash your first draft on paper, then revise and polish it until it is accurate, brief, and clear.

Lesson 17
Flowcharting Your Way toward Industrial Success

"Don't gamble: buy some good stock, hold it 'til it goes up and then sell it—if it doesn't go up, don't buy it."
— American Humorist, Will Rogers

A few years ago I ran across an impressive little flowchart on the wall of a hotel room somewhere on the crossroads of America. Thumbtacked at eye level beside the door, it was so simple and powerful that, somehow (quite by accident), it ended up tucked inside a little pocket in my garment bag. With only six boxes filled with simple notes, that little flowchart explained exactly what hotel guests should do in case a fire was roaring down the hall. A copy is sketched in Figure 1.5.

What a marvelously efficient way to communicate useful information! If you ever got trapped in a hotel fire, which would you rather have? Several dense paragraphs telling you what to do? Or a simple flowchart you could fully comprehend in a single glance? Flowcharts can provide us with a powerful and effective method for breaking a problem apart and putting it back together again to achieve improved results. Often the flowchart is hidden from public view, but, occasionally, as it was in that hotel, it is openly presented for all to see.

Eighteen years ago, when I unexpectedly became a single parent trying to raise an incredibly hungry 12-year-old, I soon discovered, to my chagrin, that cookbooks could greatly benefit from a few simple flowcharting techniques. Most cookbooks are frustratingly difficult to use. In stringy, incomprehensible paragraphs they tell you how to make pot roast or salmon croquettes. As you manage to complete each task, you have to search through the paragraph again to figure out where you last left off. Often the instructions route you to some completely different section, so you have to find some way to turn the pages with flour and sauces sticking to your hands. The cookbook itself sits in the middle of the counter, so its pages are soon stained with the meals of yesteryear. In other words, cookbooks are not very user-friendly publications.

After a number of such encounters, I began working on a different kind of cookbook. It is called *Cooking at a Glance*. Each page (see Figure 1.6) contains exactly one flowcharted recipe with all the necessary instructions clearly illustrated by color sketches. The boxes on the left-hand side list (and picture) all the required ingredients. The boxes in the middle show all the necessary steps (chopping, dicing, stirring, baking, etc.). The final box shows how the completed dish is supposed to look.

The pages are bound in a loose-leaf notebook so you can pull out the recipe-of-the-day and carry it to the local supermarket, thus eliminating the need for a separate shopping list. A magnet affixed to the back cover allows you to attach each one-page recipe to the top of your kitchen stove. This keeps it out of the way of any stray food stains.

For those who are watching their diets, three-dimensional pie charts in the lower right-hand corner of each recipe show, in a convenient pictorial format, the percentage of a healthful daily allowance of calories, salt, cholesterol, and saturated fat for each serving from the recipe.

"Originality is simply a fresh pair of eyes," said Woodrow Wilson. That is why a single parent who can hardly tell the difference between a spatula and a rolling pin can invent a simpler and more effective method for displaying and presenting cookbook recipes.

Figure 1.5   A simple flowchart.

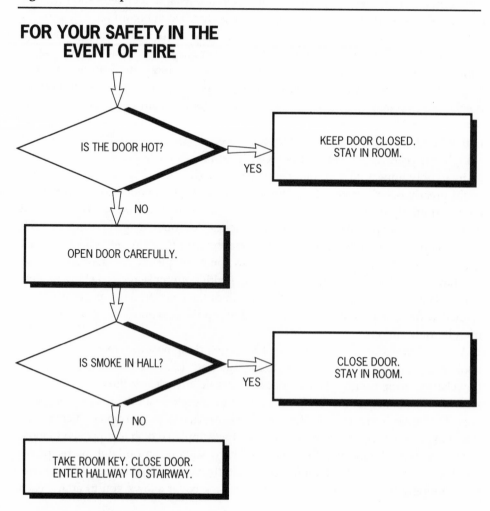

Figure 1.6   Sample page from *Cooking at a Glance.*

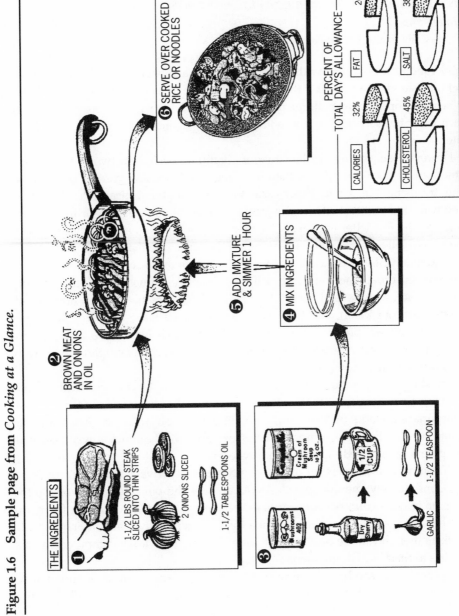

Lesson 18
Putting Your Groceries Away
in Half the Time It Usually Takes

"Man's mind, stretched by a new idea, never goes back to its original dimensions."
— Chief Justice, Oliver Wendell Holmes

Books and classes dealing with personal time management often insist that substantial time-savings can result if the reader will strive to *handle each item only one time.* When you open your mail, for instance, you are instructed to answer or discard each letter immediately, so you will not have to spend more time dealing with it later.

However, depending on the situation, handling each item two, three, or more times can be far more efficient than handling it only once. If you doubt that assertion, try using 3-in. x 5-in. index cards to create an alphabetical index for a book. You will soon find that efficiencies greatly increase if you start by sorting the index items by the first letter into 26 stacks, then sort the cards in each of these stacks by the second letter before you start arranging the cards into their final order.

Incidentally, if you decide instead to use a computer to sort the index items into alphabetical order, the computer will also do its job much more efficiently if it handles each item several times! The sorting processes used by computers—the bubble sort, quick sort, and Shell sort—are all much faster than any single-pass sorting technique, precisely because they handle each item more than one time each. In other words, the way the computer breaks its problems apart can also have an enormous impact on overall efficiency.

Transhipping operations take advantage of another efficiency-enhancing way of breaking a problem apart then putting it back together in a different way. If IBM's transportation clerks in New York can fill a train car with personal computers bound for San Francisco, shipping costs per unit will be much lower than if the computers are shipped separately in batches of one.

Of course, many orders for one or two computers arrive at shipping and receiving. Consequently, the shipping clerks can achieve shipping efficiencies only if they hang on to cross-country orders until they have accumulated a train car full bound for the same general destination. When the shipment arrives at San Francisco, the workers there break the orders apart, then ship the individual computers in small batches to their local destinations.

The next time you bring home a trunkload of groceries from your supermarket, you can try a small transhipping operation of your own. Most people put their groceries away by removing the food items one at a time as they place each one into refrigerator, freezer, pantry, etc.

Next time try breaking up the task in a completely different way. Start by taking all the food items out of the paper bags together, while scattering them across your countertop. Then scoop up an appropriate armload of items and dump them into the pantry—all at once! Another armload goes into the freezer. Another for the refrigerator, and so on. With a little practice, you will soon find that this simple "transhipping" technique will allow you to put your groceries away in half the time it usually takes.

Incidentally, your spring cleaning time can also be cut in half if you break that task into two separate parts: *cleaning* and *admiring*. Whenever you encounter some item such as an old love letter or an antique lamp that appears to require your admiration, put it aside in a special pile. Later, at bedtime, set aside a few minutes to admire—all at once—the items in your "admiration stack."

Lesson 19
Using the Standard Worksheets to Break
Your Own Problems into Smaller Bite-Size Pieces

What a gorgeous one
*   that fat sleek huge*
*   old chestnut*
I could not get at
     — Issa, 19th Century Japanese Haiku Master

The blank worksheets at the end of this lesson are provided so you can work toward the solution of the problem you formulated in the last chapter. Restate your problem clearly and concisely on page 1 of the two worksheets. Use enough carefully chosen words in your formulation to let your emotions show through. Do not write a truncated or cryptic version of your problem. Formulate it with enough simple words so a stranger would understand your problem. For some reason, when an otherwise thoughtful person formulates the same problem several times, the formulation tends to get shorter and shorter until the problem virtually disappears. Don't let that happen to you. Words are cheap, so use them liberally. Sometimes an accurate formulation of a problem in its complete form can lead directly to one or more viable solutions. Truncated versions do not usually tend to lead to anything.

On the second page of the worksheets, draw one or more balloon diagrams in which you break your problem into its component parts. Be sure to leave space at the bottom of the page. When the balloon diagram is finished, use the space at the bottom to list any solutions that suggest themselves.

Come back to the balloon diagram several times over the next few days. Think about each of its component parts, then make additional notes in the margins. If your diagram gets too messy or complicated, take out a fresh sheet of paper and draw a revised version. Engineering quadrille paper with its grid of crisscrossing blue lines can be very helpful for this kind of exercise.

Each subsequent chapter ends with one or two additional worksheets designed to help you devise other ways to solve your problem. Appendix C contains a complete set of blank worksheets. Good luck in your adventuresome quest!

What is your problem? _____
_____
_____
_____

① BREAKING YOUR PROBLEM APART AND PUTTING IT
BACK TOGETHER AGAIN IN A DIFFERENT WAY

Balloon diagrams are powerful tools that can help you break your problems apart
and put them back together again in novel and interesting ways. Draw a balloon
diagram that breaks your problem—or some aspect of that problem—into its
component parts. Relax and enjoy this exercise. Leave a little space at the bottom of
the page.

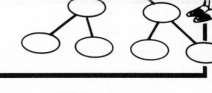

At the bottom of the page list solutions that occurred to you while you were drawing
the balloon diagram.

Is there some way to modify, combine, or eliminate some of
these parts for improved efficiency?

BREAKING THROUGH

Chapter 2
Taking a Fresh Look at the Interfaces

"It is difficult to say what is impossible. For the dream of yesterday is the hope of today and the reality of tomorrow."
— American Rocket Pioneer, Robert Goddard

In 1961 when President John F. Kennedy delivered his rousing speech asking Congress to join him in conquering the moon, our country had not yet orbited a single astronaut. Yet eight years later—largely due to the efforts of a single creative individual—Neil Armstrong and Buzz Aldrin gently lowered themselves down onto the lunar surface.

Later missions would produce far more important scientific benefits, but no one, not even the most hard-nosed geologist, could think of science at that point during the history-making trip. There was only one thought: that these daring young men get back home safely. A shimmering blast-off from the moon, a graceful rendezvous with the larger spacecraft circling overhead, and three tense days of coasting through space ended in a safe recovery in the middle of the Pacific. And suddenly, the world was ecstatic!

Londoners danced and sang at Trafalgar Square in front of giant television screens. A sign on Tokyo's tallest building read: "Three cheers for Apollo 11!"

At a New Delhi hotel, an American tourist awoke when he heard the hotel staff gathering outside his bedroom. When he emerged, they applauded while a gardener hung a garland of flowers around his neck.

The *Christian Science Monitor* commented: "We can all stand a little taller, feel a little stronger because of what these men did." And a Boston astronomer received a telegram from a Russian researcher. It read "What it must be like to be an American!"

Three hundred thousand people worked on the project, often late into the night. But in a very real sense, one man with one simple, creative idea made it possible for our country to fulfill President Kennedy's dream. One man with one idea. What had he done? How had he done it?

When President Kennedy asked his countrymen to capture the moon, Werner von Braun and his colleagues were still trying to choose between two concepts for carrying out the mission. The first called for a single 12-million-pound booster that would lift off the launch pad, then fly up to the moon dropping off increasingly smaller stages along the way. The three Apollo astronauts would then dip down to the lunar surface, explore it for a few days, then fly back to earth and reenter the atmosphere inside the Apollo capsule. The 12-million-pound booster required for this approach was roughly 100 times heavier than any booster America had launched up to that time.

Just in case building such a large booster rocket proved to be too cumbersome and difficult, a second concept was also being considered. It called for two six-million-pound boosters whose upper stages would rendezvous in earth orbit. Once the linkup had been accomplished, the mission sequence would be identical to the one used in the first concept. Both approaches would require the same total lift-off weight, but mission planners hoped that building two six-million-pound boosters would be considerably easier than building one large booster weighing twice as much.

Both of these two concepts were still being evaluated when one clever individual working almost all alone figured out how to carry out the mission with greatly improved efficiency. His name was John Houbolt, an engineer at the Goddard Research Center in Greenbelt, Maryland. For the benefit it produced, Houbolt's idea was surprisingly simple. Instead of flying the astronauts directly to the moon aboard one gigantic booster, or linking two half-sized boosters together in earth orbit, his plan called for a *rendezvous in orbit around the moon*.

When the astronauts reached lunar orbit, two of them would enter a smaller craft for their descent to the lunar surface. The third astronaut would remain in the heavier craft circling overhead in orbit around the moon where he would wait for their return (see Figure 2.1).

Because a small spacecraft would be carried down to the surface of the moon—and an even smaller one would be lifted back up again—the booster rocket could be built on a much smaller scale. In fact, according to Houbolt's careful calculations,

Figure 2.1 Taking a fresh look at the interfaces: lunar orbit rendezvous.

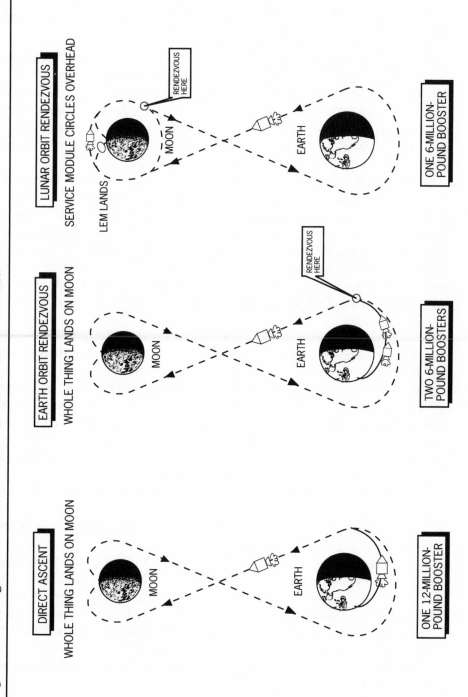

the entire vehicle would weigh only about six million pounds. In other words, with lunar orbit rendezvous, the mission could be accomplished with only *half* the lift-off weight required by the other two techniques!

Initially, John Houbolt's creative innovation met stiff resistance at NASA, so he had to be very persistent to get anyone's ear. But, eventually, von Braun ordered his best rocket scientists to compare all three techniques to see which one would deliver the best performance. Their simulations conclusively demonstrated that John Houbolt was correct; lunar orbit rendezvous was *cheaper*, *faster*, and *safer* than the other two techniques. So it was quickly adopted for use on all of the Apollo missions.

In 1969 Neil Armstrong and Buzz Aldrin touched down onto the lunar surface where they frolicked like two lighthearted gazelles largely due to one man's superb problem-solving skills. John Houbolt deserves much more credit than he has ever received, but his inspiration came from a widely used approach quite popular among aerospace engineers: *He took a fresh look at the interfaces.* By moving the rendezvous interface to a different location, he reduced the weight of the Saturn V booster by a factor of two, shortened its development time by several years, kept the astronauts considerably safer, and cut billions of dollars off the cost of each journey to the moon.

Taking a fresh look at the interfaces is the second winning strategy on the arc of creativity. Often it works wonders with little human effort—except thinking about how it should be used.

Interfaces occur where two dissimilar things come together. The shoreline forms an interface between land and water, for instance, and your front door is an effective interface that separates your cozy living room from the cold, cruel world outside. Zippers, buttons, snaps, and fasteners are also interfaces. A tin can is an effective interface that keeps the vegetables in your soup fresh and crisp. Take away the interface and the contents will gradually droop into a soggy mess.

Most interfaces are so simple, effective, and unobtrusive we seldom ever notice them at all. But they are worthy of special attention because it is often surprisingly easy—and inexpensive—to manipulate the interfaces to produce surprisingly fruitful results.

You can move an interface to a new location—as John Houbolt did for the Apollo Mission. Or you can modify it to make it more efficient. In some cases a new interface can be introduced or an old one can be deleted. Sometimes an existing interface can be adapted to a useful purpose. Henry Ford used this approach when he found an ingenious way to cut the cost of manufacturing his beloved Model T. In a later lesson you will find out exactly how he did it. But first let's go into your bathroom together where you will get an opportunity to see how important a well-designed interface can be.

Lesson 20
Discovering Some of the Interfaces
Lurking in Your Bathroom

"All our dreams can come true—if we have the courage to pursue them."
— Chief Executive Imagineer, Walt Disney

Years ago when I first heard about—but had not yet seen—the electric toothbrush, the concept sounded entirely impractical to me, in part, because I did not yet understand the interfaces. When I tried to visualize a bathroom equipped with electric toothbrushes, I saw only chaos in my mind's eye. Would each family have four or five electric toothbrushes plugged into the bathroom socket in a tense tangle of electric wires? Or would each individual have to unplug the previous occupant's toothbrush before she would plug in her own to brush her teeth? At that time small electric motors retailed for about $20 each. Would each American family be willing to spend $100 to save such an insignificant amount of manual labor? Would they tolerate a dense clutter of electric wires in their bathrooms just for the experience of owning a flashy, but largely useless, gadget incorporating the latest design?

I was convinced that the electric toothbrush could never be a marketing success until I learned how its designers had introduced a clever new interface into their automatic tooth-brushing machine. They had broken the handle in the middle so they could attach and detach stubby little brushes one at a time! This new interface allowed a single electric motor to power the toothbrushes for all the members in an entire family! It also allowed worn brushes to be replaced for less than a dollar each.

Actually, once I discovered how the electric toothbrush was constructed, I realized that, decades earlier, designers of the Gillette safety razor had embraced a similar approach. The old-fashioned straight razor it replaced came as a single unit with its metal blade permanently attached to the handle. Before each use the blade was sharpened by carefully rubbing it many times over an abrasive leather strap. Gillette and his colleagues introduced a convenient new interface so the blade could be detached from the razor. The blade could then be removed and discarded when it became dull, while the much more expensive handle could be reused. Of course, selling replacement blades soon became big business as Gillette and his backers had predicted.

If Gillette had not included this new interface, the safety razor would never have become a marketing success and he would have stayed painfully poor instead of growing filthy rich. Yet, interestingly enough, in our more affluent era, the designers of the *disposable* safety razor have now deleted that all-important interface. When a disposable razor's blade grows dull from repeated use, its owner throws the whole thing away—handle and blade!

This historical development teaches us an important lesson: Interfaces should never be regarded as frozen in concrete. If the situation changes, it makes good sense to go back and take *another* fresh look at the interface.

Lesson 21
Noticing How the Interfaces Change at Your Local Supermarket

"Never let your head hang down. Never give up and sit and grieve. Find another way."
— American Baseball Star, Satchel Paige

When I was a fidgety youngster, my father sometimes took me along with him to the A.K. Lewis grocery store at the base of Cemetery Hill beside the old train depot in Springfield, Kentucky. We waited patiently until our turn finally came. Then my father would look at his grocery list and call off the first item: "a loaf of white bread." Mr. Lewis would then waddle through the store to retrieve a big, fresh loaf for us. When he returned to the counter, he and my father would stop and exchange a little gossip. My father would then read off the second item, "a bottle of Karo syrup," which Mr. Lewis would slowly retrieve. Then he would return to the counter for a little more gossip. . . .

Their transactions moved at a snail's pace, primarily because the interfaces were all wrong. Even at that young age, I once proposed a simple change in the interfaces to speed things up a bit, but my father could see absolutely no merit in my humble proposal: "Why don't you just give the shopping list to Mr. Lewis?"

At the time, I could not imagine what could possibly be wrong with my snazzy idea, but one difficulty does occur to me at this late date. At most, my father had a fourth-grade education, so he probably could not accept the way I wanted to rearrange the shopping list interface because he felt the need to conceal his crude penmanship and his spelling errors from Mr. Lewis.

Within a few years, of course, customer/clerk interfaces were turned upside down when Krogers and the A&P finally came to town. In a self-service supermarket we hardly ever interface with clerks. Instead, we merely shovel any items we want to purchase into our supermarket carts. What a difference in the interfaces! Mr. Lewis found that he could not compete, so an empty store soon stood near the old rusty depot at the foot of Cemetery Hill as a sad monument to a more efficient interface.

The interfaces in today's supermarkets are still becoming more efficient. Supermarket scanners, self-service checkout, and vending-machine supermarkets are all bringing new changes, sometimes in totally unexpected ways.

In Bergen, Norway, I encountered a new wrinkle in customer/clerk interfaces when I went into a small food store to buy seedless grapes. The produce section was rigged with a simple electronic scale with several rows of buttons. A customer buying bananas or peanuts, for instance, pushes the "banana" or "peanut" button, then places the purchase on the scale. The scale produces a sticky label listing the appropriate price, which the customer attaches to the produce bag. At the checkout counter, the bananas are not reweighed; instead, an electronic scanner checks the label to obtain the appropriate price.

"But don't some of your customers slip a little extra produce into their bags after they have put the label on?" I asked one of the checkout clerks.

A big grin flashed across his face. "Americans always ask me that question," he replied, "but we save so much time and money with the new machine, a few dishonest customers could never pilfer enough fruits and vegetables to cancel out the gains."

Interfaces matter when you are trying to develop creative solutions. That is why the next lesson deals with concrete ways in which you can become more sensitive to the important interfaces that surround you in everyday life. In a big, stable bureaucracy, it is often impossible to make fundamental modifications, so making simpler interface changes becomes even more important. "I can't change the direction of the wind," said country singer Jimmy Dean, "but I can adjust my sails to always reach my destination."

Lesson 22
Learning to Spot and Manipulate the Interfaces You Encounter Every Day

"A man with a new idea is a crank until the idea succeeds."
— American Author, Mark Twain

In its classical meaning, an interface is typically defined as "a surface that lies between two bodies or spaces and forms their common boundary." Biologists have long known that life thrives at the interfaces. Marshlands, which were called "swamps" when I was young, support so many living creatures because they happen to be located at the triple interface between land, water, and air. Take away any one of those three elements, and two of the interfaces will disappear and many of the marshland creatures that had been thriving will no longer survive.

Creative solutions also thrive at the interfaces because that is where both problems and opportunities are encountered in large and imposing numbers. Manipulate the interfaces successfully and, sometimes, you will experience big gains in efficiency. When illegally parked cars are towed away, complicated and expensive interfaces come into play between driver, police, tow trucks, and impound storage yards. Why not "impound" the car where it is parked without moving it? A "Denver Boot" attached to the front wheel makes this possible because it renders the car undrivable. With a Denver Boot, many of the complicated interfaces automatically disappear.

A turnstile is another device that simplifies the interfaces. A turnstile is, in effect, a "people valve." It allows human bodies to pass through in one direction, but not in the other. Imagine how many extra guards we would need in subways, for instance, if subway designers had not introduced "people valves" to control the flow of paying customers. Parking lots use "car valves" in a conceptually similar manner to simplify their interfaces with drivers. Can you describe at least two completely different kinds of "car valves"?

How can you learn, as John Houbolt and King Camp Gillette did, to focus your attention on the important interfaces when you are attempting to discover simple, creative solutions? One easy way to begin educating yourself is to carefully notice and analyze some of the interfaces you encounter in the process of daily living. Start with something simple and obvious: See how many different kinds of special-purpose doors (interfaces) you can find. When you notice an interesting door, ask yourself a few pertinent questions so you can begin to feel your way toward new insights into how it works and why it has such an unusual design.

Why are so many high-rise buildings equipped with revolving doors, for instance? Why do the doors on delivery vans slide sideways instead of swinging open the way car doors do? Why do some kinds of doors open with a key, while others are secured by combination locks? What is the purpose of the "lock box" commonly used by real estate agents? What kinds of doors tend to have no locks at all? What kinds of business establishments are usually equipped with automatic doors? Why?

If you grow tired of that funny little game, try studying another kind of interface: man-made containers such as boxes and bags, cartons and cans, cellophane wrappers, and the like. Later in this chapter you will learn how the packages in supermarkets and the coat hangers in fancy hotels have been rigged with new interfaces to cut down on shoplifting and petty pilfering by customers and guests.

In the meantime, be on the lookout for some of the man/machine interfaces you encounter in your private life and on the job. What makes some machines so simple and easy to operate? Why are others so nightmarishly difficult to put through their paces? These simple exercises will be good practice for you as you begin to seek out new ways to move, modify, delete, or use common everyday interfaces for useful purposes. While you are busy pondering the mysteries of today's rather complicated interfaces, try to answer a much simpler question my father often asked me when I was in front of the fireplace riding on his knee: "Does the mortar hold the bricks *apart* or does it hold them *together*?"

Lesson 23
Making Megabucks by Designing Today's User-Friendly Machines

"Things may come to those who wait, but only those things left by those who hustle."
— American President, Abraham Lincoln

Manufacturers of today's electronic devices invariably claim that every machine they bring to market incorporates simple, user-friendly features, but, in reality, this is often little more than wishful thinking. Like Mortimer in Shakespeare's *Henry IV* they use weasel words to promise quite a bit more than they can deliver:

> *Mortimer*: I can call spirits from the vasty deep.
> *Hotspur*:   Why, so can I, or so can any man; but will they come when you call them?

Actually, many of today's wondrous electronic machines are considerably more difficult to operate than the mechanical devices they have replaced. This is a significant problem that is costing our society billions of dollars every year. It is also affecting our balance of trade because Japanese and European products often feature superior user-friendly design.

Dr. Donald Norman of the Institute of Cognitive Science at the University of California at San Diego estimates that there are "20,000 things—from cars and can openers to home computers and Coke machines—that ordinary people must learn to operate." Many of those devices—perhaps the majority—are very frustrating and demoralizing to use because their interfaces are so poorly designed.

Dr. Norman met one New Jersey physician who is completely baffled by the many controls on his digital wristwatch. But with simple, creative problem-solving techniques, he had found a way to circumvent the difficulty he has encountered. According to Dr. Norman: "He lets it read an hour later during daylight savings time." Kenneth Olsen, the computer whiz who founded Digital Equipment Corporation, courageously tells his friends that he is unable to cope with the complexities of modern machines. According to an article by William F. Allman in *U.S. News and World Report*, "Company stockholders gave him a warm round of applause when he admitted at an annual meeting that he couldn't figure out how to heat a cup of coffee in the company's microwave oven."

The cash registers at McDonald's provide us with an instructive example of how man/machine interfaces can be designed to achieve more effective results. The interfaces for a conventional cash register are not particularly user-friendly because the clerk must key in a string of digits to define the price of each item the customer decides to buy.

By contrast, the cash registers at McDonald's are beautifully designed and extraordinarily easy to use. If a customer buys a hamburger, the clerk merely pushes the "hamburger" button. The cash register, which is actually a small computer, automatically checks its memory to find the price of the item (hamburger, french fries, milk shake, etc.), then adds the proper price to its running total. If the price of an item changes—or a new dish is added to the menu—the experts reprogram the computer and, if necessary, relabel the appropriate buttons.

By simplifying the man/machine interfaces on all of its cash registers, the managers at McDonald's have greatly reduced training costs and eliminated many worrisome errors. Customer service is also faster and employees are much easier to recruit from today's gradually shrinking labor pools.

Think about the way the designers who work for McDonald's approached their task of improving the design of their cash registers. Is there some way you can adopt a similar approach in your own business or profession? Work it out in detail. Estimate the labor savings that might result, and turn it in as an employee suggestion. Each year American industry pays millions of dollars for usable suggestions.

If your company is producing and marketing a product with poorly designed man/machine interfaces, important sales may be lost as a result. Try fiddling with the interfaces to make them more user-friendly. Start by sketching your preliminary ideas on paper. Can the machine's knobs and switches be better positioned? Can summary instructions be attached directly to the machine? Does form follow function? Is the unit attractive and inviting to operate? Or does it have a hostile or forbidding look?

Each year I teach short courses and deliver lectures on various topics mostly in North America, Europe, Asia, and Australia. So far, I have not been able to find a suitable travel alarm clock. Many are too delicate to survive the rigors of travel. Most have buzzers that are not loud enough. Almost all of them are bafflingly complicated with buttons, switches, and displays that are almost impossible to decipher. After spending a fitful night sandwiched aboard an airplane bound for Munich, Sydney, or Istanbul, I am in no mood to struggle with needlessly complicated alarm-clock controls.

Why doesn't some enterprising entrepreneur develop and market a travel alarm with loud, but pleasant, chimes and two separate digital readouts, one showing what time it is, and the other showing the wakeup time? Lighted displays should also mark either "AM" or "PM." Each display should have its own dedicated single-purpose buttons and switches. Every time the user changes the setting on any button or switch, the clock would do something in response to indicate that it understands what its user is trying to do. How about voice synthesizer chips?

My dream clock would probably cost a few dollars more than the ones now available with a single multipurpose display, but it would be quite a bit easier to operate and weary travelers could check its status at a glance from anywhere in the room without touching a single button.

Lesson 24
Learning How to Modify the Interfaces with Multicolored Balloon Diagrams

"There's nothing in the middle of the road but yellow stripes and dead armadillos."
— Jim Hightower, Texas Commissioner of Agriculture

In Chapter 1 you learned how to build topic outlines, flowcharts, and balloon diagrams to partition your problem into smaller and more manageable components. Then, once you had completed a rudimentary drawing of this type, you learned how to use boxes of various shapes together with colored marking pens to modify it in various specific ways to uncover more imaginative solutions.

All the methods discussed in Chapter 1 are simple and easy to understand, but many creative people seem to prefer the balloon diagram, a free-flowing sketch that consists of notes, ovals, and branching lines. The next time you get a new assignment, try creating a balloon diagram to help you brainstorm new ideas for its efficient execution. When your balloon diagram begins to get fairly complicated, try marking some of the critical interfaces, then fiddle with each one to see if you can move, modify, delete, or enhance it to achieve improved results. Remember how easy it was for John Houbolt to save billions of dollars by moving the rendezvous interface for the Apollo Project to a different location?

Any complicated device such as a new airplane, a digital computer, or a copying machine can be broken apart in a number of different ways to highlight different kinds of interfaces. If you divide a commercial jetliner into various enclosed compartments, for instance, your attention will be focused on some of its rather large interfaces such as the doors, curtains, and walls that separate the enclosed compartments. If you divide that same airplane into major subassemblies such as wings, tail, fuselage, etc., smaller interfaces like rivets and fasteners are more likely to emerge.

Some creative individuals enjoy working with a balloon diagram so much they keep expanding and refining it until it includes dozens of balloons filled with all sorts of bizarre labels. The ideal balloon diagram, however, should include a reasonable number of important items, usually somewhere between 10 and 30.

If your balloon diagram keeps sprouting uncontrollable numbers of balloons, put down your pen for a moment and take a little time to think about what you are trying to do. Mark those balloons and their interfaces that seem to have the most relevance to the problem at hand. Then draw a simpler version that incorporates only that smaller number of balloons. Remember, the primary purpose of drawing a balloon diagram is not to divide your task into the largest possible number of parts. The purpose is to find creative solutions.

The balloon diagram in Figure 2.2 reiterates some of the problems the busy business traveler encounters in a typical hotel room: scalding showers, poor lighting, too few coat hangers, wakeup calls that never come. In this new version we have, in addition, delineated the interfaces between the members of the hotel staff and their harried guests. The problem with wakeup calls, for instance, can be solved by the hotel telephone operators so we have written "hotel operators" on that particular branching line. Housekeeping usually provides the room service menus, so we have written "housekeeping staff" on that branching line.

Once we have marked each branching line with an appropriate set of labels, we can scan the diagram to see if there is any way we could change the interfaces to make things run more smoothly. Instead of blaming the hotel operators each time they fail to complete a wakeup call, for instance, we could install alarm clocks in the guest rooms. And instead of badgering the housekeeping crew to make sure room service menus are in all the guest rooms, we could display the menus electronically on the video screen. Scan the balloon diagram for a few minutes and each time you have such an insight or idea, add pertinent sketches and notes to the margins to highlight what you have learned.

Wait an hour. Then scan your notes and sketches one at a time as you brainstorm new methods for making hotel guests more comfortable and content. How about a room service menu permanently attached to the telephone, for instance, or how about having the guest's wakeup time displayed electronically in the corner of his television screen? Develop more solutions of your own by making notes as you go along.

Now put your balloon diagram aside for a day or two and think about something else. Later, when you come back to it, see if you can expand it by adding new problems and new solutions. Play with the diagram a few minutes at a time over several days. This assignment provides an excellent opportunity for you to exercise your creativity and search for major breakthroughs the same way the experts do— by fiddling with the interfaces in various specific ways.

Figure 2.2 Problems for the business traveler (version 4).

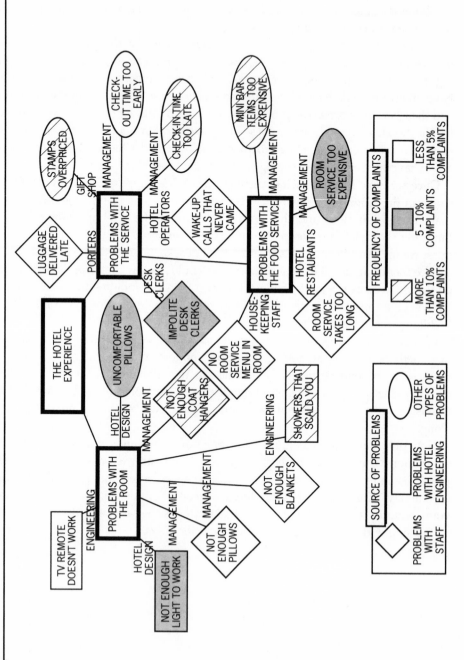

Lesson 25
Discovering the Benefits of User-Friendly Design

*"Success seems to be connected with action. Successful men keep moving.
They make mistakes, but they don't quit."*
— The Nation's Innkeeper, Conrad Hilton

Steven Jobs and his contemporaries at Apple, Inc., used a number of clever techniques when they developed the simple man/machine interfaces for their MacIntosh computer. One easy way to operate the MacIntosh, for instance, is to slide a small control device called a "mouse" over a flat horizontal surface. The "tail" of the mouse is connected to the computer. When the user moves the mouse along, it sends commands into the computer that make a tiny arrow trace out a duplicate trajectory on the screen.

The computer is operated by "pointing" the arrow at various icons (pictures). To discard a file, for instance, the user merely points the arrow toward a picture of a tin trash can then clicks a button on top of the mouse. With cleverly designed interfaces like that, computer ownership has become inviting for individuals who are baffled by the inner workings of a computer. This has opened up vast new markets for Apple's cleverly designed products.

If you are assigned to design a new machine for your company, try to make its interfaces as simple and user-friendly as you possibly can. Never assume that your customers will be interested in fiddling with your machine for its own sake. Generally speaking, they will only be interested in what the machine can do to help them in some practical way.

Responsive feedback control mechanisms help make machines user-friendly. When you do something to the machine, it should immediately respond to let you know it understands. All of its responses should be simple and logical. One of the Japanese copying machines in my office changes two different settings in more-or-less random patterns, when you push any of several different buttons. Its behavior is so illogical, office workers hate to use it. In fact, they hate it so much they will actually go to a different part of the building to search out a different machine even though they know it usually has a waiting line.

Whenever you push a button on a well-designed machine it should click, beep, light up, or take some other responsive action. Many time-sharing terminals merely sit in total silence while they are serving other clients. An occasional signal of some kind would at least let you know whether your terminal is still plugged into the system.

If you are designing a new machine, make sure it has user-friendly controls. You can do this by thinking about its operation from the vantage point of the typical user, developing simple buttons and switches, and rigging it with responsive feedback control.

Even if you never get an opportunity to design a new machine, there is another way to practice your skills for developing effective man/machine interfaces: you can design a user-friendly business form! Many of the forms we are required to fill out each day are dauntingly complicated, but they do not have to be that way.

Consider our federal income tax forms, for instance. Many people are convinced that their complexity stems directly from the complexity of our tax laws. But actually, studies have shown that the present forms could be redesigned so the average person would require only one-sixth as much time as it now takes to supply the same information. How is it possible to make our income tax forms so much easier to use? It could be accomplished by substituting flowcharts for today's tedious line-by-line accounting format.

When flowcharts of this type were tested in Denmark, their designers found that each required entry and the interaction between those entries became largely self-explanatory in the new format. Consequently, the time required to fill out each set of forms dropped by almost 85 percent!

Perhaps you can substitute flowcharts for some of the forms used in your company, or you may be able to use some other approach to redesign a form to make it simpler and easier to understand. Even if you have no intention of getting the new version adopted, this is an excellent exercise to help you learn how to develop user-friendly interfaces.

To help you get started, an extraordinarily complicated travel expense form is presented in Figure 2.3 together with an improved version in Figure 2.4 that is quite a bit easier to understand. Analyze the user-friendly features of the new form. Notice its self-evident architecture. Notice how it includes icons and arrows to help users grasp at a glance what kind of information should go in each one of its boxes. Study its self-checking features. Now see if you can make further improvements. A flowchart might help. Give it a try.

By using similar techniques, try redesigning one of the forms you are required to use at your office or one you have received in the mail. Wasted effort worth billions of dollars goes down the drain every year because the designers of our business forms do not bother to create user-friendly interfaces for the forms they are assigned to make.

If someone helps you with this effort and you end up with a monetary payment such as a suggestion award, bonus, or salary increase, find a way to share the wealth with those who helped you in your little project. A 1% "finder's fee" would not seem to be an inappropriate reward for those who provide free work or moral support. If you end up with $10,000 extra, sharing a $100 symbol of your "joint" achievement would not be out of line.

Figure 2.3 Employee expense report.

EMPLOYEE EXPENSE REPORT

(MUST BE TYPED OR FILLED OUT IN BLACK INK)

NAME	SOCIAL SECURITY #	DIVISION	LOCATION	DEPARTMENT #	MAIL CODE	PHONE EXT	TRAVEL AUTH #	WEEK ENDING

BUSINESS PURPOSE (Provide a complete description, do not use abbreviations/acronyms)	☐ INTERIM REPORT ☐ FINAL REPORT

TRAVEL	1. PERIOD	DAY/DATE								FINANCE USE ONLY
	2. TRAVEL TIME	DEPARTURE								
		ARRIVAL								
	3. CITY	FROM								
		TO								
		TO								
	4. PERSONAL AUTOMOBILE MILEAGE									
TRAVEL EXPENSES	5. MEALS	a. BREAKFAST	$	$	$	$	$	$	$	
		b. LUNCH								
		c. DINNER								
		d. ALCOHOLIC BEVERAGES								
		e. SUBTOTAL								
		f. ALLOWANCE (See instruct.)								
		g. LOWER OF 5e. OR 5f.								
	6. LODGING									
	7. INCIDENTALS	a. LAUNDRY AND VALET								
		b. TIPS								
		c. OTHER (See instructions)								
		d. SUBTOTAL								TOTALS
	8. TOTAL LINES 5g., 6, AND 7c.									$
	9. OTHER	a. PHONE/WIRE								XXXXXXXXXXXXXXX
		b. SPECIAL FEES								XXXXXXXXXXXXXXX
		c.								XXXXXXXXXXXXXXX
	10. TRANS-PORTATION	a. INTER-CITY								XXXXXXXXXXXXXXX
		b. RENTAL CAR								XXXXXXXXXXXXXXX
		c. PERSONAL AUTO @ ________								XXXXXXXXXXXXXXX
		d. LOCAL								XXXXXXXXXXXXXXX
		e. MISC. (PROVIDE DETAILS)								XXXXXXXXXXXXXXX
	11. TOTAL LINES 9 AND 10		$	$	$	$	$	$	$	$

NONTRAVEL EXP.						SUBSTANTIATED NON-TRAVEL EXPENSES IN SECTION 19 (Reverse Side)
12. FOOD						
13. ALCOHOLIC BEVERAGES						
14. OTHER	a.				$	$
	b.				$	$
	c.					
15. TOTAL LINES 12 THRU 14		$	$			
16. TOTAL EXPENSES LINES 8, 11, AND 15		$	$			

18. EXPENSES CHARGED DIRECTLY TO COMPANY CREDIT CARDS, ETC., AND NOT INCLUDED ABOVE

MEMO	DATE	DESCRIPTION	AMOUNT
			$
			$
			$
			$

17. EXPENSE RECONCILIATION

TOTAL EMPLOYEE EXPENSES (from line 16)		$
LESS: ADVANCES RECEIVED		

DATE	LOCATION	FINANCE USE ONLY	
			XXXXXXXXXXXXXXXXXXX
			XXXXXXXXXXXXXXXXXXX
			$

LESS: CO. BALANCE OUTSTANDING FROM PRIOR REPORT	$
PLUS: BALANCE DUE EMPLOYEE FROM PRIOR REPORT	$
BALANCE ☐ DUE COMPANY RCPT # _____	$
☐ DUE EMPLOYEE	$
LONG TERM ADVANCE NOT LIQUIDATED	$

HAVE UNUSED TRANSPORTATION TICKETS BEEN RETURNED TO ACCOUNTING?   ☐ YES   ☐ NO   ☐ NOT APPLICABLE

DID YOU USE COMPANY AIRCRAFT?   ☐ YES   ☐ NO   IF YES, PROVIDE DATE(S) & AIRCRAFT TYPE

REMARKS (USE SEPARATE SHEET IF NECESSARY)

ACCOUNTING DEPARTMENT USE ONLY

ACCOUNT DISTRIBUTION	AMOUNT
	$
	$
	$
	$
	$

APPROVAL (SIGNATURE AND MGMT LEVEL)   DATE

DELIVER CHECK TO

CHECK AUTHORIZATION
DRAW CHECK IN FAVOR OF ABOVE-NAMED INDIVIDUAL IN THE AMOUNT OF
$ _____   APPROVED

I hereby certify to the best of my knowledge and belief that (1) all information on this report is true and (2) all expenses claimed on this report are based on actual costs incurred and are consistent with Company/Operations/Division procedures and the instructions on the reverse side of this form.

EMPLOYEE SIGNATURE   DATE

FOOTINGS AND EXT BY	AUDITED BY	APPROVED BY

FORM M26-C REV 10-86 (FRONT)

Figure 2.4 Revised version of employee expense report.

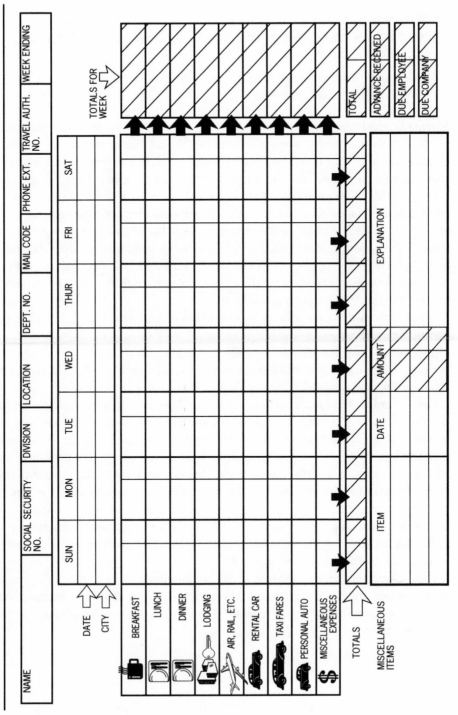

Lesson 26
Clever Ideas from the Moviemakers and Henry Ford

"Whether you think you can, or think you can't—you're right."
— Automotive Pioneer, Henry Ford

Moving or modifying an important interface can produce surprisingly productive results. But there are other ways to manipulate the interfaces: eliminating them, for example, or adapting them for a completely different purpose. The addition of sound to motion picture film provides us with an instructive example of the over-riding benefits of eliminating a bothersome interface. In a series of disastrous experiments, the voices of early actors were recorded on phonograph records, which were then played in crude synchronization with the plastic film being threaded through the projector. Movie audiences howled with laughter whenever the images on the screen got out of sync by as much as a second or two. Elaborate adjustment mechanisms were constantly being developed, but none of them worked well enough to make the howls of laughter go away.

Fortunately, a practical solution was eventually perfected by electronics expert Lee de Forest. It consisted of placing the sound track directly on the plastic motion picture film. Once this was successfully accomplished, the troublesome interface between image and sound was essentially eliminated. Consequently, the synchronization problem was solved once and for all.

Henry Ford was just as clever when he figured out how to *use an existing interface* (a wooden packing crate) in an interesting and effective manner. His vendors and suppliers thought he was just being an eccentric millionaire when he specified precisely what kind of wooden crates they were to use when they packaged their parts for delivery to his Michigan factory. He even gave them explicit instructions on the location to drill each hole in the boards. Several months later the vendors learned—from a popular magazine article—why Ford had been so finicky and precise in his packaging specifications. When the parts arrived at his factory, he instructed his assembly crews to take each packing crate apart and reuse the wood to make the floorboards for his Model T!

Think about the key interfaces in your own profession. Try to locate the specific interfaces that are causing problems. If you discover a troublesome interface, consider various possibilities for eliminating it to save money—or modifying it for use in another purpose.

Lesson 27
Building and Remodeling Today's Theft-Proof Coat Hangers

"One man with courage is a majority."
— American President, Andrew Jackson

Now that you have learned how to focus your attention on some of the important interfaces, it's time for you to take a little test. Try to think of at least a half dozen ways in which everyday, ordinary interfaces have been modified to reduce the spread of crime. One obvious example has been to put more secure locks on doors and windows. Another is to package small objects (such as lipstick and mascara) in oversized containers so they will be more difficult for shoplifters to conceal.

By thinking about this assignment for a few minutes, you should be able to list a number of other popular approaches. And, if you are truly dedicated, you may be able to devise one or two *new* ways to modify key interfaces to reduce growing crime.

Have you ever noticed how hotels try to keep their guests from stealing their expensive wooden coat hangers? They merely change the interface in the closet to allow the introduction of a hanger with no hook. Hangers designed with that funny little nub will not interface properly with the horizontal rods in an ordinary closet, so hotel coat hangers are largely useless outside the hotel.

This approach works extremely well. But it also opens up an attractive market for a new kind of interface: an inexpensive attachable hook for hotel coat hangers to adapt them for use in the home (see Figure 2.5). Hotels have been clever in the design of their coat hangers, but their managers may have failed to realize that "necessity is the mother of invention" or, as British actor Christopher Morley once observed, "High heels were invented by a woman who was kissed on the forehead."

Put on your snazziest thinking cap and perhaps you can come up with a practical way to design and build an inexpensive attachable hook to restore the interface. If you are successful in your quest, hotel managers will have to dream up another way to eliminate coat hanger theft.

Figure 2.5   America's need for a new, inexpensive interface for hotel coat hangers.

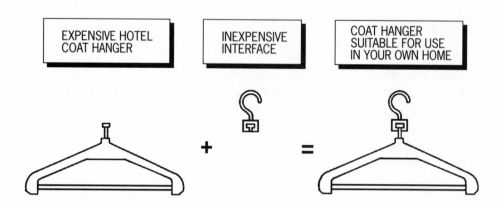

Lesson 28
Seeing the World in a Different Way

"The future belongs to those who believe in the beauty of their dreams."
— First Lady, Eleanor Roosevelt

Creativity is the ability to perceive connections between things that are not obviously connected, to notice subtle patterns others fail to see. Consider Isaac Newton, for instance. In 1665, when he left Cambridge University to escape the Black Plague, he returned to his boyhood home at Woolsthorpe. Shortly after he arrived, he noticed an apple falling from a tree. There was nothing particularly remarkable about falling apples. Others had seen the same thing millions of times before. But the young Newton looked for a new connection.

He wondered if there might be some link between the behavior of that apple hurtling down toward the ground and the pale August moon swinging across the sky. Others had failed to perceive any connection between these two seemingly unrelated events. But Isaac Newton managed to puzzle out a new connection. The force of gravity, he soon realized, was tugging on both apple and moon to govern their trajectories. The moon, however, did not fall because it was moving sideways just fast enough to avoid striking the earth. In effect, it was forever falling around a big circle.

The French mathematician Gottfried Wilhelm von Leibnitz had a long and caustic rivalry with Isaac Newton. Often they were deadlocked in bitter debates and priority battles. Yet von Leibnitz knew for sure that Newton was among the brightest men who had ever lived. "Of all the mathematics developed up until the time of Isaac Newton," he once wrote, "Newton's is, by far, the better half."

As you begin to master the six winning strategies on the arc of creativity you, too, will notice connections between things you never knew existed. That process has, in fact, already started. Before you began reading this chapter, you probably did not appreciate the subtle connection between Project Apollo, the electric toothbrush, and the floorboards in Henry Ford's Model T. But now they are intimately connected in your mind because you now realize that all of them were made more practical by clever individuals who decided to take a fresh look at the interfaces.

Lesson 29
Personal Worksheets for Taking a Fresh Look at the Interfaces

"No one would have crossed the ocean if he could have gotten off the ship in a storm."
— American Industrialist, Charles F. Kettering

Balloon diagrams can help you in a number of ways while you are attempting to learn how to take a fresh look at the interfaces. One promising approach is to break your problem apart using a balloon diagram, then write notes about the appropriate interfaces along its branching lines. Start by formulating your problem on the first of the two worksheets at the end of this lesson. Write a clear, fully defined formulation complete with human emotions in the blank space provided.

On the second worksheet, draw a balloon diagram breaking your problem into its component parts, then write notes defining the appropriate interfaces along the branching lines. If your diagram gets too messy, take a few minutes to redraw it on a fresh sheet of paper.

When you have finished the balloon diagram, write summary notes at the bottom of the page (or on a separate sheet of paper), highlighting any promising solutions that may pop into your head. During the next few days, revisit your balloon diagram and make any new additions that occur to you while you are busy doing something else or while you are studying the diagram itself.

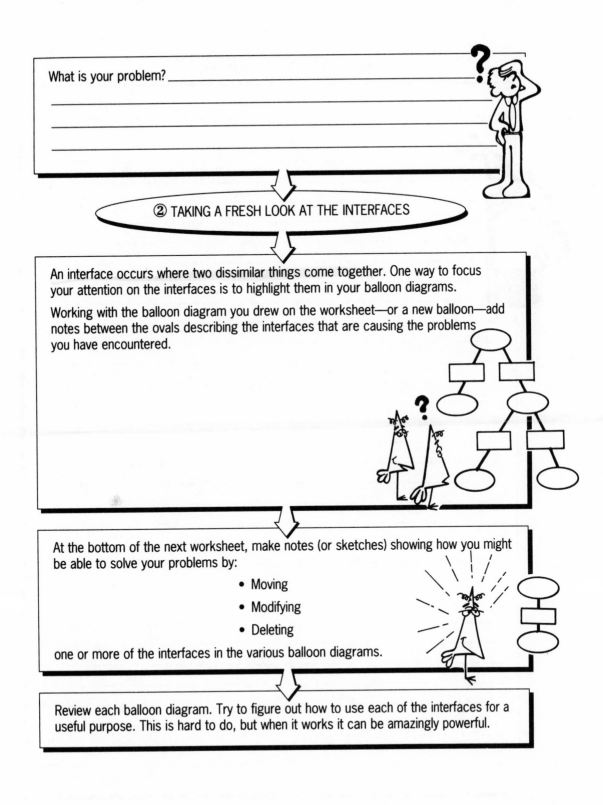

What is your problem? _____
_____
_____
_____

② TAKING A FRESH LOOK AT THE INTERFACES

An interface occurs where two dissimilar things come together. One way to focus your attention on the interfaces is to highlight them in your balloon diagrams.

Working with the balloon diagram you drew on the worksheet—or a new balloon—add notes between the ovals describing the interfaces that are causing the problems you have encountered.

At the bottom of the next worksheet, make notes (or sketches) showing how you might be able to solve your problems by:

- Moving
- Modifying
- Deleting

one or more of the interfaces in the various balloon diagrams.

Review each balloon diagram. Try to figure out how to use each of the interfaces for a useful purpose. This is hard to do, but when it works it can be amazingly powerful.

BREAKING THROUGH

Chapter 3
Reformulating the Problem

"Big shots are only little shots that keep shooting."
— British Actor, Christopher Morley

In the 1960s when trajectory experts at North American Aviation[3] were assigned to evaluate the performance capabilities of the Saturn V moon rocket, we encountered an unexpected difficulty, a difficulty that caused one of our team members—a long, lanky propulsion specialist named Bud Brux—to write an extraordinarily important interoffice memo. A few years later I published a brief account describing what he had accomplished. "If Bud Brux had sent us a map showing where five solid gold Cadillacs were buried in the company parking lot," I observed, "it would not have been worth as much as the memo he actually wrote."

To understand what Bud Brux did and how he did it, you need to know a little about modern rockets and the way we fly them into space. Most high-performance rockets consume liquid propellants from two separate tanks. One tank contains the fuel, usually kerosene or liquid hydrogen. The other contains the oxidizer, usually liquid oxygen. If there is any fuel or oxidizer left over at burnout, it cannot be burned to produce additional thrust because burning requires a mixture of the two fluids. Consequently, any residual propellants remaining at burnout represent dead-weight that has to be carried aloft by the rocket. Leftover residuals degrade the rocket's payload-carrying capabilities.

[3] North American Aviation later became Rockwell International, builders of NASA's space shuttle orbiter.

To minimize the weight of the residual propellants, the engineers who designed the Saturn V moon rocket installed special devices inside the tanks to measure the amount of fuel and oxidizer remaining throughout the flight. The system was then rigged to make small, but continuous, adjustments in the ratio at which the two propellants were being burned. This increased the rocket's performance because it helped ensure simultaneous depletion of the two propulsive fluids.

Unfortunately, whenever we attempted to simulate the rocket's trajectory, the subroutines modeling the behavior of these onboard devices caused the payload to vary by a few dozen pounds even between two, otherwise, identical simulations. These payload variations were relatively small, but they were a constant irritant to the trajectory engineers.

In an attempt to eliminate the payload variations, we convened a meeting in which we explored various methods for modifying the computer's commands. Soon it became apparent that no one in attendance was going to be able to come up with a workable solution, including Bud Brux, who sat in the back of the room without saying much of anything. Later, when he returned to his desk, he began to think about the difficulties we had encountered. Like everyone else at that meeting, Bud Brux knew that the purpose of a rocket is to carry payloads into space. Could it be possible that all of us had been attempting to solve the wrong problem? Instead of trying to simplify our trajectory simulations, perhaps we should, instead, be trying to *maximize* the payload variations. With those thoughts in mind, Bud Brux wrote a two-page interoffice memo to the trajectory experts in which he suggested that we purposely vary the mixture ratio as much as possible to see if we could increase the Saturn V's payload by a significant amount.

In those hectic days we received dozens of memos, so the one that came in from Bud Brux did not trigger a very strong response. When our simulations came back from the computer, however, the payload the rocket could carry into space had increased by nearly 3,000 pounds—each pound of which was worth about $2,000! No design changes were required to cash in on this important performance benefit. We could carry the extra 3,000 pounds of payload into space by simply adjusting a single valve in midflight! Not surprisingly, this created a sudden ripple of excitement among the Apollo engineers.

With only modest effort and a single creative idea, Bud Brux had managed to achieve a billion-dollar breakthrough. In accomplishing that beneficial feat, he had used an old trick that frequently leads to breakthroughs of major proportions: *He reformulated the problem.* While most of us were fretting about those annoying payload variations, he realized that our source of irritation might actually be a solution in disguise. By turning *problem* into *opportunity*, he found a clever new way to squeeze extra payload from the towering rocket we would soon be hurling toward the moon.

Reformulating the problem is the third winning strategy on the arc of creativity. It often works extraordinarily well for scientists and engineers, but it can also produce surprisingly large improvements in business operations too. When you are attempting to reformulate your problems, always try to view the world from an optimistic point of view. "Problems are only opportunities in work clothes," said Henry J. Kaiser.

The way we state a problem can have a crucial impact on the way we attempt to solve it. If, for instance, you spend all your waking hours trying to answer the question "How can we sort a mixture of green and red tomatoes?", you are likely to focus most of your attention on color sensors of one sort or another. But if you ask instead, "How can we sort a mixture of green and *ripe* tomatoes?", a larger variety of possibilities, such as floating them in a brine solution to distinguish their different densities, will become more readily apparent.

Similarly, if your problem is stated in the following manner "How can we crack nuts more efficiently?", you are likely to focus most of your effort on some kind of cracking device. But if your problem is stated as "How can we release more whole kernels from nuts?", you are more likely to consider various other alternatives such as drilling a hole in the shell and forcing in compressed air.

If the solution to your problem is eluding you, try several different formulations. For years researchers at the University of California at Davis tried to develop a mechanical tomato picker that would not bruise the tomatoes while they were being picked. The solution came much more quickly when one creative team member proposed a slightly different formulation: Why not breed a tougher tomato? They did. And it worked!

Brer Fox and Brer Bear of Uncle Remus fame inadvertently motivated Brer Rabbit to come up with a new way to reformulate their problem. And, when he did, he saved himself to hop through the woods another day. They had always wanted to catch a sassy rabbit so they could enjoy a big, tasty pot of rabbit stew. Unfortunately, they had been stumped by the first step in their favorite recipe: "Start by catching a rabbit." But finally the two of them developed a marvelous new plan. They would make a tar baby, then lure Brer Rabbit into getting stuck on the fake baby's sticky skin.

Brer Rabbit was so gregarious he quickly fell into their clever trap, and soon he was covered with thick, sticky tar. He was a trapped rabbit alright; only trouble was, Brer Fox and Brer Bear couldn't decide whether to hang Brer Rabbit in a tree or knock his block off with a big chunk of wood.

Brer Rabbit subtly joined in their rousing debate, desperately reformulating his problem as he went along. "Sure enough, knock my block clean off an' hang me high as the sky," Brer Rabbit pleaded. "Hang me from a *million* trees! But never, oh NEVER *throw me in that briar patch!*"

The more he insisted, the more they were tempted to take sweet revenge on that pesky rabbit. Finally, they threw Brer Rabbit in the briar patch to silence his worried pleas. When he landed, Brer Rabbit moaned and groaned, then a few seconds later he appeared at the other end of the briar patch. As he had expected, the briars pulled off the tar and Brer Rabbit was safe and free.

By reformulating his problem, that sassy rabbit had tricked the fox and the bear into throwing him into the one familiar place where he could never, ever be caught, because, as Brer Rabbit explained it, "That's where I was BORN!"

Lesson 30
Finding Out What Business You Are Actually In

"Luck is a matter of preparation meeting opportunity."
— Talk Show Host, Oprah Winfrey

In his wildly successful book, *Megatrends,* John Naisbet points out that one of the most fruitful ways to achieve commercial success is to step back every few months and ask yourself this critical question: "What business are we actually in?"

One way to do this successfully is by applying "The Law of the Situation." This law was first formulated by Mary Parker Follett, America's first management consultant. In 1904, she persuaded the owners of a window-shade company that they were really in the light-control business. When they went along with her expansive idea, their business opportunities expanded enormously.

Is IBM in the business of selling computers? Or serving their client's data processing needs? By adopting the latter philosophy, IBM's managers have captured a dominant share of the global mainframe computer market. Is Avis in the business of renting cars? Or providing transportation for car rental customers? If the Avis marketeers could convince themselves they are in the transportation business, they would no doubt find a better way to get customers from big-city airports to their downtown hotels. The skinny little strips of paper they provide printed with linear driving directions cause far more problems than they will ever solve.

In their 1981 stockholder's report, General Electric's outgoing chairman, Reginald Jones, and the incoming chairman, Jack Welch, signed a joint letter to company stockholders in which they fearlessly proclaimed that GE was "in the business of creating businesses." During the intervening decade, GE has won the coveted Baldrige Award for product quality and has vowed to become number 1 or number 2 in every business area they choose to pursue.

At a time when only 5 percent of corporate-wide sales were related to the "Office of the Future," company officials at Xerox announced that their company was in the "automated office business." In this case, company officials realized that vast changes in the business world made it profitable and prudent for them to conceptualize what business it would be useful for them to think they were in. Using a similar line of reasoning, the sewing machine giant, Singer, purposefully converted itself into an aerospace company. That reformulation was necessary because working women began to abandon their sewing machines for store-bought clothing and sales of Singer's usual product line began to flatten out to an alarming degree.

John Naisbet provides his readers with a number of other interesting examples in which a fundamental reformulation of company goals has triggered a much clearer vision for the future together with renewed growth and vigor in the corporate world.

Spend a little time reviewing your company's stated goals and the business segments your executives have decided to pursue. Then try to formulate a clear and simple vision delineating your company's role in that business. John Naisbet is correct; deciding what business you are actually in can help motivate other, more important, business decisions too.

Lesson 31
Getting Your Friends to Help Whitewash
Your Aunt Polly's Picket Fence

"The man who removes a mountain begins by carrying away small stones."
— Old Chinese Proverb

When his Aunt Polly punished the rebellious Tom Sawyer by sending him out to whitewash her wooden fence, he started toward the front gate as though he had just been condemned to spend the afternoon shoveling out all the pony stables in the state of Missouri. But during his pensive journey, he figured out a terrific new way to reformulate his problem.

Within minutes he was slapping on great swatches of whitewash with such obvious relish and enthusiasm, he began to attract a curious little crowd of onlookers. Soon the other kids from Hannibal wanted desperately to join in the fun, too. But, of course, their participation could be purchased only at a heavy price with each youngster trying desperately to outbid the others.

Tom Sawyer had started out that day smack dab on the verge of financial embarrassment. But by nightfall, he had amassed treasures beyond compare. According to Tom Sawyer's good friend, Mark Twain, these included: "a kite in good repair, a dead rat with a string to swing it on, twelve marbles, part of a Jew's harp, a couple of tadpoles, six firecrackers, and a kitten with one eye."

By skillfully reformulating his problem, Tom Sawyer gathered an almost unlimited supply of boyhood treasures, which he could later trade for other, more desirable, stuff. "If he hadn't run out of whitewash," Mark Twain remarked, "he would have bankrupted every boy in the village."

Mark Twain's rousing account of Tom Sawyer's innovative approach to life along the muddy Mississippi certainly does make exciting reading. But people today are much too sophisticated to fall for such a transparent ploy, aren't they? Don't bet on it! Read on.

When members of the Chamber of Commerce at Fargo, North Dakota, invited me to help them find new ways to reinvigorate their state's economy, I spent a few minutes reminding them of Tom Sawyer's effortless whitewashing technique. A little chuckle spread through the group but, of course, they assumed that no one alive today would ever be willing to whitewash a fence or do any other grunt work without coercion or reward. And certainly, no one would be willing to pay for the privilege of giving away their volunteer labor. Would they? As a matter of fact they would!

Each year thousands of ordinary Americans pay for the privilege of working long hours at archaeological sites. They give away their labor for free, and they pay their benefactors. "How can we set up such an enterprise in North Dakota?" one earnest young lady asked me during the break.

"Start by finding a dinosaur bone," I told her, "and, if you can't find one, *make* one!"

In 1991, a single volunteer program, Earthwatch, attracted 3,000 paying volunteers who headed off toward 111 different countries to handle a variety of assignments, most of which appeared to be at least as unpleasant as whitewashing a wooden fence: taking dental molds of baboon teeth in Ethiopia, guarding endangered sea-turtle eggs along the Caribbean, and monitoring hissing volcanoes on the Hawaiian Islands. Or how about watching the mating habits of dwarf hamsters on the colorless steppes in the Soviet Union?

An IBM marketing representative, Laura Farnsworth, from Dallas, Texas, took on some of the hamster-monitoring tasks when she accompanied biologist Katherine Wynne-Edwards on a three-week expedition bound for the harshest, windswept mountains in Soviet Asia. She worked hard, learned a lot, and shelled out $2,400 plus air fare to travel on her "dream vacation."

Most volunteers turn out to be helpful to labor-starved scientists because they are told, all along, that they are expected to serve, not play. Only about 1% turn out to be a problem. On the other hand, at least 70% are repeaters who have gone along on similar expeditions in previous years. Some travel to surprisingly mundane places to "whitewash fences" most people would choose to avoid like the plague. In 1990, for instance, eight volunteers paid big money for the dubious privilege of traveling to rural Ohio where they studied the use of human sewage as a natural fertilizer to help improve vegetable crops!

My Tom Sawyer ploy may have sounded like a ridiculous pipe dream to some of the community leaders of North Dakota intent on rehabilitating the economy of their state, but it has worked many times before. And, in the hands of a skillful "con artist," it is likely to work again—and again.

Lesson 32
Reformulating a Problem to
Put Your Most Loyal K-9 Out of Work

"Everything should be made as simple as possible, but not simpler."
—American Physicist, Albert Einstein

Throughout my teenage years, my brother loved to tell the story of a clever watermelon thief who found a way to reformulate a problem in the coolest hours of a Kentucky summer night. This is how the story goes:

> Every night a watermelon thief was stealing a melon or two from a Kentucky farmer's watermelon patch. Late one afternoon, the farmer erected a big, bright sign in his field that read:
>
> "Warning: I put rat poison
> in one of these watermelons."
>
> The next morning, when he went out to the field, there was a crudely lettered note at the bottom of the sign:
>
> "So did I."

A small-town nurse in a nearby settlement learned, to her delight, that she was on the payroll of a doctor who knew how to reformulate his problems to good effect. She got her first clue when a nun rushed out of the examining room so flustered she forgot to pay her bill. When the nurse asked the doctor what had happened, he explained that after he had examined the nun, he told her she was pregnant.

"But, Doctor," the nurse responded, "that can't be!"

"You're absolutely right," he replied, "but it certainly cured her hiccups."

Robert Crandall, the chairman of American Airlines, reformulated his security problems so many different times he ended up firing a dog. According to Crandall's account of the incident, the airline had a cargo warehouse in the Caribbean guarded all night long by a night watchman. The watchman was needed to ward off thieves but, in scrubbing down the budget, Crandall recommended that they put him on a part-time shift and rotate his nights so nobody would know when he was guarding the place. It must have worked because, during the next 12 months, no property thefts occurred. The next year, under renewed budget pressures, Crandall recommended that they substitute a dog—which they would turn loose in the warehouse. That worked well, too, because no cargo disappeared.

The following year, they needed to get costs down a little more. But the manager pointed out to Crandall that "we're down to the dog."

Crandall replied, "Why don't you just record the dog snarling?" They did. And that worked, too!

Lesson 33
Reformulating a Problem So Failure Becomes Success

"Success: the art of making your mistakes when nobody is looking."
— Old American Proverb

Sometimes reformulating a problem can be as simple as changing the definition of a single word. In his book on semantics, Senator S. I. Hayakawa gives a marvelously entertaining explanation showing how Adolph Hitler played games with the language during World War II. In his rise to power, Hitler had based his nationalistic appeals on the purported superiority of the "Aryan race"—blond Caucasians who were supposed to be of pure European stock. Unfortunately, after their sneak attack on Pearl Harbor, the Japanese were suddenly transformed into Germany's military allies. Not to worry. Hitler merely redefined the word "Aryan" to include the Japanese.

Most writers cringe whenever they receive a rejection slip. But years ago, when I was first starting to write professionally, I reformulated the rejection-slip problem for my own benefit by using failure to gain success. It took a long time, but, when I had managed to gather a bulging cigar box full of rejection slips, I wrote still another query letter to publishers pitching my latest proposed book. In that query letter, I quoted from the rejection slips I had gathered as though they were published reviews of my book. It would be nice to report that this clever ploy produced positive results. But, actually, my new query letter was rejected, too!

In a book entitled *What An Idea*, Charles "Chic" Thompson recounts an instance in which a publishing company got mixed up and printed another publisher's toll-free telephone number on more than 50,000 pieces of promotional literature. Soon the phones of the wrong publisher were ringing off the wall as misdirected phone calls came in every few minutes to disrupt the staff.

When the company president was told about this situation, he figured that, whatever he did, his company would end up paying the one-minute minimum toll on each incoming call. Consequently, he instructed his staff to take down each caller's name and address so he could mail them a copy of their catalogue. By reformulating the problem, he could relax and stop cursing the telephones. Thanks to a little thoughtfulness, his company is still profiting from those unwelcome calls.

Lesson 34
Don't Automate, Obliterate

"Trust your hunches. They're usually based on facts filed away just below the conscious level."
— Talk-Show Personality, Dr. Joyce Brothers

Heavy investments in new data processing equipment have produced disappointing results for many organizations, primarily because large companies have a tendency to use their new computers to mechanize old ways of doing business rather than striking off in new directions to find new ways of doing business. Yet the emergence of fierce global competition demands that we find more efficient approaches if we are to remain competitive in the global marketplace.

"It is time to stop paving the cow paths," says Michael Hammer in an article on computer processing in the *Harvard Business Review*. "Instead of embedding outdated processes in silicon and software we should obliterate them and start over." In his capacity as president of a prestigious consulting firm, Hammer and Company of Cambridge, Massachusetts, Michael Hammer is a master of reformulating problems so they are better suited to the modern age of computers.

Hammer freely concedes that most of the institutions and assumptions that have grown up since the dawn of the Industrial Revolution had a reasonable purpose at the time. Attempting to work with largely illiterate workers in an information-poor environment brought about its own special managerial problems, which were not always easy to handle. However, most modern workers are at least semiliterate and phones and computers are everywhere so today we live and work in a new era of "information affluence."

Every company, he believes, operates under a great many unarticulated and largely unnoticed rules, some of which have become badly outdated now that data processing machines and instantaneous communication devices are widely available. Here are a few examples of those outdated rules:

- Credit decisions can only be handled by the experts in the credit department.

- Inventory has to be stored in local warehouses if we are to provide acceptable customer service.

- Every form produced by forms control must be filled in completely and accurately.

Most of these unspoken rules could probably have been justified at some time in the past but, in Michael Hammer's opinion, we need to review our unarticulated rules periodically in today's fast-changing business environment. If we fail to revisit our unspoken assumptions, we can end up, as he puts it, "rearranging the deck chairs on the Titanic!"

When used properly, specialization brings huge dividends, but it can be carried to ridiculous extremes. In my own company if the engineers need a dozen 79-cent quadrille pads, the request goes to the purchasing department, which, presumably, is specially equipped with all the necessary information and expertise to perform that crucial role. The process works to some degree, but it is often slow, frustrating, and bureaucratic. Moreover, in many cases, according to Michael Hammer, "it is not uncommon for the cost of the purchasing process to exceed the cost of the goods being purchased."

An alternative approach consists of pushing some information-intensive processes out toward the customers (either internal to the company or external to it). Today, for instance, by using a data base approved by the vendors, a department can place its own orders directly by charging the cost to the bank's credit card. At the end of the month, the bank can then furnish a tape of all the credit card transactions, which the company reviews for reasonableness and cross-checks against its own internal accounting system. In the process, of course, internal paperwork by the ton, most of it costly and entirely useless, disappears.

An electronics equipment manufacturer advised by Michael Hammer made similar changes in the way it approaches its field service repairs. In the process, it achieved substantial productivity gains and much greater customer satisfaction. Under the old bureaucratic repair process, the manufacturer's field service operations had been plagued by the usual difficulties: slow response to customer complaints, excessive spare-parts inventory, and—most serious of all—repair technicians who were often unable to handle a needed repair because the necessary part was not carried onboard their van.

In the reformulated version of the same service, spare parts are stored at each customer's site and customers are instructed to make simple repairs themselves. When a problem arises, they call a company diagnostician who either tells them what to do on the phone or dispatches a properly equipped service technician to their site. Since the most frequently needed spare parts are already stockpiled at the customer's site, there is usually no need to stop along the way at the warehouse to pick up any additional parts. By breaking a few outdated rules, the electronics firm has built up a much more efficient approach to customer servicing with considerably faster turnaround and a much more satisfied clientele. In short, they have reformulated the problem to achieve vastly improved results.

Lesson 35
Making an Important Point the Easy Way

"The greatest discovery of my generation is that a human being can alter his life by altering his attitude."
— American Classical Psychologist, William James

When George F. Patton was in command of a hard-drinking calvary unit near Killeen, Texas, his public relations officers told him that, although local towns-people had an excellent appreciation for his troop's propensities toward Saturday-night hell-raising sprees, they had hardly any appreciation for the many positive contributions flowing to the local economy from that big military base. Staff members compiled statistics on how much money the average soldier pumped into the economy of Killeen, the largest Texas town near the camp. Then they proposed that General Patton himself, or a high-ranking member of his personal staff, make a formal presentation summarizing the results to the local Chamber of Commerce and other business-leader groups.

But George F. Patton found a way to reformulate the problem to make the benefits of the base much more readily apparent to the audience he wanted to reach. One payday he arranged to pay his troops with $2 bills. As the bills filtered through the local economy over the next few weeks, the positive economic benefits his troops provided became highly visible for everyone to see.

Lesson 36
Combining Two Problems
to Make Both of Them Go Away

"Fortunately, the wheel was invented before the car; otherwise, the scraping noise would be intolerable."
— Author Unknown

Sometimes, when you cannot puzzle out an appropriate solution to a difficult problem, you may be able to combine two problems to make both of them go away. This is seldom easy, but, when it works, it can pay off with huge dividends.

During the energy crisis of the 1970s that accompanied the Arab oil embargo, my boss asked me to help find ways to air condition big shopping centers using direct energy from the sun.[4] Our engineering studies indicated that, in regions of America with high fuel costs and abundant sunshine, sun-powered air conditioning could provide positive economic benefits—assuming that we could devise an inexpensive way to store the sun's energy for nighttime use.

Our energy experts were scratching their heads on that one, until a clever young engineer suggested that, rather than try to store the sun's energy, we might be able to handle the nighttime energy loads by burning the shopping center's trash at the site to get more energy for running the air conditioning units. Hauling a shopping center's trash away is a costly and difficult problem and it also uses valuable energy! So, by burning it at the site, we were able to solve two problems for the price of one.

For most American workers, driving to work is mostly wasted time. Direct solutions to this problem, such as switching jobs or moving next door to the factory, are definitely available. But by combining your driving problem with some other worrisome problem, you may be able to solve both problems at the same time. How about combining your driving problem with the similar problem of your coworkers? By driving a company van to your facility, with other workers inside, you can earn extra money while you are driving to work.

Or how about listening to educational tapes during your drive to help with your personal career advancement? Conventional wisdom holds that we should not try to do two things at once, but this seems like a reasonable exception.

Incidentally, many international travelers sign up as couriers whenever they travel on international trips. They help solve a problem for the airline by carrying a sealed

---

[4] Even in cold climates, we soon learned, shopping centers must be air conditioned because the human bodies and the lights inside give off so much excess heat.

pouch from one international airport to another, and, at the same time, they effortlessly cut their airfare in half! For some airlines, each international flight always includes a partially subsidized courier.

Whenever you are faced with a seemingly intractable problem, review various possibilities to see if you can combine it with some other problem of a different type. If you can do it successfully, you may be able to make both problems go away.

Lesson 37
Reformulating Your Own Problems in Searching for Simple, Creative Solutions

"Don't be a carbon copy of someone else—make your own impression."
— French Philosopher, Voltaire

Creative people can learn how to become more creative. If you doubt that assertion, pay a little visit to the Rodin Museum in Paris. There you will see Auguste Rodin's powerful style gradually beginning to emerge. Even in his early years, all the elements of his powerful style are clearly in evidence—dramatic and emotional poses, muscles in tension, stark figures emerging from raw stone—but each year, as he practiced his demanding craft, Rodin became better and more creative.

Charles Schulz, creator of "Peanuts," provides us with another instructive example of what hard work and dedication can do. His early cartoon characters showed a great deal of promise, but they were crude and undistinguished. However, with years of patient practice, he created, polished, and refined each character—and created new ones—until they became clever, sharp, and memorable. Over the years, Schulz became more creative a little at a time, right before our eyes.

Anything people can do, they can learn to do better. With proper training, you can learn to dance better, read better, speak better, play volleyball better, swim better, and, not surprisingly, you can learn how to solve creative problems better, too.

The blank worksheets at the end of this lesson are designed to help you become more creative as they guide you through various formulations of the problem you have been hoping to solve. Make a complete problem statement on the first worksheet, then fill out (as completely as you can) all of the subsequent blanks on that and the next worksheet page. If a partial solution occurs to you along the way, make a note of it in the margins or on a separate sheet of paper.

You will encounter various other helpful exercises in the next three chapters. Then, in Chapter 7, you will be urged to harvest your best ideas from all of the worksheets sprinkled throughout the various chapters of this book.

What is your problem? _____

_____

_____

_____

③ REFORMULATING YOUR PROBLEM

The way you state your problem has an important influence on the way you attempt to solve it. Restate your problem three different ways. In each new formulation change the wording and your way of looking at the problem as much as you can.

1. _____

_____

_____

_____

2. _____

_____

_____

_____

3. _____

_____

_____

_____

Review these three new formulations. Put a star (☆) beside your favorite, then make notes on new solutions.

_____

_____

_____

Play the devil's advocate. Reformulate your problem the way a vocal opponent might to make any changes in the *status quo* difficult to justify. Explain how you could quiet or circumvent that opposition. _____

_____

_____

Restate your problem so it sounds like the present situation is highly advantageous to you and your company. Be playful and preposterous in your new formulation. _____

_____

_____

_____

_____

_____

_____

Is there a small grain of truth in this way of formulating the problem? Explain how you might be able to capitalize on that grain of truth. _____

_____

_____

_____

_____

_____

_____

List three other problems that are in some way related to the specific problem you are trying to solve.

1. _____

_____

_____

2. _____

_____

_____

3. _____

_____

_____

Make notes on possible ways you might combine these various problems to make one or more of them go away. _____

_____

_____

_____

_____

_____

Chapter 4
Visualizing a Fruitful Analogy

"Ideas are like rabbits. You get a couple and learn how to handle them, and pretty soon you have a dozen."
— Nobel Prize-Winning Author, John Steinbeck

One person with one creative idea can make a big difference, but occasionally it takes two. It happened in 1905 on a lonely North Carolina beach when two brothers from Ohio wobbled into the air aboard an ungainly contraption above the sands at Kitty Hawk. Why had those two succeeded when so many others had failed? They succeeded because they had a special ability to visualize fruitful analogies in designing and building their flying machines.

Most of their predecessors had been distracted by the rapidly flapping wings of the sparrow. But the Wright brothers used the condor, a soaring bird, as the model they were trying to emulate. Their aerodynamic studies of placid soaring birds led them to design a fixed stabilizing tail and box-like wings that could be twisted (warped) by the pilot to control the trajectory of his fragile craft. By fashioning and using a simple wind tunnel, they determined the proper size and curvature for their wings. Later they figured out (again using a fruitful analogy) that their long, skinny rotating propellers were, in effect, moving wings slicing out spiraling trajectories through the air.

Orville and Wilbur Wright sold and repaired bicycles, which helped focus their attention on still another fruitful analogy: They realized that they would have to learn how to *fly* their airplane while they were learning how to *build* it—just as early European inventors needed to learn how to build and ride the first few bicycles ever assembled.

In testing their early gliders, the Wright brothers took advantage of one more fruitful analogy: They reasoned that, if they could find a good location with steady headwinds, their airplane would behave as though it were flying inside a giant wind tunnel, thus providing extra time for the pilot to practice aerial maneuvers during each flight. Steady headwinds would also reduce the ground speed during landing. So Wilbur wrote a letter to the U.S. Weather Service asking for help in finding just the right location for their summer tests. Specifically, they needed a gently sloping hill for takeoff and soft, sandy soil for landing. Steady headwinds were also necessary to produce the wind-tunnel effect that would increase the length of time in the air for each flight test. Soon the two of them had settled on Kill Devil Hill at Kitty Hawk, North Carolina, a site that just happened to have all of the desirable characteristics they had been seeking.

The first few flying machines the Wright brothers constructed were designed and built in their shop at Dayton, Ohio, then carefully disassembled for shipment on a train bound for North Carolina. Their first successful flight lasted only 12 seconds and covered barely 120 feet—less than the wingspan of a modern Boeing 747. However, when their fragile craft gently descended to the ground, the Wright brothers knew, for sure, that their world would never be the same again.

Orville and Wilbur Wright succeeded so brilliantly because they mastered the fourth winning strategy on the arc of creativity: *They visualized fruitful analogies* in building the world's first successful motor-powered flying machines. Fruitful analogies are a powerful spur to creativity that can help you solve your problems, too. Find the hidden connections between your current assignment and problems already solved by earlier inventors—or Mother Nature—and you could be on your way toward developing a billion-dollar breakthrough.

In this chapter you will learn how to cast your problem in the form of useful metaphors and similes, some of which will be fairly extensive. Your experiences with topic outlines, balloon diagrams, and cartoon captions in this and earlier chapters will also help you sharpen your ability to visualize and exploit fruitful analogies in difficult problem-solving situations.

The final part of this chapter will explain how other creative people in many diverse fields have solved their problems by making practical use of fruitful analogies. Specifically, you will learn how Fred Ferguson and his colleagues in Ottawa, Canada, are poised to capture a $20 billion market with their unique new flying machines based on the Magnus effect, the same aerodynamic principle that causes a spinning baseball to move along a curved trajectory as it zooms in toward home plate. You will also learn how modern marketeers have been saving Japanese housewives as much as 8 percent on their grocery bills by using a technology patterned after the old-fashioned automats on Manhattan Island. Finally, you will watch the work of a skilled auto mechanic as he saves himself many hours of back-breaking labor by using a fruitful analogy when he finds a new way to "sew" an old automobile engine back together.

Lesson 38
Turning Mother Nature's Raindrops
into Highly Effective Weapons

"Each of us arrives on this planet with a purpose. To fulfill that purpose is to ignite the spark in us and give meaning to our lives."
— Pop Singer, Michael Jackson

When America's early pioneers were sweeping out toward the Western frontier, they needed large numbers of spherical grapeshot to load into their shotguns and cannons. Sufficient quantities could, perhaps, have been manufactured by constructing tens of thousands of hollow molds to cast the necessary metal spheres. A simple, creative analogy, however, inspired a much better way to meet the growing need. Take a trip to Baltimore and you can see a slender brick monument 240 feet high commemorating the cleverness of early American munitions makers. Nearly every production process they perfected could, in fact, be regarded as an example of simple, creative problem-solving at its best.

When Mother Nature's raindrops fall toward the ground, they automatically form into nearly perfect spheres because of weightlessness. Would falling globules of molten metal create spheres in a similar manner?

In 1828, Baltimore's shot tower, a tall, chimney-like structure, first poked its head high up above the Baltimore skyline. Soon production of uniform metal spheres— nearly all of them intended for use as munitions—topped 10 million pounds in an average year. Metal vats filled with molten lead were carried by chain conveyors spiraling upward along the inner chimney walls. At various points along the way, workers dribbled the molten metal downward in thin, steady streams, which fell in weightlessness toward water-filled vats in the base of the chimney.

Once they had solidified, the workers rolled the spheres down inclined planes to cull out the small number that had collided in midair or, for some other reason, were ruined with surface imperfections. The discards were melted down again to make more little metal spheres. Of course, those that were perfect had to be polished and graded by size. This was accomplished by tumbling them in special machines, then sorting them into different categories by running them through sieves with holes of different sizes.

After more than a century of continuous operation, the tall, slender shot tower at Baltimore finally grew silent for the last time in 1935. Later it became a tourist museum. But other American shot towers are still operating today. Some of them are used to make the tiny spherical glass beads glistening on today's reflecting highway markers. Moreover, two other free-fall products of great value and usefulness to the people living on earth are being successfully manufactured aboard the space shuttle in the long-term weightlessness of outer space. Both of them are made from inexpensive plastics and both of them are worth millions of dollars per pound. Keep reading and you will find out what they are in Chapter 5.

Lesson 39
Trying to Build a Magnificent Contraption

"Whenever you find yourself on the side of the majority, it is time to pause and reflect."
— American Author, Mark Twain

Early in the nineteenth century an eccentric British scientist named Charles Babbage visualized a fruitful analogy that almost allowed him to build the world's first general-purpose digital computer—in 1833! Imagine how different our world would be if he had succeeded in perfecting such a computer before the start of the American Civil War!

Charles Babbage began designing his computer when he became convinced that a properly constructed mechanical device could be used to produce error-free numerical tables. After all, James Watt's steam engine could pump water for days on end in a symphony of mechanical perfection. Babbage loved to daydream about its gears and cogs rotating in perfect harmony, with its cam-driven valves opening and closing always on schedule. If a mechanical device could be made to carry out mathematical operations with comparable perfection, error-free numerical tables would be a practical reality and astronomers would no longer find themselves peering through their telescopes where incorrect ephemeris tables said Mars ought to be, only to find a patch of blank sky. Tables constructed mechanically would also allow many other professional groups to have far more confidence in the accuracy of their day-to-day calculations.

But how was he to design this new machine? Babbage had studied the intricately woven fabrics produced by the looms of Joseph Jacquard. But what did the weaving of expensive tapestries have to do with the construction of error-free mathematical tables? In 1801, Joseph Jacquard had perfected a complicated control system for contemporary weaving machines, using punched cards threaded together by strong strings. The holes in the cards—which numbered in the tens of thousands—directed the shuttles to weave animals, forest scenes, flowers, and leaves. One of Babbage's most-prized possessions was a woven self-portrait of Joseph Jacquard produced by Jacquard's looms. A massive project, the weaving had required more than 24,000 individual cards!

As Babbage fingered the multicolored threads, a fruitful analogy began to race through his brain. His new machine would *weave numbers* in the same way a Jacquard loom could weave flowers and leaves! Babbage's picturesque concept was scientifically sound, but the construction of such a gigantic mechanism was a very demanding feat. Charles Babbage spent nearly all of his time during the next 40 years trying to perfect his general-purpose digital computer. Most of his personal fortune was consumed in the process together with his earnings as Lucasian Professor of Mathematics at Cambridge University. He also used £17,000 in grants and other stipends he received from the British government. Unfortunately, difficult problems seemed to arise with every passing day.

By 1842 it was obvious to nearly everyone that the analytical engine would never be complete. Babbage felt his courage slipping away, but he plodded on hoping to find a better way. There was still some cause for hope. The plans were largely complete and some sections of the device had actually been constructed. However, the machining difficulties he encountered were much more numerous than anyone could have imagined and the government had gradually withdrawn all support for the project. Generally speaking, things had never looked so bleak. Then, suddenly, Babbage found a new friend: Lady Lovelace, the only legitimate daughter of Lord Byron, quietly joined his crusade. A mathematical genius in her own right, Lady Lovelace was later to write some of the most lucid descriptions of the functioning of the analytical engine. But for the moment, the two of them had little interest in leaving messages for posterity. Their first priority was raising money!

Their initial fund-raising scheme was simple, but farfetched. They set out to perfect a mathematical technique for winning money by betting on the horse races! Unfortunately, the horses refused to cooperate, and no amount of mathematical manipulation could produce a workable scheme.

Their next try was only a little more down to earth. Years earlier, Babbage had sketched the plans for a machine that could play a flawless game of tic-tac-toe. At the time, it had been merely an amusing diversion executed in cold steel without any showmanship, but now Babbage and Lovelace decided that the device might possibly be a gold mine in disguise. In the new, and infinitely more dramatic version, two tiny mechanical youngsters would play the game in a miniature barnyard. The winner and his rooster would crow about their victory, whereas the loser and his lamb would sob about their defeat.

Before going into final production of the device, Babbage and Lovelace investigated the profitability of similar ventures, but they were not encouraged by the results. Most mechanical devices put on display were hardly making any profit at all. The only exhibit that was pulling in the kind of money they needed to finish the analytical engine was General Tom Thumb. Sadly, the team of Babbage and Lovelace could not see any practical way to build a synthetic midget realistic enough to fool anyone, so the obvious now became clear: There was simply no way to finance further work on the analytical engine.

In Babbage's declining years, the parts of the incomplete mechanism littered his house to mock him, and the masterful drawings crammed in the corners of his desk gave him no comfort. All his life Charles Babbage had been an articulate spokesman for science and technology, but as his creative obsessions began to fade, he seemed unable to give a coherent account of the operating principles of the analytical engine. If it had not been for the lucid descriptions of Lady Lovelace, his work would probably be only a vague scientific memory.

Several factors hindered his work on the new computer: He was obsessed with redesign and he used decimal rather than binary arithmetic. He became enthralled with trivial details, and he had broad interests many of which distracted him from his work on the analytical engine. Yet, in a sense, such a critical analysis is sadly inappropriate. Perhaps a better explanation for the inability of Charles Babbage to capitalize on his fruitful analogy is that he had the misfortune of being born 100 years ahead of his time.

Lesson 40
Analogous Reasoning from the Small-Fry Set

"Disgrace: to stumble twice against the same stone."
— Roman Orator and Statesman, Cicero

As children's minds grow and mature, their words and actions gradually begin to reveal that they are learning how to reason by analogy. In simple situations, in fact, they sometimes seem more intuitive and creative than their adult counterparts. For instance, when my daughter, Donna, was five years old, she constructed a cuckoo clock of her own using the simplest imaginable materials. First she opened up her Dr. Seuss book and put it on top of her head to form a little A-frame roof, then she stuck out her tongue several times. "Coo-coo, coo-coo," she said with a toothless grin.

A week or two later, we were watching television when the show was interrupted by a prune commercial that caused her to think of another fruitful analogy. The narrator announced enthusiastically that his clever sponsor had found a way to remove the pits from their prunes. "Today the pits," he said proudly, "tomorrow the wrinkles!"

I couldn't resist asking her an obvious question: "Donna, how would you get the wrinkles out of a prune?"

"Iron it!" she replied.

On another occasion we were watching a documentary that explained how wild animals are captured alive, then flown in airplanes to zoos all around the world. "We have found that the best way to package wild animals for shipment is to put them in ordinary paper bags," the animal trainer explained. "This works well for animals up to and including small gorillas."

"Donna, how would you put a gorilla in a paper bag?"

"Fold him," she replied.

That documentary was broadcast more than 25 years ago, and in the meantime I have forgotten many things, but every once in a while, I still get a silly grin on my face when I think about that toothless little girl struggling to figure out how to put wild gorillas in big, brown paper bags. What a wonderful analogy! Always in my mind's eye, I see a big burly workman standing beside a slowly moving conveyer belt methodically folding gorillas one by one as they move past his work station.

My stepson, Chad, is just beginning to reason by analogy, which gives many of his remarks a strange and enduring charm. "What animal has the longest neck?" I once asked him.

"A snake," he replied with only the slightest hesitation.

Later, in Alexandria, Virginia, I asked a five-year-old that same question. He looked toward his mother for advice. But luckily, she refused to provide any helpful prompting. "The brontosaurus," he finally replied.

Popeye's niece, Sweet Pea, displayed a similar bent toward creative problem-solving when Popeye was playing with her in their backyard. "I'm gonna dig me an island," Sweet Pea tells him with an enthusiastic look rippling across her face. Popeye seems a bit confused. He doesn't understand how anyone can dig an island, but Sweet Pea does. She picks up her little toy shovel and digs a donut-shaped trench in the backyard. Then, after she fills it with water from the garden hose, she sits contentedly on the little island paradise she has dug!

Of course, adults can be surprisingly creative, too. The seventeenth-century Scottish mathematician John Napier always seemed to be able to come up with a fruitful analogy whenever he needed to solve a difficult problem. When a neighbor's pet pigeons kept flying onto his estate and nibbling away at his valuable grain, he announced that he would impound the birds in payment.

The neighbor agreed that Napier could keep any pigeon he could capture alive. Napier pondered the problem for a few minutes, then he scattered brandy-soaked garden peas over his grounds. Soon the pigeons were staggering about in such a stupor, he was able to collect them in a sack!

Colonel Lemuel Q. Stoopnagle devised many creative solutions which indicate that, throughout his life, he always managed to keep the child in him alive and well. Here are just three of his many creative inventions:

- An alarm clock with half a bell on it, so when two people are rooming together, it just wakes one of them.

- Carnations with buttonholes already attached to them.

- A stepladder without steps in it, for washing windows in the cellar.

People search for creative solutions because they are unhappy with the way things are:

- Sweet Pea wanted a change of scene.

- John Napier wanted to save his grain.

- Colonel Stoopnagle hated to struggle with pesky carnations.

When you hunger for constructive changes, do not stifle that inspirational feeling. Instead, get out pencil and paper and let your thoughts lead you into unfamiliar terrain. Never fight it. And don't try to guide it. Take what you get at this early stage. Later, when you are ready to polish and perfect your best ideas, you will need to cultivate a far more disciplined attitude.

Creative problem-solving entails a rich mixture of spontaneity and discipline. A hunger for change may motivate you to think creatively in the first place, but only discipline and perseverance will allow you to carry your creative ideas to completion. Still, even if you don't intend to carry out a grandiose project, daydreaming about creative solutions can be great fun. "I have a microwave fireplace," claims American writer Stephen Wright. "You lay down in front of the fire all night in eight minutes."

Lesson 41
Learning to Formulate Industrial-Strength Metaphors and Similes

"Few wishes come true by themselves."
— June Smith, Orlando Sentinel

Metaphors and similes are literary analogies that can be pressed into service as powerful problem-solving tools. They help creative individuals find simple solutions in complicated situations, and they often serve as an effective verbal shorthand. The first time you heard a camel defined as "a horse designed by committee," you may not have recognized what you were hearing as a literary metaphor, but you got the point nonetheless.

With the simplest words and phrases, metaphors and similes can focus our attention on colorful and exciting parallels. They create tension. They make diverse concepts collide, fuse, and merge, and they help us synthesize new ideas in abundance.

Some people associate fancy literary devices such as similes, metaphors, and personification with intellectual snobbishness. But Tennessee Ernie Ford was neither an intellectual nor a snob when he observed that he was "as nervous as a long-tailed cat in a room full of rocking chairs." Nor was Mohammed Ali exhibiting intellectual snobbishness when he advertised his boxing skills with this double-barreled simile: "I'm the greatest," he said. "I float like a butterfly, sting like a bee."[5]

Metaphors and similes tend to focus our attention on novel and productive similarities, contrasts, and relationships. Metaphors borrowed from nature, in particular, have always been a big help to inventors and entrepreneurs who are trying to find workable solutions to practical problems. Radar, for example, was modeled after the echo-ranging system that helps flying bats navigate through hazardous situations. The military smoke screen was patterned after the inky substance ejected by the octopus—which also provided us with the model for jet propulsion and the suction cup. Parachutes are oversized versions of floating dandelion balls and the shapes of submarines—and their gentle flexibility under hydrostatic loads—are, to some extent, crude copies of swimming dolphins, tiger sharks, and tuna fish.

Jonas Salk has long been impressed with Mother Nature's problem-solving skills. "Think like nature," he advised his students. "Ask 'How would nature solve this problem?'" His solid advice has worked well in his work and it is good advice for anyone seeking simple, creative solutions.

---

[5] Ali's opponent did not frame his reply in the form of a literary analogy, but his response was equally colorful: "My only worry," he said, "is that, after the fight, the doctor will have to cut my wrist to get my fist out of his mouth."

When Louis Pasteur was scouting around for creative ideas, he, too, turned to nature for inspiration. Early in his career, he realized that grapes ferment only when their skin is broken. Later he reasoned, by analogy, that little breaks in the skin of people might be an entryway for human infection.

Thomas Edison enhanced his worldwide reputation when he invented the incandescent light bulb. But the light bulb might have turned out to be a mere scientific curiosity if he had not also invented city-wide electrical systems in which dynamos were linked by branching power lines to enormous numbers of incandescent lamps. The analogy he used was apparently the backyard maple tree. "Nature doesn't just make leaves," he wrote, "it makes branches and trees and roots to go with them."

Enormous underground storage bins capable of holding our country's strategic petroleum reserves are also based on a clever analogy borrowed from Mother Nature's bag of tricks. The engineers responsible for the storage of petroleum quickly realized that underground caverns would be the only practical storage bins that could be made big enough to hold the enormous amounts of oil required. But they also knew that earthmoving is enormously expensive. Rooftop icicles dripping water to hollow out little indentations in fresh snow provided an instant analogy that helped provide the desired solution. By dribbling fresh water onto massive underground salt deposits, then pumping out the saltwater solution, cheap storage bins totaling hundreds of millions of barrels in capacity were formed at economical rates. But how does the salt trap the oil for future use? That part is also simple. Water dissolves salt but that same salt is impervious to oil.

Metaphors and similes seem to illuminate a room from every corner when a creative individual comes through the door. When Steven Jobs was putting together the plans for an early computer, he told his colleagues that he wanted to pattern the new machine after the household refrigerator. But what does a refrigerator have in common with a well-designed personal computer? Jobs let his metaphor hang in the air for a while before he went on to explain: "When you buy a refrigerator, you don't add anything to it. You just take it home and plug it in."

His competitors were designing their machines in modular fashion, so users could pick and choose among components tailored to their own specific needs. Their fruitful analogy was the home stereo system, which for years had been constructed from separate components.

By building a stand-alone computer patterned after the household refrigerator, Steven Jobs and his crew greatly simplified its design and reduced its price. Its lack of flexibility undoubtedly drove away a few sophisticated users. But its compensating features opened up vast new markets for millions of others who were not particularly interested in custom-level performance.

Later, when the Apple team was designing the MacIntosh computer, Steven Jobs felt his way toward another fruitful analogy when he decided to pattern that new computer after the telephone. But what did an ordinary telephone have in common with a modern computer? As Jobs explained to his stockholders: A user who makes a phone call does not have to understand what goes on inside the telephone. Operating the new MacIntosh was to be as simple as making a phone call, thus opening up vast new markets among those who were mainly interested in getting easy results without plowing through thick user's manuals or taking extension classes on computer processing techniques.

Lesson 42
Designing and Constructing the Canadian Dream Bubble

"Don't be afraid to take a big step if one is indicated; you can't cross a chasm in two small steps."
— British Statesman, Lloyd George

Frederick D. Ferguson at the Van Dusen Development Corporation in Ottawa, Canada, has been skillfully exploiting a fruitful analogy in designing a strange-looking flying machine that may someday turn out to be one of the most efficient and productive vehicles ever produced by the Canadian aerospace industry. Its strange configuration, which one reporter aptly described as "a manta ray with a golf ball on its back," is based on the Magnus effect, the same physical principle that causes a spinning baseball to follow a curved trajectory as it travels toward home plate.

The Magnus effect was first observed in the 1870s when English athletes noticed that a scuffed and worn cricket ball traveled further than it did when it was fresh and new. German physicist Heinrich G. Magnus later demonstrated that a rotating sphere creates aerodynamic forces that cause it to curve as it moves through the air.

By building a flying machine based on the fruitful analogy of a curving baseball, Ferguson is perfecting a new kind of flying machine with the speed and maneuverability of a helicopter coupled with the fuel economy and lifting capability of the old-fashioned dirigible. He is accomplishing this by constructing a hydrogen-filled gas bag penetrated by a long axle whose two ends carry powerful turbojets for forward propulsion.

Suspended from the two ends of the transverse axle is a rigid gondola draped down under the spherical gas bag (see Figure 4.1). At takeoff, the gas bag is made to rotate to create additional lift due to the Magnus effect. Through the proper combination of the Magnus effect and turbojet propulsion, the pilot can control the climb rate of his chubby little craft.

Conventional skycrane helicopters applied to heavy-lift assignments such as remote log-hauling or resupply operations for offshore oil platforms charge their customers about $2 per ton-mile for any cargo delivered. Ferguson's preliminary design, which uses a 260-foot Mylar gas bag, should be able to handle similar assignments much faster at an estimated cost of only 24 cents per ton-mile.

Frederick D. Ferguson visualized a fruitful analogy inspired by a curving baseball when he found a new way to build an innovative flying machine. Although his Canadian dream bubble would probably never win any beauty contest that had not been rigged in advance, it may succeed brilliantly in the battle for economic com-

Figure 4.1   The Canadian dream bubble.

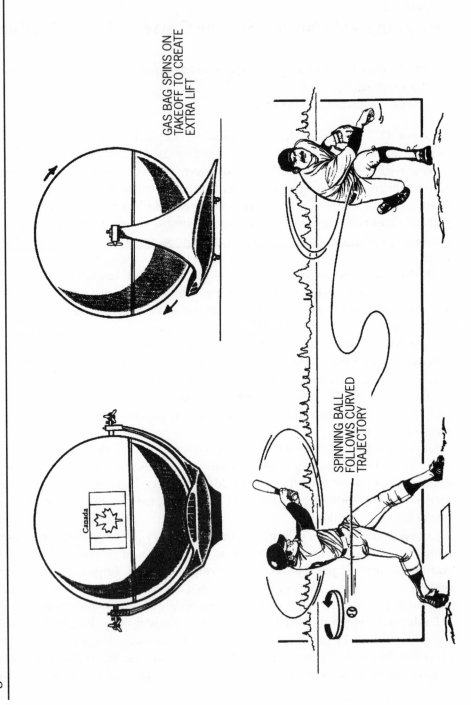

GAS BAG SPINS ON TAKEOFF TO CREATE EXTRA LIFT

SPINNING BALL FOLLOWS CURVED TRAJECTORY

petitiveness. One *Aviation Week* reporter believes that a squadron of "dream bubbles" with 90,000-pound lifting capacity could be extremely efficient in the loading and unloading of container ships in congested harbors, oil and gas pipeline construction, and in remote logging operations. During the next 20 years, he is convinced that the Magnus effect, applied on a large scale, could bring in revenues totaling $20 billion per year.

Lesson 43
Japan's Clever New Vending Machine Supermarkets

"You may be disappointed if you fail, but you are doomed if you don't try."
— Opera Soprano, Beverly Sills

During my college days, I was suddenly converted into a delighted young out-of-towner when two of my friends and I tumbled off a turnip truck that had just arrived on Manhattan Island. We wolfed down our first lunch at the automat, a room full of vending machines dispensing all kinds of snacks, tidbits, and full-size meals. For three famished young country boys that was a mighty impressive dining experience. But when we wandered back out among the neon lights illuminating Times Square, we never imagined that the automat might someday provide a perfect analogy for a flashy new concept in supermarket design.

In the new Japanese supermarkets, a special magnetic card is chained to the handle of each shopping cart. As a Japanese housewife walks around the market, she inserts the card into the slot of an appropriate machine, then punches individual buttons to select any desired food items. Each time she purchases vegetable soup, pork sausage, or edible seaweed, the computer records her purchase, then unlocks the door so she can retrieve her selection. At the checkstand, the items are not removed from the paper bags in the shopping cart. Instead, the clerk merely inserts the magnetic card into a slot in the cash register, whereupon the computer instantly spits out an itemized sales slip.

Most Japanese enjoy these "automat" supermarkets, but they do have a few nagging complaints. Specifically, the products can't be touch-tested prior to purchase and the merchandise can't be returned as easily as it can in most conventional markets. Selections are also rather limited because the automat markets are only about one-fifth as large as their full-sized American counterparts.

By way of compensation, however, the vending system provides substantial benefits. For one thing, the stores are virtually unmanned. Only 2 cashiers are needed, compared with 20 before the computerized system was installed. Moreover, the vending machines are stocked each day with only nine man-hours of labor, most of which is provided by part-time workers. Shoplifting, employee pilfering, and cashier mistakes are all but eliminated and checkout is approximately seven times faster. But the most important advantage is the one most likely to be of interest to American consumers: Food prices are 5 to 8 percent lower than those charged at competing Japanese markets.

Fruitful analogies are lurking in the shadows all around us if only we take the trouble to see. Spot something interesting this week, and 30 years from now it may be reducing the price you will have to pay to feed all the hungry people leaning on their elbows around your Sunday table.

Lesson 44
Building and Using Your Own Magic Grid

"A man who never made a mistake will never make anything else."
— British Dramatist, George Bernard Shaw

> *Synergism:* The combined action of different agents producing a greater effect than the sum of the various individual actions.

A few years ago a big, clumsy skier flew out of control and knocked me down onto the hard-frozen snow clinging to the bunny slopes at Lake Tahoe. Later that afternoon I learned that a pair of my ribs had snapped in two. For the next four weeks I was immobilized in my home in a rented hospital bed with a motor-powered sloping back. During that month of slow recuperation I had lots of time to master useful skills like learning how to pick up stray objects from the floor with my toes. Fortunately, during that same month, I also learned how to construct the magic grid.

I got interested in the magic grid quite by accident when a magazine article dealing with a new kind of spreadsheet program caught my eye. As I soon learned, a spreadsheet program is a data processing algorithm that performs some of the functions of an accountant who spreads a layer of papers and ledger sheets across the top of his or her desk while laboriously computing the consequences of various possible business decisions. The video display screen is divided into a rectangular grid like a larger version of tic-tac-toe. Each square in the grid can accept either a number or an equation defining the relationship between the other numbers on the screen. The first square, for instance, might contain a worker's hourly pay and the second the number of hours he or she has worked. The third square in the grid might contain an equation telling the computer to multiply the worker's rate of pay by the number of hours worked to determine the total weekly earnings. The other squares in the grid would hold other types of data and other equations to help in calculating taxes, deductions, contributions, etc., of all the workers on the company payroll.

A spreadsheet program is structured such that if you change any value on the screen, the computer will immediately make the corresponding changes in all the other values in the grid. This permits you to perform rapid "experiments" with various investment decisions, management policies, etc., and *immediately* determine their likely consequences. If you have a spreadsheet program, you do not have to be a computer expert to obtain impressive results. All you need is a little patience and a pioneering spirit.

When I finished the article I was anxious to experiment with spreadsheet programming. Unfortunately, I didn't have any of the software in my home. So I began to putter around with a fruitful analogy of my own. While reflecting on the power of the spreadsheet grid, it dawned on me that nearly everything I tried to accomplish in life interacted with everything else in quite constructive ways. If I changed one thing, other things tended to change automatically. If I wrote a technical paper, for instance, it might later become a chapter in one of my books. And the drawings in my books sometimes served as visuals for my platform lectures.

So I went into the den, picked up a big quadrille sheet of paper and began to make notes on some of those synergistic interactions. Soon I had arranged the various items into a grid-like pattern that was vaguely similar to a spreadsheet program. Across the top of the grid (see Table 4.1) I listed my four major professional activities:

- Engineering

- Books

- Magazine articles

- Paid lectures.

Along the left-hand side I listed the same four activities plus an extra one at the bottom of the page:

- Engineering

- Books

- Magazine articles

- Paid lectures

- Taxes and recreation.

Inside the boxes on the grid I began to write notes on how these various activities were helping one another. Then I began to think about a riddle that Paul Gillette (author of *Play Misty For Me*) had posed in one of his classes at UCLA: "What do an Eskimo, a writer, and a Jewish mother all have in common?" No one had the solution, so he answered the riddle himself: "They all *reuse* everything."

If we plan carefully enough, we can *all* reuse lots of valuable things to make ourselves and our country more prosperous without much extra effort. Of course, if you plan to sell the *same* article to two different magazines, you will have to set up a formal agreement in advance legally allowing you to do that sort of thing. But no one will object if you end up using the same research and the same thought processes in an article and later in a book or a short course. The magic grid helps you

Table 4.1   The Magic Grid

	Engineering	Books	Magazine Articles	Paid Lectures
Engineering		• Published books help reputation at work • Book research used for work projects • Writing leads to interesting job assignments (slide shows, color wallcharts)	• Magazine articles help reputation at work • Article research provides fresh expertise (atomic clocks, communication satellites, etc.)	• Lecturing builds reputation at work • Lecturing promotes short course attendance
Books	• Technical papers become chapters in books • Engineering job gives status, credibility to books • Travel promotes publishing contacts	• Material from some books can be used in other books • Self-publishing becomes tax deductible against profits	• Articles become book chapters • Book reviews help book research • Article research becomes book research • Article credit lines can be used to plug books	• Lectures/classes help sell books • Lecture topics become book topics (The Rush Toward the Star, creative writing) • University teaching leads to publishing contacts • Short courses become book topics
Magazine articles	• Technical papers can become articles for magazines • Travel for magazines promotes publishing contacts • Job provides access to library stacks, artists, photographers	• Book chapters can become articles • Book research can be used in magazine articles • Book editor articles lead to magazine editor contacts • Book reviews promote book contacts	• Magazine book reviews become magazine research • Magazine book reviews help provide magazine article contacts	• Briefing trips promote side trips to publishers • Symposia briefings can yield magazine assignments
Paid lectures	• Profession provides status for lecturers • Profession provides opportunities for after-hours lectures	• Books spark short courses, lecture tours	• Magazine articles help reputation as professional platform lecturer • Magazine topics become lecture topics (navigation in space, communication satellites)	• Platform lectures can become TV shows
Taxes and recreation	• Some work expenses are tax deductible • Classes become deductible/reimbursable • Profession provides opportunities for side trips in travel • Professional travel provides frequent flier mileage	• Home office and auto expenses become tax deductions • Writing trips become deductible	• Magazine article travel and recreation become deductible • Book reviews provide free recreational books to read • Review copies of books can be donated for tax deductions	• Lecture trips can be tax deductible • Local lecturing positions me for tennis, plays, social life • International lecturing provides recreational travel: partly subsidized, partly deductible

focus your attention on such profitable possibilities in connection with your selected profession.

One young schoolteacher who heard me talking about the magic grid at a faculty party borrowed the concept for her instructional program so everything she did in the classroom was specifically designed to help everything else. Try setting up a magic grid in conjunction with your own activities to see if you can purposely achieve more and better synergistic interactions. When it is finished, take a little time to figure out what the grid is trying to tell you, then lay out a bold plan to modify your activities to take advantage of any patterns that may emerge.

I soon found new ways to capitalize on the many connections I noticed in my magic grid, including ways to make my social life more stimulating and interesting with minimum extra cost. But I also spotted something else that suddenly turned my month of recuperation into a marvelously exciting adventure!

While reviewing the various notes in the magic grid, it suddenly dawned on me that all of my activities—engineering, writing, lecturing—would become much more efficient if I could gain access to a sampling of the latest books being published in my special fields. By coincidence, I had just written my first book review for *Technology Illustrated* magazine, so I wondered if it was possible that I might, in the eyes of some book publishers, be officially regarded as a book reviewer.

So I put together a one-page form letter indicating that I was a writer and a book reviewer interested in reviewing books on science, aerospace, robotics, and computers. From *Writer's Markets*, I selected about 70 book publishers, then sent the entire package to my typist together with 70 sheets of my letterhead stationary. She then typed the form letter, and inserted my letterhead stationary into the copying machine to produce 70 "personalized" letters.[6] When I had signed the letters and put them in the mail, I wondered if I might be wasting time—and postage, but actually, any worries along those lines turned out to be entirely groundless.

A few days later, free books began to trickle into my mailbox. Over the next few days, that trickle gradually turned into a flood. What a fun way to recuperate! The books were on all sorts of fascinating subjects and every one of them had just come off the press. Moreover, they were all free! Free books kept showing up in my mailbox, erratically, for the next three years. Over time, of course, they slowed to a trickle but, in the meantime, another marvelous thing happened as a result of my work on the magic grid. One day a letter arrived from an editor at Simon and Schuster. He was looking for a book on how computers impact the lives of ordinary people. He noted that, according to my form letter, I had published several books on similar subjects, and he wondered if I would submit a short outline of any book I might care to write.

---

[6] There is a lesson here: If junk-mail distributors keep sending you irritating form letters, don't get mad, just send them form letters of your own!

Soon I had outlined my next book, which they published the following year. It was called *The Robot Revolution* and it became a Book-of-the-Month Club selection and was translated into Italian and Serbo-Croatian.

In the meantime, my ribs have healed and I have become even more enthusiastic about the powers of the magic grid. Give it a try in connection with your own projects and good luck with any enjoyable adventures it may bring your way!

Lesson 45
Finding a Better Way to Sew an
Old Automobile Engine Back Together

"Everything has been thought of before; the problem is to think of it again."
— German Philosopher, Johann Wolfgang von Goethe

I ran across him by accident while I was riding my bike out on Bardstown Road. With only the simplest of tools, he was trying to put an old beat-up car back together so he could keep it running for a few more years. I was a youngster at the time, asking a flood of questions, happy that I had stumbled on a quick-witted mechanic dressed in faded overalls and a red flannel shirt unraveling at the sleeves.

At one point, he tied a piece of kite string to the end of an electrical wire, then pulled the wire out through the engine. He then tied a new wire to the end of the string and pulled it back through the engine again. A few seconds later, he had connected the new wire to the proper terminal and, when he tested it, the car hummed to life again.

"How did you know to tie on the string before you pulled that wire out?" I asked him with wide-eyed admiration.

"The first few times I made that repair, I didn't," he told me. "But then I found that I had to tear the engine down to put the new wire back in again. There's lots of time to think when you're tearing an engine apart!"

His clever solution surprised me but, of course, it was analogous to the hem-stitching our mothers were always doing on lazy Sunday afternoons. Then I asked him if he had learned any other tricky ways to fix the old jalopies driven by most of the poor families in that part of Kentucky.

"When I'm putting in new pistons, I keep them in the refrigerator overnight," he told me in confidential tones. "The next morning they slip right into the engine block easy as pie!"

Creative solutions tend to have a common characteristic. In behaving creatively, we often use analogies, and we plan for a future course of action, setting little traps along the way to catch prey we know will likely arrive with tomorrow's rising sun.

Lesson 46
Blank Worksheets to Help You Visualize Your Own Fruitful Analogies

"You have to kiss a lot of frogs to find one prince."
— Conventional Wisdom in the California Singles Scene

"When I was 90," Frank Lloyd Wright once told a reporter, "I was asked to single out my finest work. My answer was `My next one.'" Even in his declining years, Frank Lloyd Wright had a marvelous outlook on life and a simple way of expressing himself. Try to adopt those attitudes while you are filling out the two worksheets at the end of this lesson.

Start with a sketch or a diagram summarizing some carefully selected aspect of your problem. Below that drawing, write a description of the problem with emphasis on your feelings and attitudes toward its solution. Compose your description with enough passion so that anyone else who reviews what you have written will understand how you feel about the problem. Now try to develop a few well-chosen similes and metaphors. As you create these literary analogies, try to link your problem with other problems that have already been solved by some other creative individual—or Mother Nature! Solutions from nature tend to be incredibly powerful and effective. If you get stuck, spend a few minutes thinking about some of the clever solutions masterminded by Louis Pasteur, Thomas Edison, Steven Jobs, or someone else you admire.

In the space remaining on the worksheets, try to tease out additional lines of reasoning that may move you toward simple and useful solutions. A balloon diagram might prove helpful. Or, perhaps, you should make a flowchart highlighting the link between your problem and one of the metaphors or similes you wrote out.

When you have exhausted the various avenues of investigation in this exercise, make notes at the bottom of the page singling out any partial solutions that may have occurred to you while you were working your way through the two-page worksheet. Later you will be instructed to gather up your best solutions. Then, if you still have enough energy and enthusiasm left, you will be urged to trace your way through the arc of creativity again as you continue your search for simple, creative solutions.

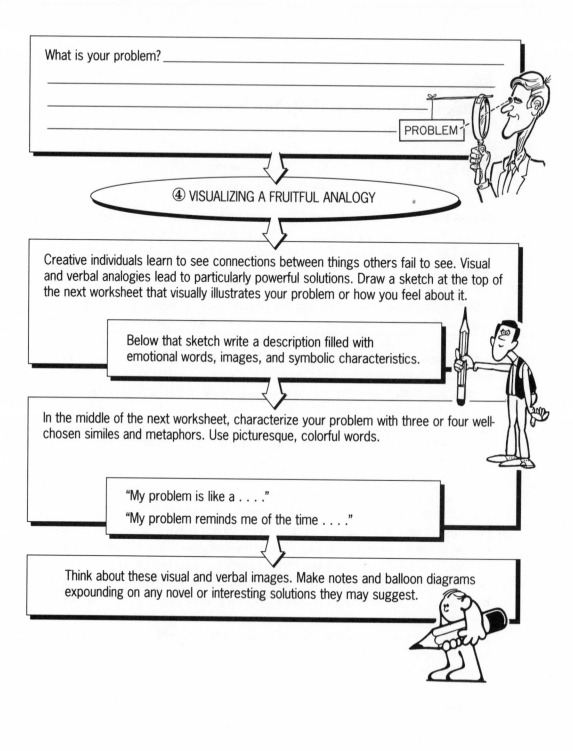

What is your problem? _____

_____

_____

_____ — PROBLEM

④ VISUALIZING A FRUITFUL ANALOGY

Creative individuals learn to see connections between things others fail to see. Visual and verbal analogies lead to particularly powerful solutions. Draw a sketch at the top of the next worksheet that visually illustrates your problem or how you feel about it.

Below that sketch write a description filled with emotional words, images, and symbolic characteristics.

In the middle of the next worksheet, characterize your problem with three or four well-chosen similes and metaphors. Use picturesque, colorful words.

"My problem is like a . . . ."

"My problem reminds me of the time . . . ."

Think about these visual and verbal images. Make notes and balloon diagrams expounding on any novel or interesting solutions they may suggest.

BREAKING THROUGH

Chapter 5
Searching for Useful Order-of-Magnitude Changes

"If you have built castles in the sky, that is where they should be; now put foundations under them."
— American Naturalist, Henry David Thoreau

During World War II front-line soldiers needed accurate artillery firing tables in ever-increasing numbers as American munitions makers developed new families of projectiles to hurl against the Nazi war machine. An artillery firing table predicts the most likely impact of a ballistic projectile by taking into account the cannon's firing angle, the current atmospheric pressure, ambient temperatures, and winds.

Huge teams of military experts were assigned to assemble artillery firing tables but, even with unlimited overtime, bottlenecks were constantly encountered as workloads continued to increase. In the hopes of circumventing these and other growing computational difficulties, two talented scientists at Philadelphia's Moore School of Engineering, J. Presper Eckert and John W. Mauchley, volunteered to build a new kind of computing machine.

They knew the Mark I at Harvard University was handling its mathematical computations using thousands of relatively simple electromechanical relays, so if they copied that approach, some level of success would have been virtually guaranteed. However, they also knew that electromechanical relays were notoriously slow and sluggish, so they made a decision to build their new computer with *electronic* switches instead.

Electromechanical relays react so slowly because, when they open or close, a little metal bar must move up or down a fraction of an inch to make or break an electrical contact. This physical movement takes at least 1/500th of a second. An electronic switch is orders of magnitude faster because, when it opens or closes, no physical object travels through space. The only thing that moves is a stream of electrons, which hurtles forward at a speed of 186,000 miles per second. Typically, a well-designed electronic switch can change states in one-millionth of a second—or even less.

In 1946, when Eckert and Mauchley's new computer finally reached operational status, they found that it could perform 5,000 mathematical computations in a single second. This meant that it was at least 2,000 times faster than its nearest competitor, the Mark I. Soon, newspaper reporters everywhere were calling it "the giant brain."

When Eckert and Mauchley decided to take a calculated risk and use unproven but highly capable electronic switches in their new computer, they placed themselves on a risky path that ended up leading them toward a billion-dollar breakthrough. By adopting a high-payoff approach, they had embraced the fifth winning strategy on the arc of creativity: *They searched for useful order-of-magnitude changes.* This strategy does not always produce acceptable results, but when it works properly, enormous productivity gains are typically achieved.

In the intervening years, other courageous innovators have made various billion-dollar breakthroughs in the same field with the introduction of transistors, integrated circuits, and parallel processing techniques. All of those innovations have triggered new order-of-magnitude improvements in modern computer design. Without their bold, but intrinsically risky attitudes, today's fastest computers could not possibly be 2,000,000 times faster than the Eniac of 1946.

Lesson 47
Magnitudes Matter!

"You always pass failure on the way to success."
— American Actor, Mickey Rooney

Magnitudes matter! A fly can walk on the ceiling, but a cat cannot, primarily because of the difference in scale. Toss that same cat from the roof of your house and it will, perhaps, live through the experience. But don't try the same thing with an elephant or giraffe.

Tiny insects called *water skimmers* can scamper across the surface of a farm pond, primarily because their total body weight is a little less than the water's surface tension. But a dull-witted sparrow attempting to imitate the water skimmer's impressive little demonstration, will sink down to join the catfish snoozing at the bottom of the pond.

Magnitudes matter! The difference between a planet and a star has everything to do with scale. Build a planet big enough, and the mass above will crush the mass below to ignite and sustain its thermonuclear fires. The difference between an atomic bomb and a pathetic little fizzle is a matter of scale, too. Below the critical mass, too many neutrons escape to keep the chain reactions firing. But if you manage to put together a ball of uranium or plutonium exceeding the critical mass, everyone in your neighborhood who manages to survive will probably complain about the noise it makes.

The Pony Express was an exciting idea, but it was doomed to failure by order-of-magnitude changes in communication technology almost as soon as it came into being—even though Alexander Majors and William Waddle invested nearly $500,000 in their ambitious venture. In 1860 they bought 500 fast horses and hired 80 young riders to carry the mail at breakneck speed between St. Louis, Missouri, and Sacramento, California. Unfortunately, less than a year and a half after their innovative service started, telegraph lines were successfully strung out across the United States along a parallel route. Horses and riders were soon trying to find some other way to make a living because of useful order-of-magnitude changes in the speed with which a message could be sent from coast to coast. Not without difficulty, horse and rider averaged a rather impressive 10 miles per hour along the entire 2,000-mile route. Even so, the service was doomed before it started because the Pony Express could not compete with the electronic telegraph signals that whipped across the countryside at 186,000 miles per second!

Be on the lookout for sudden order-of-magnitude changes in any business venture you may decide to pursue. If you can get the new technologies to work for you, your team can be a big winner, but if observant competitors beat you to the punch, you may find yourself joining those young Pony Express riders and their fast horses standing in tomorrow morning's unemployment lines.

Speed changes are especially important in the competitive world. Speed usually pays, but sometimes slower is better. Barges and pipelines are much slower methods of transportation than jet planes but for each ton-mile delivered, they are orders of magnitude less expensive. Oil and natural gas are pipeline favorites, but coal moves through pipelines, too. Powdered and mixed with water, it becomes a fluid slurry.

Slower can also be better on the factory floor. When StarKist executives learned that their tuna packers were leaving tons of meat on the bone, they slowed down operations to a more human pace. Workers were happier and more productive, and the company saved $5 million per year in reduced fish purchases when the machines were operated at a slower speed.

Lesson 48
Developing an Alice-in-Wonderland View of the World

"The brain is like a muscle. When it is in use we feel very good."
— American Astronomer, Carl Sagan

Entrepreneurs and engineers experience a sudden surge of excitement whenever they get an opportunity to change an important design parameter such as temperature, pressure, power, or velocity by an order of magnitude or more. Sometimes changes in that magnitude range can be achieved simply by making a piece of equipment extremely large or extremely small. The Water Pic, for instance, is a miniature version of the devices used in hydraulic placer-mining to wash flecks of gold from the rugged hills sticking up above the Sacramento River. The gyroscopic stabilizing device that helps smooth the ride for passengers aboard ocean-going cruise ships is a gigantic copy of the toy gyroscope balancing itself on the point of a pencil or along a horizontal string. Similarly, some practical tunneling devices are, in essence, grossly enlarged versions of the carpenter's brace and bit.

Whenever you notice an interesting device, think about how it might be used for some completely different purpose if it could be made a thousand times bigger—or a thousand times smaller. One easy method for getting yourself into the proper frame of mind to exploit such large changes in physical scale is to adopt an Alice-in-Wonderland view of the world. What would you do if you woke up tomorrow morning only to find that your body was suddenly 100 times smaller? Or bigger? Under these magical conditions, how might you use the objects littering the top of your desk to aid in your quest for survival? Can you think of some unusual way to employ an electric razor or a toothbrush that is hundreds of times bigger than the one sitting in your bathroom? Could a volleyball be of some use if you suddenly found that you were 60 feet tall? Or 3 inches tall?

Hollywood's *Incredible Shrinking Man* used a sewing needle to defend himself against playful spiders and bugs. He even wore it in his belt like a thin, but deadly, sword. The Lilliputian youngsters in *Honey, I Shrunk the Kids* zoomed through the air clinging to the back of a wildly agitated honey bee, and they ended up using Cheerios as life preservers to stay afloat in a big, fat bowl of milk.

Early in his career, Sam Walton figured out how to exploit order-of-magnitude changes in physical scale when he was searching for the most favorable locations to build and open new Wal-Mart department stores. As soon as he had earned enough money, he bought and learned how to fly a small private plane. Buzzing through the sky a few hundred feet above Main Street America, he got a marvelously clear view of empty lots, residential housing patterns, competitors' locations, and the flow of traffic along the shady, small-town streets sweeping past him down below.

Wal-Mart is much bigger today, but company executives still shy away from corporate jets, because jet-powered airplanes cannot fly low enough and slow enough for the aerial scouting missions on the scale Sam Walton first found to be so useful so many years ago.

Lesson 49
Building Big Pneumatic Tubes to Transport Human Passengers

"Impossibility: most of the things worth doing."
 — Chief Justice, Louis Brandeis

Thirty years ago, salesclerks in department stores routed money and paper receipts to different departments encased within little metal capsules sucked through long, skinny pneumatic tubes. My brother and I loved to trace the route of the tubes in each store, but we would never have imagined that creative engineers might be able to construct enlarged versions of those little tube-encased capsules big enough to carry *human* passengers from one location to another.

The concept of propelling a big, lumbering passenger train with air pressure forces may seem like a fanciful daydream swirling through the brain of some bubble-headed entrepreneur. That is why most people are surprised to learn that pneumatic (air-powered) subway trains were successfully operated in a number of locations even before my father was born.

America's first air-powered subway train was constructed on Manhattan Island in 1870 by Alfred Ely Beach, one of the early editors of *Scientific American*. His tunnel was only a little bit more than 200 yards long. Despite its small size, his underground subway rides were quite popular among the cultured gentry of Manhattan Island who came in enthusiastic swarms to ride the single block from Warren to Murray deep under the gaslights of old Broadway. Decked out in their pinstriped suits and stovepipe hats, bankers, haberdashers, and chimney sweeps alike arrived each day to inspect the richly-upholstered "motorless carriages" and to try to puzzle out the mysterious source of their motive power.

To the casual observer, the train had no obvious means of propulsion. It hissed no steam and no one ever came to feed it oats or hay. Yet it could transport endless streams of human passengers back and forth through its underground tunnel. Small wonder many of the onlookers mistook the new contraption for some kind of perpetual motion machine. But Alfred Ely Beach had absolutely no interest in fraud or sham, so he spent too much of his valuable time explaining how a large, stationary fan "shoved" the 18-passenger car through the tunnel in one direction and then "sucked" it back in the other.

They came. They gawked. They giggled. They asked silly questions. They believed everything they were told by anyone who happened to be on the scene. They were a constant delight to Beach and his many friendly colleagues. Unfortunately, however, the swarms of curious tourists did very little to help solve the project's most serious problem: money. Beach tried, in every waking moment, to attract the serious interest of Wall Street financiers. Unfortunately, in the end, it was hopeless. In 1871, after twelve months of intermittently successful operation, the tunnel went silent for the third and final time. A few weeks later Manhattan's lucrative transit franchise was awarded to a more conservative entrepreneurial team who promptly installed a conventional system of electrically powered elevated trains.

The subway train built by Alfred Ely Beach less than a decade after the end of the American Civil War was not by any means the world's first air-powered vehicle. Nor was it the largest or most successful. Thirty years earlier, in a remote corner of Northern Ireland, a far more efficient pneumatic system had sent commuter trains swishing along a carefully prepared guideway. The trains were propelled by a piston that extended from the bottom of the train car into a subterranean pressure tube 15 inches in diameter. Commuters who rode onboard the Irish trains reported that they displayed "speed, power, efficiency, smoothness, and cleanliness far superior to the (finest) steam locomotives in existence." Moreover, at first, they paid their own way, without government subsidies.

Functional copies were soon installed on the English mainland. At first they, too, worked surprisingly well; but within a few years, every one of them had either been replaced or abandoned. The major problem centered around a flexible leather flap running the full length of the pressurized tube, which could not survive the dismal British winters nor the knife-hard teeth of the energetic sewer rats who thought of it as a tasty midnight snack!

Applied over a large surface, air pressure forces can exert an amazing amount of propulsive power. If, for example, a train is 13 feet in diameter, the air pressure will ram it through a 13-foot tunnel with a force of 140,000 pounds—approximately five times the pulling power of today's largest diesel locomotives. Yet the vacuum pumps installed in the tunnel can be operated with less than a half dozen 2,500-horsepower motors. Such surprisingly small motors are practical because they can be operated continuously to store energy even when no trains are hurtling along through the tunnel.

Air pressure forces can be used to propel a commuter train over relatively short distances. When the trip stretches beyond a few dozen miles, however, air pressure gradually begins to lose its propulsive efficiency. Fortunately, in theory, for longer trips, the earth's gravitational field can help pull the train through the tunnel, furnishing propulsive forces almost for free.

The concept of propelling a subway train through a subterranean tunnel with a combination of air pressure forces and gravity was patented in 1968 by Lawrence K. Edwards of Palo Alto, California. Edwards and his team learned the engineering trade in the aerospace industry, so they tended to think on a very large scale. In fact, one of their first published studies seriously reviewed the practicality of installing a subway tube over a 3,000-mile route stretching from New York to San Francisco!

In those days petroleum products were just about the cheapest fluids in existence, so only a black-belt oracle with a Ph.D. in ESP could have foreseen that America's diplomats would soon be kneeling on the Sahara pleading for a few thousand barrels of oil. Nevertheless, Edwards realized that the world's fossil fuel supplies would not last forever, so he gurgled with delight whenever he daydreamed about the intrinsic efficiencies of his cleverly designed gravity trains. "If one ignores the losses due to the circulation of air through the tube," he wrote, "and the trifling amount of rolling friction, the train achieves a free trip!" By contrast, a commercial jetliner slurps its kerosene like a ravenous fuel hog as it "consumes billions of foot-pounds of energy in climbing to cruising altitudes, all of which is wasted by the descent at the end of the trip."

The Edwards engineering team was planning to install two gravity tubes side by side on the interior of each tunnel. Such an arrangement has two important advantages: Tunneling costs are reduced and the pressurized gases can be vented back and forth between the two tubes, thus providing extra energy savings on nearly every trip. Their concepts were developed to a high level of sophistication but, unfortunately, they were never able to raise the billions of dollars necessary to build a workable system on the scale they proposed.

"Scale up! Scale down!" might well be the rallying cry for today's creative entrepreneur. Enlarge a department store's pneumatic tubes to make them a thousand times bigger, and you may have a superior design for a nation-wide system of subway trains. Magnitudes matter—they matter more than ever in our modern large-scale industrial world.

Lesson 50
Venturing into the Heart of a Slow-Motion Computer

"Every great and commanding moment in the annals of the world is the triumph of some enthusiasm."
— American Poet, Ralph Waldo Emerson

Motion picture cameras allow us to observe and study events that were nearly impossible to view in the days when filming techniques had not yet been perfected. Film shot at normal speed can be quite revealing, but when we use film cameras to speed things up or slow them down, whole new worlds of action and adventure can suddenly come into sharp focus.

Slow-motion images of a dripping water faucet reveal, for instance, that falling raindrops are not tear-drop shaped or spherical as many speculators had previously believed. Actually, they are round on the top and slightly flattened on the bottom. With similar technology, time-lapse photography shows us in detail exactly how a sunflower stem pivots throughout a cloudless day to track the sun.

Even without actually making such a film, we can use the *concept* of slow motion to gain new insights into how objects in the real world behave if we change the time scale by a vast amount. This trick was used with great success by computer expert Dr. Ivan E. Sutherland at Harvard University to direct the attention of his colleagues toward the enormous speed variations in some of the hardware devices they were installing in modern data processing centers.

By human standards, all data processing operations seem to proceed at uniformly phenomenal speeds. Cards disappear into metal hoppers at 20 per second. Storage drums hide themselves in whirling blurs. Magnetic tapes twitch back and forth like jet-propelled nervous breakdowns. In seconds, high-speed printers spew out enough pages to bury a covey of speed-reading experts over the Christmas holidays. In our everyday lives we are not attuned to such impressive speeds, so it is easy to conclude erroneously that the various data processing devices perform at more or less the same pace. But from the processing unit's point of view, the peripheral devices exhibit vast variations in speed. Nearly all of them are maddeningly slow by electronic standards, but a few of them hardly seem to move at all.

To illustrate the enormous variations in speed, we adopt a trick first suggested by Sutherland in his Ph.D. dissertation. We imagine that we have slowed everything in a computer system down a million-fold. Instead of performing a million additions per second, our slowed-down computer will perform at a more human pace: one addition per second. If the auxiliary devices are also slowed proportionately, we begin to comprehend just how fast the computer's processing unit routinely operates. For example, an input typewriter that types 10 characters per second would type only about *1 character* per day in our millionth-speed model. (A computer receiving inputs from a fast typist would be like a worried investor receiving a telegram from his stockbroker in installments. Every morning before breakfast he receives one new letter of the message!)

A few input/output devices are orders-of-magnitude faster than typewriters, but most of them cannot come close to keeping pace with the computer's high-speed processing units. A chain printer that can print 20 lines a second is astonishingly fast from our human point of view. But it would print only *1 character every four minutes* in our millionth-speed model. Magnetic tapes that supply 100,000 characters a second would supply only *6 characters a minute*. However, since it takes about 1/500th of a second to get the tape up to speed, our slowed-down model would require half an hour to deliver its first character!

Human beings are so lethargic by electronic standards our millionth-speed computer would probably conclude that all of us are inanimate objects. A technician nervously pacing the floor as seen from the computer's point of view would take only *one step every four days* and blinking his eyes would require about 16 minutes. (Putting it another way, a modern computer can add 1,000 eight-digit numbers in the time it takes a flirtatious sailor to wink his eye.)

Some auxiliary devices, however, operate at a rather brisk pace even in the computer's reference frame. High-speed magnetic drums and cathode-ray-tube displays, for example, can nearly match the electronic speed of the processing unit. This simplifies some design difficulties, but it makes the overall problem of coordinating the various devices even more demanding and difficult. Juggling the many devices—with their extraordinary variety of operating speeds—is like trying to design an efficient freeway system that can accommodate a random mixture of race cars, covered wagons, family Chevrolets, and three-toed sloths! It can be done, but it requires a complicated variety of clever design tricks.

Whenever you are puzzled and confused by big variations in speed, try setting up a variable-speed model of the process you are attempting to study. One way to accomplish this is to film the procedures with a movie or video camera set at one film speed, then project the film at an entirely different speed. This will speed the action up or slow it down, so you can study it from a different time perspective.

Another productive approach is to use the thought-model first suggested by Dr. Ivan E. Sutherland. Merely adjust the speed upward or downward conceptually by making a few simple pencil-and-paper calculations.

If you are a whiz at data processing techniques, a third promising possibility also suggests itself: Do a computer simulation complete with animated graphics. Then play the animation at several different speeds so you can study the process from different time perspectives. If you are lucky, you will gain powerful new insights into how the process under study actually operates.

Lesson 51
Using Logarithmic Graphs to Depict Large-Scale Conceptual Ideas

"The difficult: that which can de done immediately.
The impossible: that which takes a little longer."
    — Spanish/American Philosopher, George Santayana

Graphs and charts, properly constructed, can help us portray complicated situations with amazing clarity and effectiveness. A picture may be worth a thousand words, but a skillfully drawn graph can be worth a thousand pictures! If you doubt the truth of that assertion, get a copy of Edward R. Tufte's exciting book, *The Visual Display of Quantitative Information,* and read his interesting commentary on the construction of the beautifully crafted six-dimensional graph put together by graphics expert Charles Joseph Minard. On a single sheet of paper, his graph summarizes the terrible fate of Napoleon's army during the invasion of Russia in the bone-chilling winter of 1812.

A thick band at the top of Minard's graph represents the size of Napoleon's army (442,000 men) as they crossed the Niemen River on the Polish-Russian border. Along the way, the width of the band gradually shrinks at each location on the map as Napoleon's forces fitfully melt away. By September they finally managed to reach Moscow with a much smaller army of 100,000 men.

Napoleon's retreat is depicted by another steadily shrinking band as the merciless Russian winter cuts down the rest of his troops. A temperature scale at the bottom of the diagram quantifies the horrible human suffering his soldiers were forced to endure during their desperate retreat. A big drop in the number of survivors is depicted at the crossing of the Berezina River, the last great calamity before they finally limped back into Poland. At that point only 10,000 soldiers remained from the 442,000 who had so confidently initiated the Russian campaign.

Minard's superb graphic depiction also highlights the movements of auxiliary forces routed to various locations to cover the rear and the flanks of Napoleon's ragtag army. All together, six different variables are successfully represented on a single page: the size of Napoleon's army, its physical location on a two-dimensional map, the date they were at each location, the general direction the army is moving at each point along the way, and the temperatures on various dates during Napoleon's devastating retreat.

In preparation for his intriguing book, Tufte studied thousands of published graphs, but he reserves the highest praise for the one depicting Napoleon's Russian campaign. "It may well be the best statistical graphic ever drawn," he quietly concludes. Graphs and statistics have somehow gotten a bad name with many American students and private citizens alike. In sufficiently skilled hands, however, graphs can be a big help as you try to formulate simple, creative solutions. "If your statistics are boring," Tufte concludes, "then you've got the wrong statistics."

A well-designed graph can definitely be a work of beauty and sometimes it can save lives, too. Such a graph was constructed in September 1854, by Dr. John Snow who was struggling to pinpoint the cause of a deadly epidemic raging through central London. On a city map he marked the locations of eleven public water pumps surrounded by 500 dots representing the living quarters of each British citizen who had died of cholera. Soon an obvious pattern began to emerge: the homes of all the victims were clustered around the Broad Street pump. At this point Dr. Snow did not call for the formation of a committee. Nor did he start a new ecology movement. He merely pulled off the pump handle, thus ending London's cholera epidemic.

Order-of-magnitude changes are sometimes difficult to portray on an ordinary rectilinear graph but another approach is available that can be surprisingly effective: Try using logarithmic scales or scales that increase by a factor of ten at each new major division. To illustrate the fundamental utility of logarithmic scales, we consider the various modes of transportation that could be used on a journey from St. Louis, Missouri, to San Francisco, California. Early covered wagons were able to complete such a journey in about three months compared with 10 days for the Pony Express. Today you can drive a private car on that same 2,000-mile trek in about 50 hours, whereas a commercial jetliner can get you there in 4 hours or less. The astronauts sweep across the sky paralleling the route from St. Louis to San Francisco in 7 minutes (although manned capsules usually travel in the opposite direction!).

These travel times span several orders of magnitude, so how can we hope to depict them accurately on the same graphical scale? The simple bar charts at the top of Figure 5.1 show why a rectilinear graph (one with evenly spaced scales) is a bad choice. As you can see, all the bars on the right are essentially coincident with the horizontal axis. No height difference can be discerned on the scale being used. The graph at the bottom shows why a properly constructed logarithmic scale works so much better. Notice that each horizontal line running across the logarithmic version is a factor of 10 (one order of magnitude) larger than the horizontal line immediately below. In this case, all the information is clearly depicted on the same graph even though the data values vary by more than five orders of magnitude!

Another interesting logarithmic graph is sketched in Figure 5.2. It depicts historical advances in timekeeping accuracy over the past 1,000 years. Notice that each major division on the vertical scale represents a hundred-fold improvement in timekeeping accuracy.

Figure 5.1   Travel times for various methods of travel.

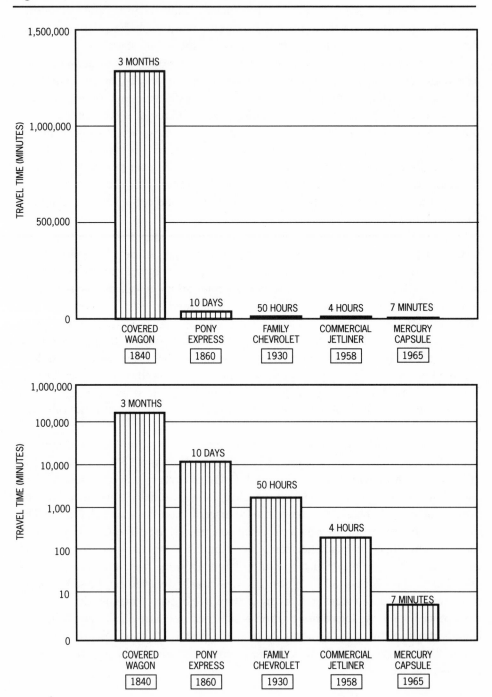

Figure 5.2   Historical improvements in timekeeping accuracy.

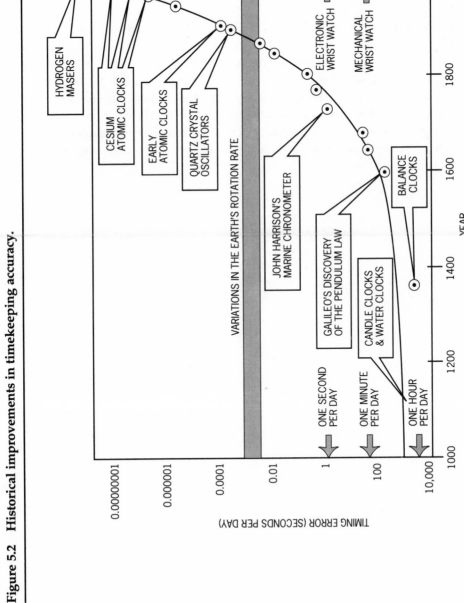

A thousand years ago the best available timekeeping devices were candle clocks and water clocks which, on average, lost or gained about 15 minutes per day. In the intervening centuries, scientists and technicians have gradually perfected mechanical balance clocks, pendulum clocks, marine chronometers, quartz crystal oscillators, and atomic clocks. Today's best commercial atomic clocks (hydrogen masers) are so stable and accurate that they lose or gain only one second every 8 million years.[7]

The logarithmic graph in Figure 5.2 depicts a 12 order-of-magnitude improvement in timekeeping accuracy. If we tried to plot that same data on an ordinary rectilinear graph, all the parts except the two on the far right would be sitting on the horizontal axis. Logarithmic graphs are a bit harder to construct but, in many situations, they are essential for producing consistent and readable results.

If you are working on a simple, creative solution involving an order-of-magnitude improvement in some important performance parameter such as speed, strength, weight, or power, you may discover big benefits if you experiment with logarithmic graphical scales.

---

[7] If the first cave man had had such a clock strapped to his wrist on the day he was born, it would not yet have lost a single second!

Lesson 52
Trying to Predict the Future in a World Where Everything Is Changing at a Breakneck Pace

"High expectations are the key to everything."
— Billionaire Marketeer, Sam Walton

Whenever technology is moving at a rapid pace toward some kind of order-of-magnitude advancement, the task of predicting what will actually happen becomes incredibly difficult. In the face of big changes, even world-ranking experts who are attempting to make predictions in their own field of expertise sometimes make incredible mistakes.

"Making predictions is always difficult," nuclear physicist Hans Bethe once told a lecture audience, "especially when they involve the future." Other knowledgeable experts have not always been quite so cautious in their assessment of the soothsayer's thankless task. Maybe that is why they have so often made embarrassingly incorrect assessments and evaluations:

"The Americans may have need of the telephone, but we do not. We have plenty of messenger boys."
— Sir William Preece, Chief of the British Postal System, 1876

"No mere machine can replace a reliable and honest clerk."
— Remington Arms Company Executive on being offered the rights to manufacture the typewriter, 1898

"Radio has no future."
— Lord Kelvin, President of London's Royal Society, 1904

"The public will never accept artificial silks."
— Bradford Silk Mill Directors upon being offered the rights to manufacture rayon, 1912

"There is no likelihood that man can ever tap the power of the atom."
— Robert Milliken, Nobel-Prize-Winning Physicist, 1923

"We must not be misled to our own detriment to assume that the untried machine can displace the proved and tried horse."
— John K. Kerr, Major General of the U.S. Army, 1938

"Television won't last. It's a flash in the pan."
— Mary Somerville, Radio Technologist and Pioneer, 1948

"I think there is a world market for about five computers."
— Thomas Watson, IBM Executive, 1958

Contemporary experts of world-class stature made these and many other grossly inaccurate predictions. But history records one prediction that is even more incredible still. In 1899 officials at the U.S. Patent Office sent a rather worrisome evaluation of future technologies to President William McKinley. "Everything that can be invented has been invented," it concluded without qualification.

Of course, we should not be fooled into believing that all the difficulties inherent in making accurate predictions have arisen with the rapidly emerging technological advancements of the twenty-first century. Confident predictions made by respected experts have been going awry for at least 2,000 years. This is what Cicero had to say about futuristic prognostication when he was addressing the Roman Senate: "It seems to me that no soothsayer should be able to look at another soothsayer without laughing." Soothsayers are better paid in our more affluent era but Cicero's caustic remarks apply just as well today as they did 20 centuries ago.

Lesson 53
Building Fairy Castles in the Sky

"Failure: not falling down, but staying down."
— American Film Actress, Mary Pickford

In 1957 when Russian rocket scientists launched the first Sputnik, I was a junior in college on a beautiful green campus in the bluegrass region of Kentucky. That next Friday afternoon when my class in differential equations was finally dismissed, I hitchhiked 60 miles along a dusty country road to my hometown, Springfield, Kentucky, populated by 2,000 placid souls.

The next morning I was walking along Main Street when a high-school buddy, chubby freckle-faced Johnny Hardin came walking up to me in front of Milburn's shoe repair shop. "Hey Tom, I hear the Russians launched a new artificial earth satellite," he said with wide-eyed amazement. "They have one, do you think we should have one?"

It's a little embarrassing to think about it now, but at the time I couldn't think of a single reason why our country should launch a man-made satellite into space. But before I could say anything, Johnny Hardin answered his own question: "I don't think we should be willing to spend all that money," he said. "After all, there's *nothin'* out there."

Neither of us realized it at the time, but Johnny Hardin was precisely right. There is nothin' out there. In fact, *there are three kinds of nothin' out there* and all three of them involve profitable order-of-magnitude changes that are destined to enrich our lives in a hundred dozen different ways. Space, it turns out, is a marvelous place to obtain useful order-of-magnitude changes.

The first kind of nothin' in outer space is no gravity, or what we sometimes call *microgravity*. Travel upward from the surface of the earth into a low-attitude orbit and the gravity pulling on your body will decrease by a factor of a million. Here on earth gravity keeps you and your cornflakes from drifting up to the ceiling. It also causes your coffee grounds to sink to the bottom of your cup, and, if you cool your coffee with a cube of ice, it makes the ice float on top.

These three physical properties—weight, sedimentation, and buoyancy—are virtually nonexistent in space. If an astronaut mixes oil and water, the oil will not float to the top. If he lights a match, the smoke will not drift upward. If he flips a coin, it will not fall back into his hand. Instead, it will travel in a straight line until it slams into the ceiling of his spacecraft.

Surprisingly, short-term microgravity here on earth was being used to make useful products even before the start of the American Civil War when munitions makers opened up the free-fall shot tower in Baltimore that we discussed in Chapter 4. Today weightlessness is still being used for that same purpose, and in the formation of the tiny glass beads for use on reflecting highway markers. Microgravity is also helping the space shuttle astronauts produce two useful products in outer space that are already being used by the people living on earth.

Tiny latex microspheres one-tenth the diameter of a human hair were the first successful product made in space. On each mission on which they are made, the space shuttle astronauts produce four ounces of the spheres with a retail value exceeding $5 million per pound—1,000 times the value of 24-karat gold. Scientific laboratories purchase the microspheres in $400 vials, each of which contains 15 million microspheres.

Smaller latex spheres have long been used by scientists and technicians to calibrate optical microscopes and to measure the holes in high-precision filters and porous membranes. Laboratory technicians sprinkle them into the field of view of optical microscopes to serve as tiny "yardsticks" so they can gauge the size of the other objects in the field of view. Precisely calibrated microspheres help ensure uniformity in the production of finely ground powders such as paint pigments, cooking flour, explosives, and toner particles for copying machines. Medical practitioners use them when they are counting human blood cells and in glaucoma and cancer research.

For many years, latex spheres ranging from 1 to 3 microns in diameter (1 micron = 1/25,000th of an inch) have been "grown" in a bath of heated water in ground-based laboratories. Random Brownian motion of the water molecules buffets the small spheres to hold them in suspension while they are growing to the desired size. Unfortunately, for larger spheres, gravity causes the material to sink to the bottom of the container where they settle into a gooey cream or solidify into spheres with nonuniform sizes and shapes. Much larger microspheres can be produced in the weightlessness of space because there are practically no gravitational forces to pull them out of suspension from the liquid in which they float.

Incidentally, my friend Johnny Hardin now owns and operates a self-service supermarket in Springfield, Kentucky, called the Downtown Supermarket. There he sells several products whose production benefits from the use of space-age microspheres for precise granule calibration. These include small cans of spray paint, cooking flour, and women's face powder.

The second successful space-made product is a motion picture film called *The Dream Is Alive*, a 37-minute adventure filmed by the astronauts riding aboard the space shuttle. Tickets are sold for $4 each at 40 specially equipped IMAX theaters throughout the Western world. Exhibitors are delighted with the film's money-making potential, which came as no surprise in view of the popularity of Hollywood's *Star Wars* trilogy and the millions of enthusiastic tourists who crowd into the Smithsonian's Air and Space Museum.

In the opening sequences of the film, Walter Cronkite supplies the commentary as the shuttle thunders upward into outer space from Cape Canaveral, Florida. Once the astronauts reach orbit, they deploy a 105-foot solar array, capture and repair an ailing satellite, gulp floating shrimp directly from the air, and frolic around in zero gravity. These sequences successfully portray the ingenuity and enthusiasm of the men and women we pay to travel into space.

Recently when Johnny Hardin was a delegate to a marketing convention in Washington, D.C., he took his family down to the Washington Mall to watch *The Dream Is Alive* at the Air and Space Museum. His wife's favorite part was watching the astronauts sleeping in their bunk beds. Their bodies are restrained, but their hands and arms are floating up toward the ceiling in eerie weightlessness.

The second kind of nothin' found in abundance in outer space is no air—the hard vacuum. For decades vacuum technology has been used here on earth to produce useful products for largely oblivious consumers. Every incandescent light bulb houses a man-made vacuum; so does the picture tube in every color television set. Vacuum technology is also used in refrigeration equipment, in the freeze-drying of foods, and in the welding of certain dissimilar metals. Two hundred miles above your head, the air experiences a dramatic order-of-magnitude reduction: It is only one-trillionth as dense as the air now filling your lungs. At the Rockwell International facility where I work in Seal Beach, California, we spent $8 million building a new 40-foot vacuum chamber to simulate the ambient vacuum found in outer space. But the pumps in our vacuum chamber must work for several hours to produce a vacuum that is not nearly as good as the one the astronauts can obtain free in space. Open the door of a spaceship, and the vacuum outside becomes instantly available for many kinds of space-age research.

The virtual absence of air in space will allow tomorrow's aerospace engineers to develop surprisingly inexpensive inflatable structures. In the late 1950s, several giant Echo balloons 135 feet in diameter were inflated in space a few hundred miles above the earth. They reflected radio messages from one ground transmitter to another. In one experiment, a crude television image was bounced from coast to coast. It originated from the Massachusetts Institute of Technology in Boston and it read "M-I-T." Inflation of those enormous silver bubbles was possible only because of the natural vacuum of outer space. On the ground, working against atmospheric pressure, 80,000 pounds of gases were required to inflate an Echo balloon. But in the vacuum of space, only 30 pounds of gases were needed to do the same job just as effectively.

Large geodesic domes, parabolic mirrors, and other inflatable structures can be erected in space with comparable efficiency. Unenclosed television picture tubes and klystrons (extremely efficient microwave energy transmitters) may also be possible in any orbit about the earth. In addition, scientists are investigating the practicality of processing rare metals and biological materials in the wispy atmosphere on the space frontier.

The third kind of nothin' found in outer space is nothin' to block your view, or what space-age researchers sometimes refer to as the *wide-angle view*. Here on earth a fairly big wide-angle view is important for firefighting towers, military reconnaissance, and aerial crop surveys. Move upward from the surface of the earth into outer space and the amount of the earth you can see increases by a factor of 500,000 or more. These order-of-magnitude changes in the wide-angle view are already being used in a number of important ways to enrich the lives of the people who live on the surface of earth.

For instance, the cloud-cover maps you see on the evening news, which are broadcast from orbiting satellites, have greatly improved long-range weather forecasts. The Landsat earth-resources satellite, which also capitalizes on the wide-angle view from space, provides us with valuable information on cropland use, snow cover, mineral deposits, and hidden sources of pollution. Such a satellite picks up reflected light from the surface of the earth with a sensitivity to color far surpassing that of the human eye. By enhancing the resulting images with computers, experts can detect subtle features spread over huge areas they would fail to see even if they walked the land. Colorful clays, for instance, are associated with deposits of uranium, and certain plants are unusually healthy when they grow over hidden treasures of tin and molybdenum. The aerospace trade journals are crammed with stories of minerals and other valuable deposits discovered from space, including diamonds, petroleum, copper, and geothermal steam.

Communication satellites are today's most profitable application of the broadranging view from space. Annual revenues currently exceed $3 billion, with annual growth rates of 20 to 30 percent. Twenty-four countries, including Indonesia and Brazil, own and operate their own communication satellites. At last count, 140 nations had ground antennas capable of receiving voice and video messages from space. While you are reading these words, 50,000 telephone calls are passing through communication satellites for relay to distant locations. So are at least 200 color television shows. Religious sermons, video conferences, computer data, stock-market quotes all depend on instantaneous space-age transmissions through orbiting satellites.

Most of today's communication satellites are launched into *geosynchronous* orbits 22,300 miles above the earth. At that particular altitude, a satellite's orbital motion exactly matches the earth's rotation rate. Thus, to the people living on earth, the satellite appears to hang motionless above a particular point on the equator. Some modern satellites can handle as many as 20,000 telephone conversations plus several channels of high-quality color TV. Within a few years, improved versions will be providing world-wide "pocket telephone" service to busy travelers and beaming international television programs broadcast directly into our homes. Incidentally, the building that housed Milburn's shoe repair shop today contains a new business, B & E Television, that sells and installs satellite dishes for the people living around Springfield, Kentucky.

One easy way to achieve useful order-of-magnitude changes in important design parameters is to move our production facilities from the surface of the earth upward into the space flight environment where profit-making opportunities are beginning to sprout at an amazing rate. Already, today, space industrialization is bringing in $5 billion per year to farsighted American entrepreneurs and, despite the current recession, annual revenues have been growing at 20 to 30 percent. Small wonder space industrialization expert Art Dula feels his excitement growing whenever he ponders the commercial opportunities that have been emerging along the space frontier. "The next generation of billionaires," he believes, "is going to come from the business of space."

Lesson 54
Big Hopes for Tomorrow's Micromachines

"Genius: the capacity for seeing connections where lesser men see none."
— American Psychologist, William James

"An ant can carry many times its own weight," notes William Trimmer, editor of the *Journal of Microelectromechanical Systems*, "not because it's so much stronger than we are, but because the scaling laws of nature make small things relatively stronger and faster." By applying a highly refined version of the same technology used in producing silicon computer chips, today's experts in nanotechnology have been fashioning tiny silicon grippers, generators, and electric motors with moving parts no bigger than the period at the end of this sentence.

Many tiny devices of this type are being developed in the laboratory, and a few of them are already being sold in today's commercial marketplace. One of them, for instance, is used to measure abrupt decelerations for air-bag triggering units. It costs only about $10, less than one-sixth as much as the larger units it has been replacing.

Someday, a tiny little drill may be crawling through your bloodstream where it will search out and destroy any plaque deposits building up inside your arteries and veins. Some advanced versions may even be equipped with a pair of nanotechnology tweezers to snatch up globules of dangerous cholesterol along the way, thus reducing your chances of suffering from heart disease and strokes. Another device built on a similar scale may someday be placing human eggs among sperm precisely enough to enhance success rates for *in vitro* (test tube) fertilization.

Many research firms around the world are finding new ways to integrate the new devices with tomorrow's electronic miracle chips to provide awesomely efficient cooperative arrangements: tiny brains feeding signals into tiny muscles. "We want to give computers the means to interact with the real world," explains Berkeley Professor Richard S. Muller, "using the equivalent of hands, noses, ears, and eyes."

Many of today's microelectronic devices are, in fact, being developed as miniature sensors to detect motion, beams of light, or changes in chemical composition. Some of them are made from parts smaller than the cross section of a human hair. Because of their small size, they can be operated by even the tiniest hint of pneumatic or hydraulic pressure. Many of them are several orders of magnitude smaller than their full-size counterparts. They also tend to be cheaper, less power hungry, more precise, and more reliable, too.

Lesson 55

Structured Worksheets to Help You Uncover Useful Order-of-Magnitude Changes

"Wit has truth in it; wisecracking is simply calisthenics with words."
— American Author, Dorothy Parker

I was born and raised in a little wooden house on Armory Hill in Springfield, Kentucky, looking down on the tree-lined streets below. We played in the woods finding birds' nests and honey bees, swinging on old grapevines, pulling frisky sunfish from gurgling streams. Our family was gravel-driveway poor, but at meal-times, we always had enough to eat. We had warm clothes. We had good friends. We had almost everything a family needs. But in those early childhood years, we never had enough store-bought toys.

Fortunately, at an early age, we learned how to make zeechers. My brother and I invented them in our backyard, where we made them by the dozens. Sometimes we dismantled old zeechers to make new ones. Incidentally, we also invented the name.

A zeecher is a handmade machine constructed by kludging together bits and pieces from other devices with a maximum possible number of moving parts. Our zeecher-of-the-week, for instance, might include a small electric motor, assorted roller-skate wheels, chains and sprockets from an old Singer sewing machine, the illuminated dial from a busted radio, and even my mother's snazziest egg timer (if we could manage to sneak it out of the kitchen unnoticed).

Zeechers usually do not perform useful functions, but in my mind's eye, they have always represented the essence of creativity. They turn the problem inside out—or stand it on its head. They combine unusual components in fresh, new ways. They emphasize novelty and surprise and they trigger excitement and curiosity even among those who do not fully understand how they work.

Watch out for funny combinations—at home or on the job—because an amazing number of creative solutions are actually zeechers in disguise. In his book, *A Whack on the Side of the Head*, Roger von Oech explains how Johannes Gutenberg combined two devices, the wine press and the coin punch, to make a powerful new zeecher:

> The purpose of the coin punch was to leave an image on a small area such as a gold coin. The function of the wine press was . . . to apply a force over a large area in order to squeeze the juice out of grapes. One day Gutenberg playfully asked himself: "What if I took a bunch of coin punches and put them together under the force of the wine press so that they left their images on paper?" The resulting combination was the printing press and moveable type.

John Landis Mason of Vineland, New Jersey, never heard of a Zeecher. Nevertheless, he managed to build a highly profitable version in 1832. From his early childhood years he had seen local farm families struggling to preserve enough nutritious food to carry them through the long New England winters. Mostly they pickled, salted, or dried vegetables, meats, and fruits. Or they buried the food in cold cellars under heaps of charcoal, corn husks, or sawdust in the vain hope of holding at least some of the worst bugs and rodents at bay.

Some daring individuals packed items in glass bottles and jars, then tried to seal out the air as best they could. Cork stoppers or paper-wrapped corncobs provided a fairly good seal for narrow-mouthed bottles. But wide-mouthed jars had to be sealed with wax or lard which seldom worked well.

For years Mason had been running a machine shop where he made and sold screw-top metal cans. Sealing problems aside, he knew that glass jars were ideal for food preservation. Glass tends to be chemically inert, impervious to air, transparent, and easy to reuse. So he decided to combine two familiar objects: the metal screw cap and the glass jar. Soon he had perfected a new kind of Zeecher that solved nearly all of his neighbor's canning problems: the Mason jar. Within a decade, men, women, and children everywhere had also become his neighbors.

When he was a 27-year-old graduate student matriculating at Philadelphia's Drexel Institute of Technology, Norman Joseph Woodland kludged together a new kind of Zeecher for use in modern supermarkets. After a few weeks of work, he perfected the linear barcodes now found on nearly all of today's food items.

According to Woodland's personal account, his contribution consisted of combining two established technologies: the movie soundtrack and the Morse code. "I just extended the dots and dashes downward and made narrow lines out of them," he later told a reporter. "Then I figured out how to decode the black and white stripes using a modified version of the movie sound system developed by Lee de Forest.

In the 1920s de Forest had affixed a voice-generated stripe consisting of varying shades of grey to the side of a strip of celluloid motion picture film. He then sent a beam of light through the film as it was threaded through the projector. Photoelectric cells on the back side of the film translated the variations in brightness into a corresponding waveform which was then converted into sound by loudspeakers strategically spaced around the theater.

Woodland adopted the same basic principle, but the light-intensity variations in his supermarket scanners were created by reflecting bright beams of light from the alternating black-and-white stripes on his binary barcodes.

Americans don't yet realize it, but they definitely need to learn how to make more and better zeechers. Unfortunately, today, zeecher expertise is becoming a vanishing skill. It has begun to disappear because our younger generation is almost always neck-deep in store-bought toys that would have turned my brother and me snake-green with envy. Today's youngsters seldom need to make, modify, or repair their own zeechers. If they did, our country's future competitive posture would probably be assured.

The worksheets scattered throughout this book are purposely designed to unearth and develop your innate zeecher-making skills. The ones at the end of this lesson will help guide you toward discovering useful order-of-magnitude changes. Write your current problem formulation at the top of the first page, then follow the instructions on the next two pages as you attempt to discover, use, and refine large-scale changes in important design parameters. Hopefully, this will help lead you toward new ways of teasing out better solutions.

As you play with this exercise, try to get your emotions to work in parallel with what you are trying to do. Cultivate a passion for your fondest dreams. Find a better way, then improve it. Stick like glue. Learn to ignore your harshest critics. Eventually, they too may share your dreams for the future.

What is your problem? _____
_____
_____
_____

⑤ SEARCHING FOR USEFUL ORDER-OF-MAGNITUDE CHANGES

An Alice-in-Wonderland view of the world, in which things change by a factor of 10 or more, often helps us tease out useful solutions. Describe how your problem would be affected if you or some of the objects involved were suddenly 10 times larger. _____
_____
_____
_____
_____

What if you or some of the objects were 10 times smaller? _____
_____
_____
_____
_____
_____

Review these observations and make notes on any new solutions they may suggest. __
_____
_____
_____
_____
_____

How would your problem be affected if things were suddenly speeded up 100-fold? ___

_____

_____

_____

What if things were slowed down 100-fold? _____

_____

_____

_____

Radio waves, video images, and electronic devices such as computers can speed things up or slow them down. Make notes on how electronics might help solve your problem. _____

_____

_____

_____

Gravity, atmospheric pressure, and viewing areas change dramatically when we move into space. Brainstorm ways in which space technology might help. _____

_____

_____

_____

_____

People make a big difference. How could you solve your problem if you suddenly had 100 times more people? _____

_____

_____

What would you be forced to do if you suddenly only had one person part time? _____

_____

_____

_____

Review the notes on this page. Make more notes in the margins on any new solutions they may suggest.

Chapter 6
Being Alert to Happy Serendipity

"The difference between the impossible and the possible lies in a person's determination."
— Baseball Coach, Tommy Lasorda

One person with one simple, creative idea can change the world forever. It happened in 1581 when Galileo Galilei was resting on a wooden bench in a lovely little Italian church near the Leaning Tower of Pisa. While he was sitting there enjoying that soft, summer afternoon, he focused his attention on something many other churchgoers had noticed a thousand times before: a candle hanging on a chain, gently swaying in the breeze. But Galileo was far more intuitive than any of his predecessors, so he figured out something all of them had failed to see. The amount of time required for the candle to swing back and forth was independent of its swinging arc. If it traveled along a short arc, it moved more slowly; if it traveled along a longer arc, it moved faster to compensate.

Galileo carefully recorded his observation, but he never attempted to build a clock based on the pendulum principle he had managed to discover. He did, however, suggest that others do so, and soon timekeeping accuracies had improved to a remarkable degree. Moreover, the construction of precise clockwork mechanisms quickly led to the building of other precision machines. Soon technological improvements began to sweep across Europe in wave after wave. Some historians have, in fact, credited Galileo's simple observation with the spawning of the Industrial Revolution.

Galileo had not wandered into that pretty little Italian church with revolution in mind. But, once inside, he was fortunate enough *to experience happy serendipity,* the sixth winning strategy on the arc of creativity. Serendipity occurs when we are seeking one thing, and end up finding something completely different, or when we stumble on a creative solution almost entirely by accident.

Of course, some people manage to place themselves within sight of a major technological breakthrough and then, without stopping to evaluate, walk right past it toward something else. "Chance favors the prepared mind," observed the French scientist Louis Pasteur. His assertion contains a distinct measure of practical truth, especially if we bear in mind that the thing we are looking for almost never comes our way, at least not in the form we had expected.

Life is a pinball machine, not a Swiss watch. With some effort, we may be able to urge that shiny metal ball to roll in some preferred direction—where targets of opportunity seem more likely to occur. But we can never plan in advance the precise trajectory the ball will follow. "No plan survives contact with the enemy," observed Major General Chaim Herzog of the Israeli army. That is because in battle, as in everyday life, unforeseen contingencies tend to spoil the intended results. Of course, if you end up with a simple, creative solution worth several billion dollars, no one will much care whether it was the one you originally set out to pursue.

Serendipity has played a big role in many of mankind's most important discoveries. These have included vulcanized rubber, the self-starter for automobiles, Raytheon's microwave oven, the Daguerre photographic plates, the cotton gin, and many, many others. In this chapter you will learn how a few of these important discoveries came to be, and how you can increase your chances for experiencing serendipity, which even today plays a crucial role in the major breakthroughs that occur in our modern technological world.

Lesson 56
The Practical Benefits of Taking a Bath

"You'll never be a loser until you quit trying."
— Football Coach, Mike Ditka

Serendipity typically occurs when we are distracted, relaxing, or even taking a bath. Two thousand years ago, Archimedes was sitting in his favorite tub when suddenly he realized that he could measure the volume of any solid object by the amount of water it displaced. Without stopping to write anything down—or even put his boxer shorts back on—Archimedes raced through the streets of Athens letting his neighbors know what a marvelously clever man he had turned out to be. "Eureka! Eureka!" he shouted at the top of his lungs. "I have found it! I have found it!"

History does not record what fellow Athenians thought Archimedes, red-faced, wet, and naked, had suddenly managed to discover, nor if any of them stopped what they were doing to snicker up their sleeves. We do know today, of course, that immodest Archimedes had accidentally stumbled on a method for determining if the king's crown was made of pure gold—without cutting into it or melting it down!

Even in these tolerant times, running through the streets in your birthday suit may not be a paticularly good idea, even if you do happen to stumble on a creative solution. Nevertheless, when serendipity comes your way, you will probably share some of the excitement Archimedes felt on that glorious day. Heartfelt emotions can, indeed, constitute a reliable guide that can help us identify creative solutions worthy of further consideration. Solve a practical problem creatively, and you will almost always feel a sudden surge of excitement. Learn about a creative solution masterminded by someone else, and you are likely to feel a slight tinge of jealousy instead!

Lesson 57
Adventures in Serendipity

"The person who makes a success of living is the one who sees his goal steadily and aims for it unswervingly."
— Hollywood Film Producer, Cecil B. deMille

In the early 1900s a young man named Earl Dickson accepted an executive position with a medium-sized company that produced and sold most of the surgical tape being used by American doctors. A few months earlier, he had married a pretty young lady who was just learning how to cook on an old-fashioned wood-burning stove, so he got plenty of practice wrapping her hands with bandages whenever she cut or burned herself.

Of course, he worried about her every time he had to leave for work, so he began experimenting with various ways for combining gauze pads and tape so that, when she was alone, she could bandage one hand with the other. Unfortunately, while his simple bandaging kit sat around in the kitchen to await his wife's next accidental injury, the tape dried out and the gauze pad became a bit dirty. After experimenting with various protective covers, Dickson found that ordinary crinoline did the trick quite effectively. Soon his company, Johnson and Johnson, began to market the new product, which they called the *Band-Aid*. In this case, marriage, injury, and concern had made a winning combination. Serendipity had struck again!

Years later, an engineer at Raytheon had a similar experience. When he was assigned to work on a new piece of radar equipment, he noticed that candy bars in his pockets melted when he was near active radar transmitters. Intrigued by that unexpected phenomenon, he went out and bought some popcorn and found that radar beams could cook that, too. Over the next few months he and his fellow engineers gradually figured out how to perfect the Radarange which is sold today as the microwave oven!

When Alexander Fleming noticed an old petri dish in his laboratory contaminated with a rather disgusting slimy green mold, he resisted the temptation to dump its contents down the drain—as other, less inquisitive researchers might have done. Instead, he studied its curious growth patterns only to find an unusual ring-like structure surrounding the contamination at the center of the dish. Something mysterious, and quite unexpected, was killing the microbes that were taking a nap on his petri dish. Later he learned that it was a powerful germ-killer, penicillin, which might not otherwise have been discovered—at least not then and not by him.

In 1948 an equally inquisitive citizen of Switzerland, Georges de Mestral, went for a walk along the pleasant Swiss countryside. That night when he got back home, he noticed a clump of sticktights clinging with great tenacity to the sleeves of his winter jacket. Most other hikers would have been mildly irritated by the fuzzy mess he found. But de Mestral wondered what made them stick so tightly, so he pulled off a few and put them on a glass slide under his microscope. Soon he learned that they were covered with tiny curved hooks that snared themselves in the loops in his jacket. The powerful curiosity of de Mestral eventually led him to the creation of Velcro, which has become a universal fastener with a multitude of practical applications.

When a chemist at G. D. Searle accidentally spilled an experimental fluid on his laboratory workbench, he tried to clean it up as best he could. Later, when he was reading a book, he licked his finger to turn a page and his finger tasted curiously sweet, even sweeter, it seemed, than sugar. Aspartame soon became a laboratory curiosity and went on to become big business in the diet food market; today we know it under its trade name as NutraSweet.

Serendipity later paid a most welcome visit to 3M's laboratories when a young researcher dropped a glass beaker on the floor filled with a new industrial compound. Several days later she noticed clean spots on her sneakers wherever stray drops had landed. Out of that accidental spill emerged a dirt-repellant substance now marketed with great success as Scotchgard fabric protector.

Pursuing accidental discoveries of this type almost always involves a rather large and worrisome calculated risk for any courageous innovator. That is why forward-looking managers need to find good ways to take the sting out of research-related failures among the researchers who live and work on the firing lines. Jim Burke, head of the New Products Division at Johnson & Johnson, tries to cultivate such a professional stance toward the members of his staff. He was initiated into that magnanimous attitude by General Robert Wood Johnson, who once summoned Burke into his office immediately after one of Burke's first stabs at innovation—a new children's chest rub—had failed miserably in the competitive marketplace.

"Are you the one who just cost us all that money?" he asked Jim Burke, who had been struggling to come up with some way to defend himself. Before Burke could formulate a defensive response, Johnson went on with his mock tirade: "Well, I just want to congratulate you. If you are making mistakes, that means you are making decisions and taking risks. And you won't grow unless you take risks."

Long ago, General Johnson realized that success and failure are almost always two sides of the same coin. Thumb through the biographies of supposedly successful leaders: Napoleon Bonaparte, Harry Truman, Abraham Lincoln, Ulysses S. Grant—pick anybody you consider to be successful—and you will almost always find numerous failures threaded among their more commonly reported successes.

Lesson 58
Watching an Apple Fall from a Tree

"Fall seven times. Stand up eight."
—Old Japanese Proverb

In 1665 serendipity graciously entered the life of Isaac Newton shortly after he left Cambridge University to escape the ravages of the Black Plague. Safely back among the people of Woolsthorpe, he seemed reinvigorated by the familiar surroundings of his boyhood home.

Although the young Newton had reportedly been a rather poor student in the early grades, his powerful intelligence and creativity asserted themselves even before he reached his teenage years. When he was still a tow-headed youngster, for instance, he managed to construct a charming little windmill backed up by one mouse power for times when the wind refused to blow. Later, he made a paper kite rigged to carry a little lantern high above the British countryside. The people of Woolsthorpe had never seen flickering lights floating across the nighttime sky, so Newton may have been responsible for some of the earliest unofficial sightings of UFOs.

At the age of 23, while relaxing near his mother's home, Newton saw an apple fall from a tree. That simple incident represents serendipity at its best, because it suddenly caused him to wonder why apples always fall down while the moon continues to sail overhead. Soon he theorized that the force of gravity tugging on apple and moon falls off systematically with increasing altitude. Newton had no sure way of knowing what kind of mathematical law it followed, but he surmised that gravity's strength declined in the same way a light beam dissipates when we move farther away from its source. Double the distance and its intensity falls off by a factor of four.

Thus, by Newton's reckoning, the force of gravity pulling on the moon should be about 1/3,000th as strong as the gravity we experience at the surface of the earth. In one minute a falling apple would be pulled downward about 10 miles by the earth's gravity. In that same minute, the moon would fall down toward the earth only about 16 feet. During that one-minute interval, its orbital velocity also carries it sideways 38 miles. Consequently, its combined horizontal and vertical motion bring it back onto the same gently curving circular path over and over again.

Newton figured all this out because of a serendipitous encounter with his mother's favorite apple tree. Armed only with his inverse square law of gravitation, three deceptively simple laws of motion, and one of the most powerful intellects that ever pondered anything, Newton quietly began unraveling many of the hidden secrets of the universe.

Lesson 59
Following Serendipity's Golden Rule

"A critic is a gong at a railroad crossing clanging loudly and vainly as the train goes by."
— British Actor, Christopher Morley

No one can give you precise guidelines on how to become the fortunate beneficiary of serendipity. To some extent, as we have seen, serendipity tends to come when you least expect it. But you can increase your chances for such an experience by taking the time to expose yourself to unusual situations, by leading a rich and varied life, and by studying informative examples of serendipity from the past. Studies of this type teach us one rather interesting thing about serendipity: It is most likely to occur when you are working on a job you truly enjoy—or when you are doing something unrelated to your usual occupation.

Study Michael H. Hart's book, *The 100: A Ranking of the Most Influential Persons in History,* and you will soon learn something else interesting, too. Almost every important discovery in recorded history was masterminded by people living in cities.[8] Many of history's most influential power brokers traveled city to city during the formative years of their chosen professions. Whenever they arrived at a new destination, they were no doubt exposed to fresh stimulation.

"Cities remain the cradle of civilization's creativity and ambition," says Eugene Linden of *Time* magazine. ". . . the catalytic mixing of people that fuels urban conflict also spurs the initiative, innovation, and collaboration that move civilization forward."

The late social critic and creativity spokesman Lewis Mumford echoed precisely that same sentiment when he argued with great conviction that "the city is a place for multiplying happy chances and making the most of unplanned opportunities."

It may not seem particularly noteworthy that urban dwellers develop most of today's creative solutions. After all, in the Western world at least, most educated people—creative or not—live and work in urban areas. But this has not always been the case. Early in the eighteenth century, for instance, only about 6 percent of the people in Europe were city dwellers. But why does it matter where we live? Why can't we just stay in one place while we ponder new and exciting solutions? Creativity is synthesis, and to synthesize new ideas we need raw materials, facts, people, attitudes, and, most of all, interactions. City dwellers and travelers become accustomed to seeing and masterminding change. They also tend to be unusually sensitive to their surroundings and more receptive to new ideas. Build your alert-

---

[8] Muhammad, who ranks at the top of Hart's list, is almost the only exception.

ness around an occasional outing to some new place, especially some exciting city filled with new ideas such as Los Angeles, London, or Milan, but don't schedule your trips to the same locations over and over again.

Most of us are more in tune with our surroundings when we are not insulated by our own preferred circle of friends. Thus, a good way to raise your alertness is to travel by yourself on selected occasions. This, then, is serendipity's golden rule:

GO SOMEWHERE YOU USUALLY DON'T GO,
TO DO SOMETHING YOU USUALLY DON'T DO.
ALONE.

The novelty of it—and the fact that you are not surrounded by a thick security blanket of friendly faces—will force you to study your surroundings from a fresh perspective while watching out for novel and interesting concepts and attitudes at your new destination. The fact that you are there alone will force you to interact with the new people you find there, if only to seek directions or find a good place to eat.

In the past 10 years, as a part of my lecturing career, I have made 40 international trips to all sorts of exotic locales, most of the time traveling by myself. On many such occasions, I have experienced the joy of serendipity and I have also picked up some marvelous tidbits and advice along the way.

On one occasion, for instance, a flight attendant gave me this intriguing recommendation: "Whenever you are traveling in some strange land, try to view *everything* as an adventure," she told me. "Your positive attitude will show on your face, others will notice it, and they will reach out to help you every way they can."

Lesson 60
Harvesting Fresh Ideas from Your Television Screen

"I can give you a six-word formula for success: Think things through—then follow through."
— Airplane Pilot, Eddie Rickenbacker

The distinctive joy of serendipity has visited me many times during my long professional career. Once it happened while I was watching a telecast of the Apollo 11 astronauts coming back from the moon. During an animation sequence showing the trajectory of the Apollo capsule coasting back toward earth, the commentator happened to mention that the three astronauts were sharing their crowded spacecraft with 85 pounds of lunar rocks.

Suddenly, in a flash, it occurred to me that if they tossed one of those little moon rocks out of their window, it would become a synthetic meteorite—a "meteorite" of known size and composition that would also be traveling at a known reentry speed!

The next morning I went over to our company library where I did a little research on meteorites to see if that idea might produce scientific benefits. Soon I learned that 185,000,000 meteorites career into the earth's atmosphere every day from outer space and that they add 600,000 pounds of new material each year to the mass of planet earth. Meteor trails (shooting stars) have been studied for many years using photographic techniques in which whirling shutter blades systematically interrupt time-exposure photographs to make little white dotted lines on the photographic plate. These dotted lines allow researchers to determine meteorite entry speeds.

Most "shooting stars" are created by thumbnail-sized flakes of stone or metal moving at extremely high velocities as they breach the earth's atmosphere. Over the years vast numbers of meteorite fragments, large and small, have been recovered but, with the exception of a few tiny micrometeorites, none had ever been retrieved prior to its searing journey through the earth's atmosphere. Until the age of space, there was no way to calibrate the size and composition of a meteorite and then measure its fiery death during reentry.

Another intriguing problem associated with meteorites concerns the origin of billions of strange button-shaped objects called *tektites*. Scattered over continent-sized regions on the earth's surface, tektites have a strange glassy composition and are composed of materials not otherwise found in the region where they are discovered. They have apparently fallen on the earth many times in big, intense "swarms," each of which is composed of uncounted billions of individual tektites. Some tektites carry evidence of melting and surface scratches, indicating that they have moved at extremely high velocities through the earth's atmosphere.

Their broad-ranging distribution, and the fact that their chemical composition does not seem to vary with location, indicates that tektites may be associated with meteorite falls rather than natural geological processes. One theory holds that they came from the moon when big meteorite impacts splashed material from the lunar surface. Having reached escape velocity, the moon rocks then coasted through cis-lunar space until they hit the earth.

The papers I submitted to NASA proposed that future Apollo astronauts create a swarm of synthetic meteorites by flinging several moon rocks out of the Apollo capsule while they were on their way back to the earth. Similar moon-rock samples would be returned to the earth for later analysis. The entry of each moon rock into the earth's atmosphere could be observed from the earth and, perhaps, from the Apollo capsule (see Figure 6.1). Reentry speeds would be about 25,000 miles per hour, well within the speed range of naturally occurring meteorites. Tossing the stones in pairs or larger groups would allow scientists to distinguish them from natural meteorites, which, on a typical clear night, can be seen with the naked eye about every 20 minutes or so.

Figure 6.1   The synthetic meteorite experiment.

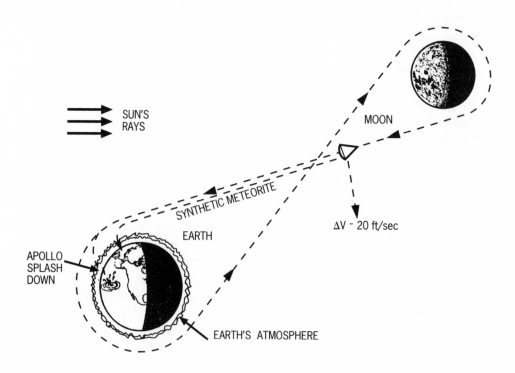

Stones purposely ejected from the Apollo capsule during its long journey back from the moon would serve to calibrate many previous astronomical observations. A tektite experiment could be performed in similar fashion by flipping out several moon rocks of the appropriate chemical composition aimed at a shallow sea or a sparsely inhabited desert region on earth. Fortunately, the entry speed of tektites has been established through wind-tunnel tests to be nearly identical to the speed of the synthetic meteorites.

For several months NASA experts reviewed the possibility of conducting the synthetic-meteorite experiment. They knew it would work—and that it would produce valuable scientific results—but in the face of growing budget cuts, they reluctantly deleted it from future plans.

Lesson 61
Finding New Ways to Enjoy a Rich and Varied Life

"Nature has given man one tongue and two ears, that we may hear twice as much as we speak."
— Greek Stoic Philosopher, Epictetus

In 1936 low moaning sounds rumbling through the lower decks of a big cruise ship traveling from Europe to New York created happy serendipity for a bearded passenger named Theodor Geisel. Soon Geisel became intrigued with rhythmic sounds of the propellers mingled with the sounds coming from the ship's engines. So he began writing silly rhymes to mimic those intriguing harmonic beats.

After he arrived at the docks of New York, Geisel revised and polished his catchy rhymes. Then he bundled them together into a children's book describing the strange happenings a little boy imagines are taking place on the street where he lives. Soon Geisel managed to get his book published under the title *And to Think I Saw It on Mulberry Street.*

Eventually Theodor Geisel—or Dr. Seuss as he called himself on the covers of his books—managed to sell 200 million volumes intended to amuse and delight the children of the baby-boom generation. His various books were jam-packed with silly rhymes and strange phrases, all of which ultimately sprang from the happy serendipity Geisel was lucky enough to experience during that long sea voyage of 1936. If he had not taken the time to listen to the rhythm of the ship's propellers rotating in perfect harmony with the sea, a generation of disappointed children would have missed sharing the joy and whimsy of Dr. Seuss.

Twenty years after Geisel started his highly productive writing career, Bennett Cerf, cofounder of Random House, bet him $50 he could not write an interesting and coherent children's book containing fewer than 50 words. The final book, which turned out to be only 49 words long, is entitled *Green Eggs and Ham.* The simple words inside are used quite sparingly, but it is one of the most successful children's books ever imprinted with the pseudonym of Dr. Seuss.

The one-page worksheet at the end of this lesson is purposely designed to help you increase your chances for experiencing happy serendipity in much the same way Theodor Geisel did on that noisy cruise ship in 1936. The brief exercises outlined on the worksheet are based on serendipity's golden rule:

GO SOMEWHERE YOU DON'T USUALLY GO,
TO DO SOMETHING YOU DON'T USUALLY DO.
ALONE.

The exercise involves only five simple tasks. First you are instructed to formulate a problem you are hoping to solve. You then discuss how serendipity has already helped you in the past to solve a portion of this or some other, similar problem. Next, you map out a plan for visiting at least two unfamiliar places—alone. Finally, you explain what you plan to do when you get there, and how you plan to get away without taking any of your family or friends along.

Serendipity is, by nature, an unusual or even an extraordinary event, so you can never be sure you will experience the personal joy of happy serendipity. But you can increase your chances of experiencing such a joyous event by purposely putting yourself in strange and unusual situations with a positive attitude. When you get there, stay alert to your surroundings and receptive to new ideas!

Even if serendipity retreats to some distant frontier while you are living up to your commitments, you can still learn a lot by going to a couple of places you don't usually go to do a few things you don't usually do without a bunch of friends going along. Try it. When you do, you are practically assured of having some kind of new adventure.

What is your problem? _____

_____

_____

_____

⑥ BEING ALERT TO HAPPY SERENDIPITY

Serendipity is most likely to help you solve your problem when you are doing something completely unrelated to your usual occupation. Watch out for happy serendipity. Has serendipity already helped you solve a portion of this or some other problem? If so, explain: _____

_____

_____

_____

_____

Your chances of experiencing happy serendipity will increase if you go somewhere you don't usually go to do something you don't usually do—alone.

In the spaces below plan two visits that are at least vaguely related to the problem you are trying to solve.

☆ Where are you planning to go?   (two places)

1. _____

2. _____

☆ What are you planning to do?   (two tasks)

1. _____

2. _____

☆ How do you plan to get away alone?   (two plans)

1. _____

2. _____

Chapter 7

Getting Your Ideas Accepted in a Gangling Bureaucracy

"It's not whether you get knocked down, it's whether you get up."
— Football Coach, Vince Lombardi

Those who win big in today's competitive world of business engage in broad-ranging campaigns to get what they want—they fight their battles on many fronts. One good way to get such a campaign rolling is to develop and polish a large number of creative ideas, not just one or two. Practical experience indicates that when a creative individual generates a large collection of ideas, the quality of those ideas does not decline as more of them are produced.

In previous chapters you learned how to develop creative ideas in abundance. In this one, you will learn how to screen your ideas so you can select the most practical and exciting samples for further revision and refinement. You will also learn how to make persuasive proposals and presentations to help get your ideas adopted by the leaders of your organization.

Many young professionals seem amazed that when they say something in a staff meeting, no one seems to listen to what they have to say. However, they need to realize that, in fact, the participants at a meeting seldom pay much attention to *any* unprepared statement. That is why you must learn how to come to those meetings fully prepared with the proper winning strategy.

Among other things, you must learn how to use informal caucuses to gather advanced support for your ideas, how to put together colorful and effective presentations, how to capture the full attention of everyone in a meeting with a single sheet of paper, and how to handle—or deflect—any tricky questions they may pose.

Finally, you will learn how to handle even the most demoralizing disappointments if and when some of your best ideas are rejected. Only three simple lists are required, each of which can be written on a single sheet of paper. Once you have compiled those three lists, your spirits will be restored, and you will have ample courage and confidence to develop a fresh batch of creative ideas, to package them for public consumption, and to come back and fight another day.

"Happiness is mostly a by-product of doing what makes us feel fulfilled," remarked Dr. Benjamin Spock of baby-book fame. He spent a solid fraction of his life dreaming up ways to make our world a better place to live. So did Cliff Clavin from the television show "Cheers." "Having a dream isn't stupid, Norm," he told his bar-stool buddy. "It's *not* having a dream that's stupid."

Lesson 62
Finding the Most Affordable Way
to Live Better Than King Henry VIII

"You do what you can for as long as you can, and when you finally can't,
you do the next best thing. You back up but you don't give up."
— Military Test Pilot, Chuck Yeager

The key to a full, rich, abundant life has always been technology, skillfully applied. Modern technology can sometimes be grindingly complicated, but many of mankind's most spectacular breakthroughs have come from dirt-simple ideas applied in a dirt-simple manner.

With the gradual emergence of today's superb technologies, even the semiskilled workers straddling the production lines in Youngstown and Cincinnati live better than King Henry VIII did at the pinnacle of his sumptuous reign.

Sixteenth-century castles were cold, dark, uncomfortable places to live—and surprisingly unsanitary! Every few weeks King Henry and his entourage had to shuffle from castle to castle because whenever a castle was heavily occupied for a month or more, the stench became unbearable. Finding decent medical care was another worrisome problem even for ruling monarchs of the day. For years, King Henry had a painful ulcer on his leg that could not be cured by any of his court physicians. Today, of course, a cure would probably come with a single visit to any street-corner medical clinic.

British dramatist Oscar Wilde lived and worked during some of the most brutal years of the Industrial Revolution, when mechanization could have been a tempting target for his barbed pen. He soon realized, however, that advancing technology has always been the key to a more cultured and prosperous style of living. "Civilization requires slaves," he wrote. "Unless there are slaves to do the ugly, horrible, uninteresting work, culture becomes almost impossible. Human slavery is wrong, insecure, and demoralizing. On mechanical slavery—on the slavery of the machine—the future of the world depends."

In any slave-holding era, ancient or modern, few masters enjoyed the services of more than a dozen slaves. Today, however, even those clinging to the bottom rungs of our economic ladder are served by more slaves than that. Based on our country's annual per-capita energy consumption, each of us has, in effect, 250 mechanical slaves devoted to making our lives easy and interesting.

Simple, creative ideas applied on a massive scale have pushed the standard of living of the average American citizen up to a level King Henry would hardly be able to understand. Small wonder creative individuals command such a premium in today's world of expansive technology.

How can you develop, refine, and exploit the winners from among the many creative ideas resting among the clutter on top of your desk? At the Del Monte cannery we sorted out the smallest, most delicious "party pack" peas by running all of the peas that came into the factory through a series of sieves (filters). You can do exactly the same thing with your bulging stack of creative ideas.

The first and most important filter for any new idea is how much excitement it causes you to feel. If it doesn't excite you, throw it into the inactive bin. Don't throw it away because, at some future date, you may be able to combine it with some other idea to synthesize a real winner. Or you may find a way to adapt it for a different purpose.

The second filter is the amount of excitement your idea arouses among your colleagues, family, and friends. The world's best idea will languish unless you can find someone else who shares your passion for its real-world implementation. Of course, passion and enthusiasm are not enough. Any marketable idea must be useful and practical as well as exciting.

If it passes both excitement tests, continue your systematic quest by creating a persuasive one-page marketing kit. Summarize the salient features of your idea on a 17-in. by 22-in. (oversized) quadrille sheet. Cut and paste problem statements, verbal descriptions, supportive graphs, tabular data, sketches, and photographs onto that single sheet of paper. Then add color to give it pizzazz.

Among other things, your compact marketing kit should state the problem you are attempting to solve, explain how your simple, creative idea will help provide the desired solution, and summarize the practical benefits with such simplicity that any intelligent person can figure out why your idea is worthy of further attention.

Study the summary sheet, then run it through another excitement filter. If it still excites you—and at least one other person—revise, polish, and redo it as many times as necessary. Add color for clarity and sketch in big, bold arrows to emphasize the logical flow. In short, make that one page sing!

Now put your big sheet aside for awhile. Come back to it later when you are fresh and rested and can reevaluate it and revise it some more. Early in my writing career I relied on this simple slogan: "Write when you're hungry, revise when you're well fed." Yearning and passion are totally appropriate when you are first formulating a new idea. But when you approach the implementation phase, it must be able to survive on its own merits in the cold light of day.

Work on several ideas at the same time so if one of them turns out to be a dud, you will have others to fall back on, polish, and refine. Choosing the best idea from among a group of viable candidates is much easier on your psyche than investing all your energies in a single idea that might fail at any point.

Once you have put together a few one-page summary sheets, show selected samples to supportive colleagues to get their preliminary reactions. Listen to what they have to say. Ask questions. Take notes. Later, when you are alone, expand and refine your notes and try to figure out how you can further improve and strengthen your ideas and your one-page summary sheets. If your colleagues help in a big way, find a way to reward them with a 1% commission for their helpfulness and support.

As your summary sheets become better and better, and you begin to fill in any gaps and holes, take your ideas to less optimistic colleagues. Meet with them one at a time or in small groups. At each of these meetings listen, take notes, and improve! In the early formative stages, when your idea is delicate and fragile, you should avoid pessimistic critics if possible. But, when your idea is strong enough to stand on its own merits, any pessimists you know should be actively cultivated. By injecting a bit of realism into your thinking, a good pessimist can perform a valuable service.

Why should you go through such an elaborate process? You are getting ready to reveal your hatchling ideas to the real world. Never regard this portion of the creative process as a worrisome burden. Influential people (even dictators) have always had to sell their ideas to others. Almost all of them did it with written reports, oral presentations, or persuasive conversations.

Christopher Columbus, for instance, in striving for the opportunity to lead his own flotilla toward westward exploration, for instance, needed all the persuasive powers he could muster over many, many years. Nor did he skimp on visual aids. He used astronomical observations, models, and the latest maps to argue that the earth was a sphere and that it was not as large as some had surmised. He also gathered driftwood and big, brown nuts said to have floated to the shores of Portugal and Spain from the far east. During his long selling phase, Columbus made many presentations before his daring voyage was finally approved by Ferdinand and Isabella.

As a modern entrepreneur, you must also learn how to make forceful presentations. They serve many useful purposes; in particular, they are necessary to raise money from banks, venture capitalists, and sometimes supportive family and friends.

Lesson 63
Taking Over a Meeting with a Single Sheet of Paper

"I like the dreams of the future better than the history of the past."
— American President, Thomas Jefferson

Formulating and implementing simple, creative ideas is almost always a rather haphazard process with many bends and turns along the way. Random targets of opportunity also abound when you are selecting your best ideas for public consumption. However, when some of your ideas have finally been refined enough for exposure to a wider audience, you will need to display total discipline in packaging and presentation. Fortunately, your one-page summary sheets will help you get ready for these more formal presentations.

Incidentally, if it serves your purpose, you can take over a small meeting—at least temporarily—with a one-page summary sheet. Take it to the meeting neatly packaged inside a thin manila folder. When the opportune moment arrives, say a few appropriate words by way of introduction, then unfold it and begin referring to it as though it constitutes a big, colorful briefing chart. If you have developed even a fleeting reputation for creativity, every person in that meeting will stop to see what your big, colorful sheet illustrates and what you have to say. Your goals should be strictly limited, but be sure you know what you want from the audience before you start, and be sure your mini-presentation ends with some kind of simple call to action. Bigger, more important meetings, of course, require a more structured approach.

Lesson 64
Working toward a Popular Groundswell of Support

"Successful person: one who goes on looking for a job after he has found one."
— Traditional Definition

"Nobody listens to what I have to say at staff meetings. When I make a comment, everybody else just goes right on talking." This popular lament often contains a big element of truth. Even if it happens to you regularly, though, don't take it as a personal affront. Instead, go to a meeting or two with no intention of speaking, then sit quietly and watch what happens.

As you will soon notice, hardly anyone listens at meetings except to a few specific individuals who have done their homework in advance. Notice who they are and notice that they have rich ideas usually backed up with colorful and interesting pieces of paper or simple, but effective, transparent viewgraphs.

If you investigate further, you will probably find that those individuals also tend to be the ones who have informally caucused their ideas in advance with some of the other attendees. With patience and hard work, they have already spent a little time refining, polishing, and promoting their ideas. Usually, in addition, they have written their ideas on paper, revised them, flowcharted them, and carefully exposed them to a few selected friends. In other words, by the time you are hearing about their creative solutions in a public meeting, they have already built up a popular groundswell of support.

Many years ago, when early civil rights leaders were demanding more political power, America's home-grown philosopher Eric Hoffer could not hold his tongue any longer. "Power doesn't come in a can," he said. "It comes from careful organization and attention to detail. Nobody can *give* you power."

Does Eric Hoffer's remark suggest something to you? Is it possible that you, too, might someday walk into a meeting with a few key supporters already locked in place? Some people seem to think there is something morally wrong with caucusing, but actually it is a time-honored approach in the political arena. Caucusing, in particular, allows a small organized splinter group to thrash out any agreements, positions, and compromises before they expose their ideas to a larger, more disorganized group.

Once you have made a few one-page summary sheets of some of your best ideas, you will be in an excellent position to hold caucuses with a few trusted colleagues. You may also want to expose your ideas to some of the people who may turn out to be resistant to your proposals. One of the most influential political leaders of the twentieth century, President Lyndon Johnson, often held long, rambling conversations with political enemies. When an aide asked the president why he invested so much time in one particularly disagreeable politician, Johnson quickly replied: "I'd rather have him *inside* my tent pissing out, than *outside* my tent pissing in!"

President Johnson was always amazed by how much genuine influence he could wield with a sincere compliment or two. This seemed to work even with the most powerful and sophisticated politicians in Washington. Giving compliments is a people-skill you should also be willing to cultivate if you want to have your ideas put into practice. But don't wait until you need a favor *before* complimenting some-one, and never give a compliment that is not entirely sincere.

Fortunately, there are simple ways to get into the proper frame of mind to de-velop complimentary feelings toward other people. When I was in college, Dr. George W. Crane and his brothers published a textbook on applied psychology that included a marvelous appendix describing an informal organization called "The Compliment Club." That book, incidentally, was a publishing phenomenon. Al-most immediately, it was adopted as a textbook by well over 1,000 colleges and universities.

Dr. Crane stumbled onto The Compliment Club when he was teaching an exten-sion course in social psychology for Northwestern University in downtown Chi-cago. Most of his students worked in local department stores, offices, and factories and attended his class at night. Their average age was about 25.

One night a student named Lois stayed after class for a conference. "Dr. Crane, this may seem like a trivial matter," she began, "but I am so lonely, I could just end my life right now." She then began to cry. "I come from a little town in Wisconsin . . . [and] I don't know anybody except a few girls at the office. . . . Millions of people surround me in this great city, but I feel as desolate as if I were Robinson Crusoe." Her sobbing subsided a little, as she kept spinning out her story, which ended with this poignant observation: "If I only were as nonchalant and sophisti-cated as that Miss Miller who sits across the aisle from me."

At this point, Dr. Crane interrupted to make a rather startling revelation: "I'm glad you mentioned the poise and self-assurance of Miss Miller [because] two weeks ago she came in here and began to cry because she was so lonely and devoid of friends."

When that conference was over, Dr. Crane concluded that if he could not come up with some way to mitigate the pain of his students, his class in social psychology would have to be regarded as a farce.

The next week he gave his students an assignment purposely designed to help minimize their isolation and loneliness. "Each day you are to pay an honest compli-ment to each of three different persons . . . every day for 30 consecutive days." As part of the exercise, he required that they keep accurate records describing each recipient of their compliments as "sales clerk," "streetcar conductor," and so on. In addition, they were instructed to record what they said to the person and any response they received from each compliment.

What a difference three daily compliments can make! Soon all loneliness among the students had disappeared and they all looked forward to their class each week, especially Lois! As Dr. Crane described it, she could hardly get into the classroom before she and a half dozen other students would be conversing gaily. "This Compliment Club has removed my terror and loneliness and given me new zest," she later explained. "It has altered my entire outlook on life."

Some of his students felt a bit hypocritical until Dr. Crane told them that, when we compliment someone, we don't have to like or admire that person. A compliment is a strictly limited remark with a very narrow focus. Consequently, we can compliment our enemies as well as our friends. We can, indeed, pay totally sincere compliments to people we do not like at all. As Dr. Crane explains it: "We [can] divorce ourselves from our own petty prejudices and size them up in a scientific, detached fashion until we find a good point. Nobody is so devoid of merit that he doesn't have some good qualities!"

The Compliment Club still has a few openings. You can become a volunteer member by complimenting at least three people each day for 30 days. Keep records on the results and do not confine your compliments to your office environment. Give it a try and, someday soon, you may find that your former enemies are all standing inside your tent aiming out, instead of standing outside aiming in.

Lesson 65
Pitching Your Ideas in a Formal Written Report

"If at first you don't succeed, try, try again. Then quit. No use being a damn fool about it."
— Hollywood Film Star, W. C. Fields

Sometimes a good idea is informally adopted after it is proposed at the copying machine or at a small staff meeting. However, most of the time, if you want to sell your ideas to the people who work in a modern bureaucracy, you will have to learn how to make forceful and effective presentations. Occasionally, a written report alone will suffice, but swaying powerful people will more typically require a well-organized oral presentation. Combined packages are often the most effective of all: an oral presentation followed by a written summary, for instance, or a written report handed out at a meeting where you are making an oral presentation.

"The purpose of writing is to communicate." My students invariably agree with that introductory statement. Yet many of the interoffice memos they compose fly in the face of that stated purpose. In particular, their writing is often laced with cryptic abbreviations and acronyms:

> The overall budget from the SDIO shows a 7.6% liftoff PL margin, but the OBDH, RCS, and sunshield SVM subsystems and PLM are above specs.

Cryptic acronyms are not compatible with the purpose of writing, which is to communicate. Acronyms tend to confuse and alienate even the most dedicated reader. Avoid them in your writing. Learn to communicate with your reader, instead. Never purposely try to muddy the water the way Alexander Haig did in a 1983 television interview: "That is not a lie," he argued, "it's a terminological inexactitude."

But how can you slant and structure your writing so it is simple, readable, and persuasive? One productive approach is *to write for an audience of one*. Instead of writing for an invisible multitude, choose one specific person as your target audience. Always pick a likable, optimistic person who will be interested in what you have to say. As you are writing, direct everything you put on paper toward your one-member target audience. Visualize his or her responses in your mind's eye as you set each sentence down on the printed page and as you revise your write-up too.

For an important report, you may want to compose a page or two summarizing the salient characteristics of your target audience with emphasis on how he or she is likely to respond to the ideas you are presenting. Appendix B contains an analysis of this type, centering around the target audience of my book, *Striking It Rich in Space*.[9] As you will see in Appendix B, I tried to communicate with my target audience, Anthony Ralyea, even though I had talked to him only one time in my life. Incidentally, with Anthony Ralyea in my mind's eye, can you imagine one of my chapters containing something baffling and cryptic like:

> The overall budget from the SDIO shows a 7.6% liftoff PL margin, but the OBDH, RCS, and sunshield SVM subsystems and PLM are above specs?

When you are starting to put together a written proposal, you will need to devise some sort of structured plan. During the early planning phases, capture your thoughts on paper as quickly as possible by constructing a balloon diagram. For a logical well-organized presentation, however, some other, more refined, organizational tool will probably turn out to be more effective.

An outline can be a big help, but don't abbreviate the individual topics too much. Insert a few words into each subtopic to allow your attitudes and emotions to show through. Here is a short portion of the topic outline I used in putting together an early draft proposal for this book:

- Using visual aids to bring a superior architecture into sharp focus
    1. Dynamic outlining and flowcharting techniques
    2. "Mind mapping" with balloon diagrams

- Smashing everyday things apart
    1. How to write more powerful and effective interoffice memos
    2. Cutting down on the cost of getting to work
    3. Discovering a simpler way to cook a nourishing meal

As you write, you will probably find better ways to organize and structure your presentation, and better ways to make personal contact with your reader. If your writeup becomes overly complicated, you may want to pause periodically and revise your outline.

When we attempt to solve a problem, we usually formulate the problem first, then work toward its solution. But for some reason, many beginning writers present their solution first, then they discuss the problem their solution is intended to solve. One way to avoid this trap is to construct a simple problem-solution diagram. Figure 7.1 presents a sample from the introductory chapter of this book. Once you have assembled your problem-solution diagram, follow along in it as you formulate

---

[9] *Striking It Rich in Space* was later given a new title: *Space, Inc., Your Guide to Investing in Space Exploration.*

Figure 7.1   Probem-solution diagram for more powerful writing.

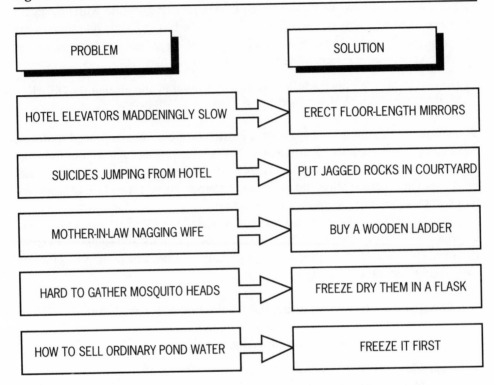

your most persuasive arguments. Start by describing the problem. Make it real and important to your reader. Then describe the solution, which—by some amazing coincidence—you just happen to have available at your fingertips!

The problem-solution approach to writing leads to heavy reader involvement because your reader also gets a chance to think about the problem. In fact, it is a good idea to introduce a problem, then present some background information before you reveal the amazingly clever solution you have devised. The various problems in Chapter 1 were all handled using that technique. Notice how much reader interest would have been lost if I had presented the solutions first like this:

> The manager of a San Francisco hotel put mirrors inside and next to the elevators in his hotel. He did this to distract his clients so they would not notice how slow the elevators were.

> The manager at another hotel put jagged rocks in the courtyard below the observation deck. He did this to scare off potential suicides who might otherwise jump from the observation deck on the top of his hotel.

Whenever you are working on a fairly big writeup, break your overall task into three separate and distinct parts:

1. Planning what you want to say

2. Writing a rough draft

3. Revising and polishing your writeup.

Always do these tasks *one at a time*. Writers tend to get very frustrated whenever they try to do two or more of these things simultaneously.

When you plan your writeup, do nothing else. Start with a balloon diagram, if you like. Then outline your story line or flowchart it. Or make a fairly complete set of problem-solution diagrams. If possible, put your plan aside for awhile before you start writing your rough draft.

When you write your rough draft, do nothing else. Never stop to look up words in the dictionary.[10] Get everything down on paper first. If possible, put your rough draft aside before you begin to make revisions.

When you revise and polish your writeup, do nothing else. Polish the sentences and fill in any missing gaps. If possible, put it aside before it is finished. Come back to it later. When your writeup is approaching its final form, try reading it aloud. A well-written passage sounds good to the human ear. Further revise any rough sections, sentences, or phrases as you read them aloud repeatedly.

End your writeup with something conclusive, a summary of its contents, a call to action, an indication of what you plan to do next. If possible, combine your writeup with some kind of oral presentation. If nothing else, hand out the copies in person and, as you do, summarize with a few well-chosen words why you wrote it and what it concludes.

---

[10] No one will see your rough draft but you, and you already know you don't know how to spell.

Lesson 66
Learning to Appreciate the Amazing Power of the Spoken Word

"You can't build a reputation on what you are going to do."
— Detroit Automaker, Henry Ford

Influential people have always had a special knack for presenting powerful ideas using simple spoken and written words. Consider the three most influential leaders during World War II—Adolph Hitler, Winston Churchill, and Franklin Roosevelt.

Americans often view Adolph Hitler as a fanatical monster who seized power by brutal force. A more accurate characterization is that he seduced the German people into following him with his remarkably effective speaking skills. With just the proper touches of drama and nationalism, he gave riveting speeches in major German cities and over national radio. Many knowledgeable experts place him near the top of the list of the greatest orators of the twentieth century.

Winston Churchill was remarkably witty with carefully prepared remarks, but he also spoke well extemporaneously. "If you were my husband," a matronly lady once told him in a fit of irritation, "I would put poison in your tea."

"Madam, if you were my wife," he replied, "I would drink it."

Franklin Roosevelt was actually a wealthy aristocrat, but the common people in small-town America loved to hear him talk because he spoke their language with such dramatic skill. Before America's entry into World War II, he needed congressional approval to ship large quantities of arms to England. Many Americans resisted the hazardous involvement those supplies would bring, but Roosevelt's simple argument made it hard for organized resistance to solidify. "If my neighbor's house was on fire, I would lend him my garden hose," he said simply. Soon, enormous convoys of ships loaded with military supplies were sailing toward the docks of London.

If you want your ideas to be accepted by others, you must learn how to state them clearly and simply. When Walter Cronkite's fellow newscaster, Chet Huntley, suddenly passed away, Cronkite began his next broadcast with six simple words that touched the nation: "A friend of mine died today."

With similar simplicity, CBS reporter Reid Collins added an intriguing twist to a story about the swallows that arrive annually on St. Joseph's Day at the Mission of San Juan Capistrano. "Sure enough, the mystery continued for another year," he reported. "Some 38,000 human beings were gathered down there on the ground. The swallows find them in droves every March 19th."

When Beau LaBarre in the television series "Welcome Back, Kotter" needed to highlight the pain of a broken heart, he did it with this simple explanation: "There are three things you don't get over in a hurry," he said, "losing a woman, eating a bad possum, and eating a good possum."

In your own presentations always strive for similar simplicity. Put your ideas out in the open for all to see. You may get shot down anyway. But at least make sure your critics understand what it is they are rejecting.

Lesson 67
Making Effective Technicolor Presentations

"I take a simple view of life; keep your eyes open and get on with it."
  — British Actor, Sir Lawrence Olivier

According to my graphic arts professor in college, a reporter once asked a well-known artist if oil painting was hard to do. "It's *hard* if you know how," he replied, "*easy* if you don't."

Anyone can learn how to slap paint on a canvas. But slapping it on so it will trigger a meaningful response from museum-goers is a much more difficult thing to do. Public speaking is quite similar. Anyone with sufficient courage can use puffs of air to make sounds in a crowded room. But consistently successful public speaking comes only with meticulous preparation.

The first step toward success begins when you analyze three things:

1. Your audience and their special needs

2. What you want to say to them

3. How you want them to respond.

Start by finding out all you can about your audience. How many people will there be? What do they do for a living? How are they related to one another? What are they hoping to learn from your presentation? Write out a short analysis of these and various related factors on a single sheet of paper.

Now think about what you want to say to the audience and how you are hoping they will respond. If, for instance, you are pitching one of your creative ideas, you may want them to provide some kind of endorsement for you to proceed. Perhaps you want them to form a study group to further research the implementation of your idea. If you cannot figure out what you want from the audience, cancel your presentation. "The human brain starts working the moment you are born," said George Jessel, "and never stops until you stand up to speak in public."

If possible, visit the room where your presentation will take place to check it out in advance. Equipment breaks. Microphones go on the fritz. Bulbs burn out in overhead projectors. Test every piece of equipment you are planning to use.

Visualize what the room will look like during your presentation. Try to think of the audience members as specific individuals with separate hopes and dreams. Many presentations fail because the speaker thinks of the audience as a vast multitude. In conversation, we direct our remarks toward one person at a time and we maintain (intermittent) eye contact. If you do the same thing in a public presentation, it can be much more effective and persuasive.

Lock the door. Now imagine that there is one friendly person in the room. Rehearse your opening remarks to that person's empty chair. Visualize a positive and supportive response. Now add a second person to your imaginary audience. Direct your next few remarks to those two listeners alternately by maintaining eye contact back and forth between them. Use words and phrases similar to the ones you use in casual conversation. Continue to use your imagination to fill the room gradually as you rehearse a larger portion of your talk. As you rehearse, maintain eye contact sequentially and try to stick to a conversational tone of voice in all of your remarks.[11] The purpose of any oral presentation is to communicate. Unreasonable nervousness comes mostly when speakers think of it as a public performance instead.

Now that you have had an informal rehearsal that approximates the speech you intend to give, go back to your desk and begin a much more systematic preparation of the real thing. Start with a balloon diagram or construct a topic outline, flowchart, or a set of problem-solution diagrams. Relate all the materials you compile to the characteristics of your target audience and the response you hope to receive.

Most modern presentations involve visual aids such as viewgraph transparencies or 35-mm slides. Make a few samples and take them back to the room where your presentation is to be made. Test your visuals carefully on the projection equipment. Walk to different parts of the room to see how they look from various angles. Make sure you can read everything that appears on the screen. Notice where all the electrical plugs and light switches are located.

Now go back to your desk and begin to design a complete set of briefing charts. Avoid acronyms; use ordinary, everyday words liberally, even if your presentation is scientific or technical. Make the story line as simple as you can without compromising its content or accuracy. Develop a catchy title and a dramatic opening statement. Here is the opening I use in my short courses dealing with the space-based Navstar navigation system:

> Ever since the days of World War II we have been using ground-based radio-navigation transmitters to fix the positions of ships and planes. Many of these ground-based systems have been highly successful. But, in recent years, we have been *moving* the navigation transmitters from the surface of the earth upward into outer space.
> There must be some compelling reason for doing this. After all, it costs something like $40 million to build a spaceborne transmitter and another $40 million to

---

[11] Some college speech teachers use a similar technique. During a student speech, they have other students quietly file into the room one by one until the room is full.

launch it into space. This is about five times what it costs to build and install a ground-based navigation transmitter. What is it about the space flight environment that is so attractive to navigation engineers? Later, we will answer that question. But first, let's begin with a few simple definitions. . . .

Notice that this introduction involves no cryptic acronyms or fancy five-dollar words. Notice also that it pulls the members of the audience into a little mystery, acknowledging that they are intelligent human beings who may be able to figure out something challenging and interesting.

Once you have formulated your story line and determined what response you are hoping to get from your audience, prepare the final version of your briefing charts. Design them so they are as rich, varied, and interesting as your one-page summary sheet—from which many of them can be taken. Include a mixture of sketches, graphs, colorful words, and interesting diagrams.

If your lecture is more than 15 minutes long, include a "roadmap" chart, like the one in Figure 7.2, that shows the structure of your presentation. This so-called "waterfall" chart should be shown six times during your presentation, each time with a different box colored in. Charts of this type can lend cohesiveness to your presentation because they show your audience what you have discussed so far, what facet of your argument is currently under discussion, and what portions remain to be discussed.

In structuring your oral presentation, make it tell an interesting story. Every visual should advance and support your story line in some concrete and constructive way. If it doesn't help the story, throw it out. Avoid monotonous word charts; strive to make your visuals more interesting than mere strings of words. If you feel compelled to include a word chart, add sketches, graphs, and photographs around the edges to make it more visually interesting and informative. You need not discuss every item in every visual, but be prepared to answer questions about anything that appears on the screen.

Adding color to your briefing charts will make them more attractive and persuasive. Some computer graphics packages are rigged with color capabilities, but the necessary equipment is expensive. If you use 35-mm slides, adding color is easy. Simply color the hard copies you are planning to photograph with marking pens or colored pencils.

Coloring 8 1/2-in. x 11-in. viewgraph transparencies is also relatively easy. Make them in black and white, then use Sharpie marking pens to color small areas of a transparency. Larger areas can be colored with sticky-backed transparent cellophane, which can be placed directly on the plastic transparency. You then cut off the excess with an Exacto knife. Sticky-backed cellophane and Exacto knives can be purchased at any art supply house that caters to commercial artists.

Figure 7.2   A typical "waterfall" chart for structuring an oral presentation.

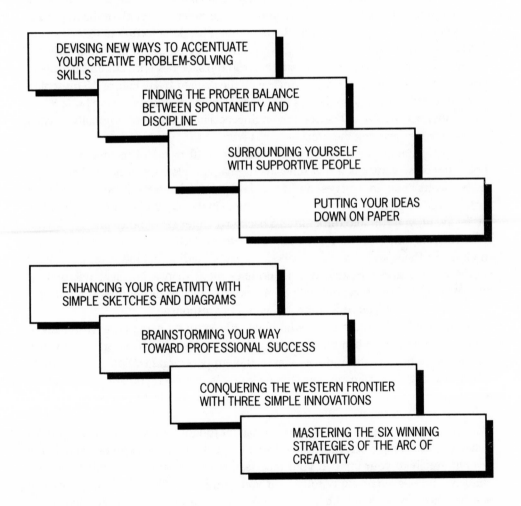

When everything is ready to go, rehearse your presentation a few times, preferably in the room where it will later be delivered. Rehearse the opening and the closing several extra times until you feel completely comfortable with the words and phrases. Don't memorize your presentation; tell your story sincerely in your own words. You may want to bring a few selected friends to the last rehearsal if you feel comfortable with their presence.

If you are doing a presentation *without* visual aids, it will be far more effective if you do it without notes. But how can you manage to remember all of the important things you have to say? Try using "the incredible shrinking lecture notes."

Make a fairly complete set of lecture notes with key phrases and little sketches to prompt you on what comes next. Add color to the sketches with colored pencils so your eye can keep track of where you are on the printed page. Figure 7.3 presents a portion of the notes I used when I presented the keynote address at the Long Beach Convention Center for 400 petroleum engineers. The notes were originally in color but here we are printing them in black and white.

For a 45-minute presentation, start with about 10 pages of technicolor lecture notes. Rehearse your talk a few times using that complete set of notes. Then summarize your notes in 3 pages, and try a few more rehearsals. Next, reduce your notes to only 1 page and rehearse a little more. Finally, try it with no notes at all. If, at any point, you run into difficulty, go back to a larger set of notes and work your way back down again. As a professional platform lecturer, I have tried this little trick many times and it always works. Instead of hiding behind a big podium, I wade into the audience armed with nothing more than a lavaliere microphone strapped around my neck, but with all the necessary facts and figures at my fingertips. Without fail, that daring approach gets a big response.

Many people, especially those who have little lecturing experience, worry about all the wrong things when they are preparing for a big speech. Mostly they worry about questions from the audience—even though poor organization ruins far more public presentations than any question ever can. If, however, you are worried about embarrassing questions, there are a few things you can do to protect yourself in advance.

First of all, be prepared. Know your topic thoroughly. Read a few extra articles when you are doing research. Realize also, though, that no one expects you to know everything about your topic. If your talk itself is well organized, members of your audience will be surprisingly tolerant if you simply say: "I don't know, but I will get back to you on that." Or even if you flub a question or two. Another good confidence-building approach is to plant a question or two in the audience in advance. Unless you are very dumb, the answers to those questions should sparkle with factual information, clever wording, and wit.

Figure 7.3   Typical set of technicolor lecture notes.

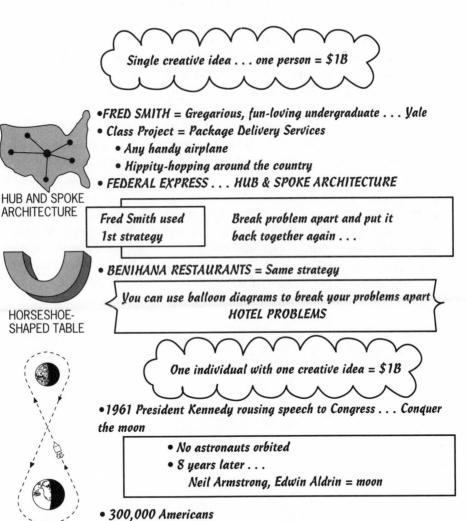

Deflecting a few questions also works well most of the time: "George Peterson is our resident expert on that. . . . George, do you have anything to add?" Another way to deflect a question is to defer it to a postmeeting session. At an aerospace conference on the UCLA campus I once heard a speaker deflect a question that way with amazing skill and tact. One member of the audience insisted on peppering the speaker with question after question. "I'm not sure everyone here today is as interested in this issue as you and I are," the speaker said finally. "Why don't we meet for a drink when this meeting ends? Then we can go into all of your concerns as deeply as we like."

When I was about 11 years old, I saved up my allowance and sent off for a ventriloquist's dummy listed in a mail-order catalog. I never learned how to operate that ornery critter with any noticeable degree of skill, but I still remember a wonderful bit of advice from the instruction booklet that came in the package: "Never let 'em see your dummy dead!"

Before you show up to make an oral presentation, always *check out everything in advance*. Never try to learn how to operate a microphone or a cranky slide projector while your audience members are squirming impatiently in their seats. Whenever you are doing a presentation, strive to project the image of a consummate professional, and always dress the part. If you send your audience the message that the presentation is important to you, it will also be important to them.

Lesson 68
Finding a Way to Muddy the Distinction between Failure and Success

"Don't go around saying the world owes you a living; the world owes you nothing, it was here first."
— American Humorist, Mark Twain

If you take a few risks in attempting to get your ideas adopted in today's bureaucratic society, disappointments will inevitably occur. On the other hand, if you always play it safe, your chances of having any great success will shrink to the vanishing point. "Those who dare to fail miserably can achieve greatly," said American Senator Robert F. Kennedy. King Camp Gillette made a fortune with the world's first safety razor, but he struggled through eight disappointing years before he had his first product ready for market. Ultimately, he sold 50 billion packages of razor blades with his portrait printed on the front. But during those first eight years, he lived with many shattering disappointments. Often he was on the verge of quitting. What a sad thing that would have been for him—and his many satisfied customers.

In attempting to polish, package, and market your best ideas, you will inevitably suffer a few deep disappointments. So how can you keep your spirits up? One promising approach is to find a way to redefine the task at hand so that, with a little twist, you can blur the distinction between failure and success. This is possible only because you are the one who is keeping score!

Several years ago I found a way to redefine success when a book deal I was working on suddenly fell through. That disappointing chain of events began when my publisher called me in for a one-to-one meeting at his office a few days before Thanksgiving. When I arrived, he handed me some shattering news. I was about halfway through a textbook I had been writing for him called *Computers in Controversy*, and when he called the meeting, I figured something bad was about to happen.

"I'm sorry to tell you this," he began, "but we have decided we can't market the book you are writing for us."

I was stunned by the news, but I managed to ask him if I was free to sell it to someone else.

"You're free to sell it to anybody you want," he told me softly. As I walked out through those stiff swinging doors to their parking lot, my head was spinning. What should I do now?

Driving back home, I began to formulate a tentative plan. Experience had taught me that losers tend to fight their battles piecemeal. They interview for a job; then sit around waiting for the results. Winners don't wait. Winners almost always engage in systematic campaigns to get what they want. I knew I could strive to sell a book. But most responses from publishers tend to be decidedly negative. Even for published authors, the mail coming in from publishers is mostly rejection slips.[12] So I made a vow: Between Thanksgiving and Christmas I would work as hard as I could to get 100 rejection slips!

A few days later, I began sending out proposals to publishers, making phone calls to editors, attending book fairs, and the like. It can be quite unnerving to send out one manuscript, wait three or four weeks, and then get rejected. But if your goal is to get 100 rejection slips in one month from a variety of projects, you can come home each night to find many interesting pieces of paper stuffed into your mailbox. Each day I counted up all the rejection slips, then added a new dot to my graph. Rejection slips were flooding in, but my whole attitude toward them had suddenly changed. Once they had represented failure, but, by redefining the problem, I had converted *failure* into *success*.

So what happened? Did I reach my goal? Three days before Christmas I had managed to gather only 70 rejection slips. At that point, my quest was interrupted by an unexpected phone call. An editor vacationing in Florida phoned to say that she wanted to publish the social controversy book. As soon as that contract was signed, I would have to go back to writing, so I would never reach my goal of 100 rejection slips. However, the news was not all bad. This new offer raised my royalty rate by more than 50 percent!

When you are trying to sell your ideas in the competitive marketplace, engage in well-planned campaigns to get what you want. Attack on a broad front. Try many ideas at once, not just one or two. If possible, try to slant your thinking so you can muddy the distinction between failure and success.

Friends and counselors of Angel Ragins, a 19-year-old from Macon, Georgia, told her that financial help for college was almost impossible to obtain, so she set up a broad-ranging campaign to maximize the number of chances she had for failure or success. Although she worked 30 hours a week while attending high school, she set aside enough time to send out more than 100 applications. When the responses came back, she applied for scholarships from seven colleges and more than 30 foundations, institutions, and companies.

Even though she was a good student and a campus leader, her friends still thought her chances were pretty slim. But Angel did a bit better than any of them thought she would—she was offered $315,000 in college scholarships at various institutions. Of course, she was not able to keep all the money she was offered, but she did get enough to cover all of her expenses at the college of her choice, Texas A&M.

---

[12] This is true even if you have an agent, as I do now. Most of the mail from agents is either rejections from them or rejections from the publishers they contact.

Lesson 69
Restoring Your Courage to Come Back and Fight Another Day

"A truly wise man never plays leapfrog with a unicorn."
— George Peppard in the title role for "Banacek"

Even if you cultivate the world's most positive outlook, you will find at times that in attempting to sell your ideas, you may still become a little discouraged when opportunities fail to materialize. Don't slink away or dwell on your depression. Get on with the business of life.

How do you go about doing that? Surprisingly, it is just as simple as all the other solutions discussed in this book. Once you learn how, you can dispel your depression with three simple lists, each less than one page long. My own short intervals of depression, I have found, come most often when I get home from a long trip. Waiting for me in my mailbox or on my phone-answering machine are a sampling of life's little problems magnified by the fact that, invariably, I'm tired when I get back home.

Depression comes when nagging difficulties advance toward us from all directions, when we feel we can't get our arms around all of our problems. It also comes when we feel we are not in control, and when we lose perspective. So how does knowing all of this help rid us of depression? It helps because we can use pencil and paper to attack and eliminate all of these unwanted conditions.

The next time you are feeling depressed, try making three simple one-page lists:

List 1: Make a list of all the things that are bothering you, large or small. Number each item as you write it. Don't go on to the second list until the first list is complete.

List 2: Item by item, with numbers beside them, write down a simple plan highlighting what you intend to do about each of the things that are bothering you on List 1. Some of your action items may include doing nothing. Do not go on to List 3 until List 2 is completed.

List 3: Make a list of all the things that are going well in your life.

At odd moments over the next few days, reread these three one-page lists. Soon you will begin to feel your depression melting away. And why is that? Because you have now managed to get your arms around all your problems and you now have a comprehensive plan of action. And because you now see your problems—and their solutions—in the proper perspective laid out against the other good things that are happening in your life.

Try it. If it works, it will give you fresh courage to come back and struggle some more for the things you have been hoping to accomplish.

Lesson 70
Spending a Little Time Harvesting Your Best Ideas

"Don't confuse fame with success. Madonna is one. Helen Keller is the other."
— Syndicated Columnist, Erma Bombeck

"All men who achieve greatness have been dreamers," said Orison Marden, editor of *Success* magazine. Great men are also considerably more courageous than the average person. Newspaper reporters who nicknamed him "Lucky Lindy" concluded that Charles Lindbergh was taking foolish chances, but actually he was a master of the calculated risk.

After carefully evaluating risk versus gain, he devised a simple, creative solution: He plunged into the darkness over the Atlantic all alone in a single-engine plane with no radio and no heavy survival equipment. He reasoned that extra engines would make the trip riskier because, if any one of those engines failed, he would inevitably splash down in the Atlantic. Thus, by his estimate, a three-engine plane was about three times riskier than one with a single engine.

He also concluded that, since his navigation capabilities were so crude, a radio would be largely symbolic and survival equipment would merely prolong his ordeal in the chilly waters of the North Atlantic. So his best bet was to fly alone in a small plane powered by a single engine carrying an absolute minimum of unnecessary weight.

Thirty-three hours after takeoff, when he finally touched down at Le Bourget Field, one hundred thousand Parisians were there to greet him and snatch souvenir chunks from his plane. When he returned to New York, two million came, and the sky over Fifth Avenue was a storm of confetti.

During his long journey, Lindbergh built up a strong rapport with "The Spirit of St. Louis," the machine that carried him across the Atlantic. Later he titled his autobiography *We.*

"What kind of man would live where there is no daring?" Lindbergh later wrote. "I don't believe in taking foolish chances, but nothing can be accomplished without taking any chances at all."

Marshall your courage whenever you are hot on the trail of a creative idea. Ignore the critics. "Go for it!" urged Rocky Balboa when Clubber Lang expressed a strong desire to smash Rocky and successfully defend his heavyweight title. Financier Donald Trump voiced similar sentiment when he told a group of fledgling entrepreneurs: "As long as you're going to think anyway, think big!"

Of course, thinking up daring solutions is only the first step. Implementing them in the real world is also vitally important. The one-page worksheet at the end of this lesson is included to help move you in the direction of practical implementation of some of your best ideas.

First you are instructed to formulate the current version of your problem. Then you are sent back through the worksheets you have been filling out as you worked your way through the previous chapters of this book. As you review the various worksheets, pick out a sampling of the best creative solutions you have managed to develop so far. Write those solutions in the spaces provided. Then go on to the exercise at the bottom of the page.

In that section you are instructed to formulate specific ways in which you plan to research, refine, and improve your best ideas. These activities might include going to the library, for instance, or contacting specific people or organizations that may be able to help you with your proposed solutions.

If it is appropriate, you may want to make one-page summary sheets highlighting the salient characteristics of one or two of your creative ideas. The preparation of a written or an oral report may also be helpful at this juncture.

Finally, you may decide to try something that often proves to be quite fruitful. Using just the ideas you have written on this summary sheet, or a subset of them, go back through the entire set of worksheets and brainstorm refinements to your creative solutions to flesh out the details and bring them closer to implementation. For this purpose, additional blank worksheets are provided in Appendix C.

What is your problem? _____

_____

_____

_____

HARVESTING YOUR BEST IDEAS

Review your notes on all the previous worksheets. In the spaces below list a
sampling of your best ideas. Reword them as necessary to make them clearer,
cleaner, and more self-contained. _____

_____

_____

_____

_____

_____

A
BRIGHT
IDEA

_____

_____

_____

_____

In these spaces list the specific things you intend to do to further research, refine, and
improve the ideas in the box above. _____

_____

_____

_____

_____

_____

_____

The Problem   **The Solution**

Hint: One way to improve your ideas is to take the best ones and quickly go back
through the previous worksheets to make a new set of sketches and notes. Try it. You
may be surprised at the results.

Chapter 8
Case Study: Applying What We Have Learned

"You may be disappointed if you fail, but you are doomed if you don't try."
— Opera Singer, Beverly Sills

In 1989, as I mentioned earlier, I was invited to present a professional platform lecture on simple, creative problem-solving techniques at the 109th annual meeting of the Fargo Chamber of Commerce in Fargo, North Dakota. The 400 members who heard my presentation that night were attempting to rehabilitate the economy of their state. To help you learn how to handle the creativity worksheets, sample copies dealing with their problems are filled out in this chapter. The following is a summary of the problems faced by the state of North Dakota extracted from the materials they sent me a week or so before my presentation:

> *North Dakota's economy is based on agriculture and light manufacturing. The state has cold winters and mild summers. For decades its population has held steady and, in recent years, has begun to decline. The state has a good educational system, but college-educated young people tend to leave when they graduate. Telecommunication systems and surface transportation are highly developed.*
>
> *The state borders Canada, but there are no large population centers near its Canadian-American border. Fargo is the largest city in the state.*

High technology has largely passed by North Dakota although the state does have large, well-financed medical research centers. Pollution levels are low, housing prices modest, congestion largely nonexistent. The people in North Dakota are friendly and cordial. Labor rates are fairly low.

North Dakota leaders see several problems with their state: out-migration of young people, a stagnant population, a narrow economy mostly concentrated in farming and the processing of farm products, a lack of high-technology industries, unreliable markets for farm products, and the like.

In an attempt to make their state more prosperous and secure, political leaders commissioned a consulting firm to do a "Visions 2000" study intended to characterize the state and to advance plans for making it function more efficiently. Town-hall meetings were also held statewide to obtain input from community leaders and private citizens.

On the basis of this brief summary, I have formulated the problem statement on the following worksheet. At this point, no attempt is being made to solve the problem. Solutions are proposed and evaluated in the next few lessons. In the final lesson the best available ideas are harvested and future plans for improved solutions are carefully formulated.

BREAKING THROUGH

CHOOSING THE PROPER PROBLEM

Simple, well-formulated problems lead to practical, creative solutions. Choose a simple problem that bothers or concerns you. In the box below, state your problem clearly and concisely in ordinary, everyday language. Use action words and personal pronouns in complete sentences like this:

> *Injuries costing $2 billion each year are caused by amateur baseball and softball players sliding into second, third, and home plate. How can we reduce these costly injuries?*

Don't try to solve the problem yet. Just state it clearly and simply.

What is your problem? _North Dakota has a stagnant population with valuable young people streaming out of the state. The economy, which is largely based on agriculture, is not expanding. How can we help the state?_

PROBLEM

Restate your problem whenever you are asked to on subsequent worksheets.

Lesson 71
Using Balloon Diagrams to Break North Dakota's Problems into Smaller Bite-Size Chunks

"There are three ingredients for a good life: learning, earning, and yearning."
— British Humorist, Christopher Morley

Once I had read some of North Dakota's "Visions 2000" study, I filled out a set of worksheets summarizing their problems with preliminary ideas on a few productive solutions. The balloon diagram on the worksheet at the end of this lesson is one result. Notice that one of the ovals in the balloon diagram says "Attract Retirees." Since I made that little note, I have learned that the nearby town of Wheaton, Minnesota (population 1,615), has rolled out the red carpet for senior citizens from other states. City fathers are hoping that their safe streets, friendly neighbors, and affordable housing will attract older residents from other, nearby communities.

During the last decade, Wheaton's population dropped by an alarming 18 percent and, as a part of their survival strategy, town leaders are attempting to attract "Golden Oldies" with every inducement they can muster. So far, their strategy includes:

- Thirty-second ads on Twin Cities TV touting Wheaton's wonders

- A booth at the annual Twin Cities Expo in Minneapolis

- A free bus tour of Wheaton departing from the Twin Cities 180 miles away.

If you were assigned to write a short report summarizing the state's problems together with a few proposed solutions, you could work directly from the balloon diagram sketched on the worksheets or you could use the balloon diagram to make a topic outline summarizing the issues in more detail:

A sampling of North Dakota's economic problems

Narrow farm-based economy

- Problem Statement and Historical Roots

- What Can Be Done to Broaden the State's Economy?
    1. De-emphasize Farming: Expand toward Value-Added Manufacturing
    2. Encourage High-Tech Industries
        - Computer Chip Manufacturing

- Large-Scale Software Development
- High-Tech Film Animation

- Revising the State Tax Codes
  1. Tax-Free Startup Intervals for New Companies
  2. Property Tax Relief
  3. Investment Tax Credits for High-Tech Research.

Notice that, for simplicity, only the first one-fourth of the topic outline is presented here. Notice also that the outline amplifies some of the concepts presented in the balloon diagram. Various errors in format, punctuation, etc., have also been corrected.

The three-step procedure of starting with a balloon diagram, followed by a topic outline, followed by a brief writeup is easy to execute and it provides a convenient format for recording your most promising thoughts.

What is your problem? ___*The economy of the state of North Dakota*___
___*is becoming less competitive and less productive relative*___
___*to the other American states and other countries in the rest*___
___*of the world.*___

① BREAKING YOUR PROBLEM APART AND PUTTING IT
BACK TOGETHER AGAIN IN A DIFFERENT WAY

Balloon diagrams are powerful tools that can help you break your problems apart
and put them back together again in novel and interesting ways. Draw a balloon
diagram that breaks your problem—or some aspect of that problem—into its
component parts. Relax and enjoy this exercise. Leave a little space at the bottom of
the page.

At the bottom of the page list solutions that occurred to you while you were drawing
the balloon diagram.

Is there some way to modify, combine, or eliminate some of
these parts for improved efficiency?

BREAKING THROUGH

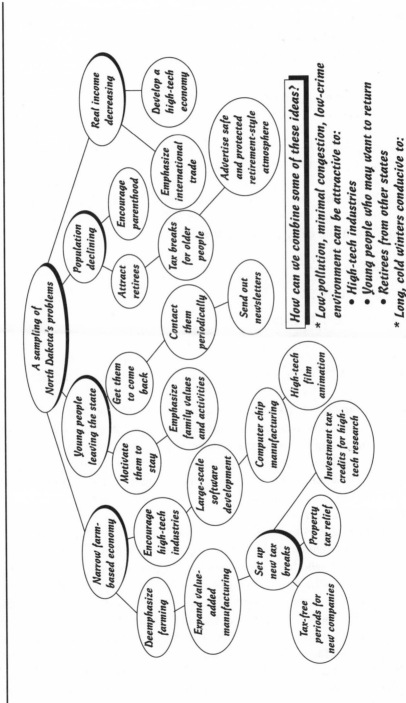

Lesson 72
Modifying the Interfaces to Help
North Dakota Become More Competitive

"The best way to have good ideas is to have lots of ideas."
    — Nobel Laureate, Linus Pauling

Within easy walking distance of my home in Southern California is a small mom-and-pop pizza parlor that always sends out inviting smells to entice anyone who may be passing by the shop. The aroma it produces makes pizza seem like a delicious thing to eat. But as soon as customers peek through the door, their eyes are assaulted by big, bold signs that cancel out any otherwise favorable inducements to come in and enjoy a tasty pizza meal:

"NO SLICES"

"NO SANDWICHES"

"NO PUBLIC RESTROOMS"

"NO CHECKS"

"PLEASE DO NOT COMB YOUR HAIR INSIDE THE PIZZA HOUSE"

No member of my family has ever eaten a pizza at that little family restaurant, nor have we met the people who own the place but, if I had to guess, I would say that they have never thought much about the best way to interface with their customers.

Is every one of those negative warning signs really necessary? Couldn't they, for instance, just refuse to accept a personal check? Couldn't they just gently tell any customer who takes out a comb to put it back in pocket or purse? And why not sell pizza by the slice if the price is right?

"The money is always there, only the pockets change," said Gertrude Stein. First impressions are tremendously important, especially when you are interfacing with potential customers who have money you are hoping to move from their pockets into yours. That is why you should always strive to put your best foot forward, especially when you are interfacing with large numbers of money-laden customers.

Customs inspection stations provide some of the worst interfaces ordinary people are ever unlucky enough to encounter. It is hard to quarrel with the need for guarding and securing international borders. Someone has to be responsible for keeping out illegal intruders, drugs, and contraband, but why do border guards everywhere have to make *all* of their guests—good and bad—feel like they are suspected of some heinous crime?

The worst border crossing I have encountered was on the Greek island of Rhodes. I came at night on a big ferry boat that had just arrived from Marmaris, Turkey. The harbor was almost pitch black with only a few scattered lamps illuminating small patches of the docks. As I lugged my suitcases down a long black pier with the other passengers, it was not clear to any of us where we were supposed to go or what we were supposed to do. Finally, we came upon a small wooden shed manned by an armed guard who gestured for us to go inside using his automatic weapon as a big, long pointer! Inside there was no place to sit down and no one came for 20 minutes or so.

Finally, a big, abrupt woman in uniform walked in and began gesturing for everyone to open their bags. She said nothing to me specifically, but she did make white X's on the sides of my suitcases with big pieces of chalk. Then, after a while, she indicated gruffly that I could leave. I never got any clue as to why my suitcases were being singled out.

Tourists bring lots of money into a country. Why then are they so often treated like unwelcome intruders? Clearly, key tourist countries should pay more attention to this important interface with the outside world.

If I ever have my own country, I will find a way to welcome all arriving international guests. Picnic tables with cut flowers and checkered tablecloths will be set up at the borders. Tea and cookies will be served while the document inspectors circulate from table to table. Some individuals may be excluded or even detained, but the ones who do get in will know for sure that they are welcome to my country.

A similar attitude could help the state of North Dakota build up attractive interfaces with the rest of the world. As the worksheets and the balloon diagrams at the end of this lesson indicate, there are a number of ways to work with North Dakota's interfaces to encourage more people to visit the state. Promising possibilities include playful welcoming signs and "Winter Wonderland" train rides.

A few locales have already executed some of these suggestions. Colorado, for instance, features snow-country train rides and Maine makes tourists feel that state officials are concerned about their comfort and survival by wording their "Fasten Seat Belt" signs so it appears that somebody cares. Many signs in England are written as reasonable requests instead of harsh, legalistic commands.

Notice that the best ideas have been listed at the bottom of the second worksheet. Now that those best ideas have been isolated, we can concentrate on any practical ways in which solutions might be teased out by modifying, moving, deleting, or using one of the relevant interfaces for a practical purpose.

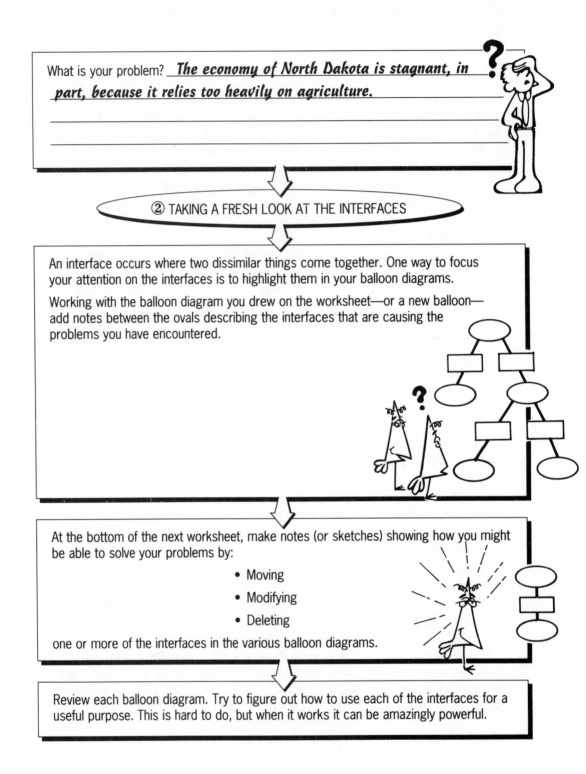

What is your problem? _**The economy of North Dakota is stagnant, in part, because it relies too heavily on agriculture.**_

② TAKING A FRESH LOOK AT THE INTERFACES

An interface occurs where two dissimilar things come together. One way to focus your attention on the interfaces is to highlight them in your balloon diagrams.

Working with the balloon diagram you drew on the worksheet—or a new balloon— add notes between the ovals describing the interfaces that are causing the problems you have encountered.

At the bottom of the next worksheet, make notes (or sketches) showing how you might be able to solve your problems by:

- Moving
- Modifying
- Deleting

one or more of the interfaces in the various balloon diagrams.

Review each balloon diagram. Try to figure out how to use each of the interfaces for a useful purpose. This is hard to do, but when it works it can be amazingly powerful.

BREAKING THROUGH

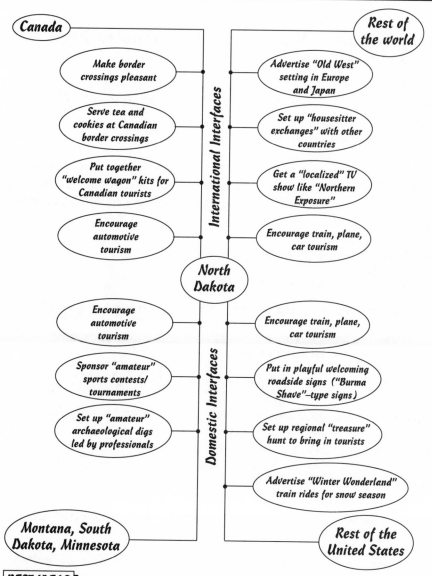

Canada

- Make border crossings pleasant
- Serve tea and cookies at Canadian border crossings
- Put together "welcome wagon" kits for Canadian tourists
- Encourage automotive tourism

Rest of the world

- Advertise "Old West" setting in Europe and Japan
- Set up "housesitter exchanges" with other countries
- Get a "localized" TV show like "Northern Exposure"
- Encourage train, plane, car tourism

International Interfaces

North Dakota

Montana, South Dakota, Minnesota

- Encourage automotive tourism
- Sponsor "amateur" sports contests/ tournaments
- Set up "amateur" archaeological digs led by professionals

Rest of the United States

- Encourage train, plane, car tourism
- Put in playful welcoming roadside signs ("Burma Shave"–type signs)
- Set up regional "treasure" hunt to bring in tourists
- Advertise "Winter Wonderland" train rides for snow season

Domestic Interfaces

BEST IDEAS

☆ Clever and appealing signs on the highways (some puzzling and mysterious). Publicize them.

☆ "Winter Wonderland" train rides to attract visitors during snow season

Lesson 73
Using Structured Worksheets to Reformulate Even the Stickiest Problems

"Get a good idea and stay with it. Dog it, and work at it until it's done, and done right."
— American Imagineer, Walt Disney

How can you learn how to reformulate your problems to tease out simple, but elusive, solutions that will pay big dividends? One effective approach is to pause periodically and ask yourself—and your colleagues—a standard list of penetrating questions:

- "What are we actually trying to do?"

- "What business are we actually in?"

- "How can we restate our problem in a half dozen different ways?"

- "What beneficial results can we expect if we do manage to solve the problem as we have formulated it so far?"

- "What bad things will actually happen if we fail to solve it?"

Another approach is to restate your problem in an extreme or opposite formulation. For example, the business leaders of North Dakota are hoping to keep young people from leaving their state. But what if they decided to *encourage* them to leave, instead? Would there be some hidden benefits stemming from that opposite outcome? Here are some possible benefits:

- Since teenagers and young adults commit the most serious crimes, crime rates might fall even lower.

- Young people have more babies, so hospital overcrowding and traffic congestion rates might eventually further decline.

- With less demand for housing, houses might become even more affordable for those who remain.

These answers are not likely to cause the opposite formulation to replace the original formulation, but they may cause certain modifications in the problem you are trying to solve. Instead of concentrating on getting *all* young people to remain in the state, for instance, perhaps North Dakota's leaders should concentrate on keeping only those young people who are well educated. Or those who already hold steady jobs. Or perhaps they should concentrate on getting those young people who have already left the state to come back again, bringing with them their newfound skills and expertise.

What is your problem? _Intelligent, well-educated young people are_
leaving the state of North Dakota. How can the state leaders
get them to stay, instead?

③ REFORMULATING YOUR PROBLEM

The way you state your problem has an important influence on the way you attempt to solve it. Restate your problem three different ways. In each new formulation change the wording and your way of looking at the problem as much as you can.

1. _Young, well-educated people become even more valuable_
   to the state once they have left and gained more
   experience. How can North Dakota get them to come
   back once they have left?

2. _Valuable young people are leaving the state. How_
   can state officials get old, less desirable, poorly
   educated people to leave, too, so things will
   balance out?

3. _When young, well-educated people leave the state can_
   they be encouraged to ship money back to their friends
   and family they left behind?

Review these three new formulations. Put a star (☆) beside your favorite, then make notes on new solutions.
Set up an "Expatriot's Newsletter" mailed to them monthly. Put in
job ads, housing announcements, stories about low pollution and
congestion levels in the state.

Play the devil's advocate. Reformulate your problem the way a vocal opponent might to make any changes in the *status quo* difficult to justify. Explain how you could quiet or circumvent that opposition. _People who want to leave the state should be_
encouraged to leave. If they do not want to stay, we should say
"good-bye." Survey them. See if they really want to leave.

Restate your problem so it sounds like the present situation is highly advantageous to you and your company. Be playful and preposterous in your new formulation. *As more and more people leave the state, we could turn it into a national park. The few that remain would then have very pleasant and prosperous lives.*

Is there a small grain of truth in this way of formulating the problem? Explain how you might be able to capitalize on that grain of truth. *As some rural parts of the state begin to get more thinly inhabited, we could turn them into green, grassy parks. Abandoned towns could become "ghost towns" outfitted like the Old West. They could become important tourist centers like Chautauqua, New York.*

List three other problems that are in some way related to the specific problem you are trying to solve.

1. *Everywhere throughout the world people are flocking to large cities. In 1800 3% of humanity lived in urban areas. Today it is 30% or so.*

2. *Young people have always been prone to pull up stakes and go somewhere else.*

3. *Rural America's population all over the country has held steady for nearly 100 years. All of our population growth has gone into the cities.*

PROBLEM NO. 1
PROBLEM NO. 2
PROBLEM NO. 3

Make notes on possible ways you might combine these various problems to make one or more of them go away. *How about trying to attract the young people from other, nearby states to live and work in North Dakota? How about setting up youthful recreation programs and apprenticeship programs?*

Lesson 74
Seeking Fruitful Analogies

"I'd rather be a failure at something I enjoy than a success at something I hate."
— Comedian, George Burns

While I was fiddling with the worksheets at the end of this lesson in the hopes of helping the economy of North Dakota, I tried to visualize as many fruitful analogies as possible. My initial image of the state was represented in my mind's eye as a big, flat sheet of ice with a sprinkling of people huddled around its icy borders.

Other people who might otherwise be willing to come to North Dakota probably view the state as frigid and forbidding, too. How can state leaders hope to circumvent that decidedly negative image in the popular imagination? In their pamphlets and TV commercials, North Dakota's spokesmen could claim that their state does not have a cold climate, especially in the summertime. At most, however, only a few people are likely to fall for that trumped-up version of the story. Perhaps there is a better way.

The main difficulty is that, to most people, cold weather triggers a variety of negative connotations: colds and sickness, aches and pains, bad driving conditions, slippery sidewalks, big heating bills. Who would voluntarily move into a place like that?

As I note on the second page of the worksheets in this lesson, Vance Packard discussed an analogous situation in his popular book, *The Hidden Persuaders*. According to his account, when Manhattan admakers were assigned to develop a new advertising campaign to sell more prunes, their focus groups told them that prunes conjured up extremely negative images among American consumers. Prunes were associated, for instance, with poverty, boarding house food, and constipation. Moreover, they had a black, ugly color and an unpleasant texture. No direct ad campaign seemed likely to overcome all of those negative images, so the admakers simply filmed colorful commercials in which eating prunes was portrayed as healthful good fun. The party atmosphere spread throughout America and soon prune sales were shooting through the roof!

North Dakota's admakers could possibly decide to try an analogous approach. Rather than attempting to conceal North Dakota's cold climate or claim that it is not cold in the state, they could film happy North Dakota families laughing together and having fun in their "winter wonderland." This is more or less what Australia has done with the Paul Hogan tourist campaigns in which they take a continent that is mostly covered with deserts, and make it very inviting with good-natured fun. "We have lots of water," Hogan says, "the place is surrounded by it!"

Two other promising analogies are also highlighted in my two-page worksheets: Scotland and Ireland. Scotland has long been plagued by a stagnant economy, so a government bureau called the "Scottish Development Agency" was instituted to help stimulate large-scale economic activities. The main objective of the Scottish Development Agency is to study and evaluate emerging technologies and to encourage modern industries to come to Scotland and set up shop. High-level cooperation is also stimulated between the excellent colleges and universities in the Glasgow/Edinburgh area and local business leaders working there.

The government of Ireland has set up a vaguely similar program to help encourage excellence in education and to market Ireland's superbly trained work force to high-value industries who might be interested in moving to their country. With that positive action-oriented attitude, Ireland has managed to attract software development firms, computer chip production, and a number of companies that produce and distribute high-technology film animation sequences for television advertisements and motion picture films.

North Dakota could benefit from these excellent models of motivated industriousness. By using Scotland and Ireland as fruitful analogies, industry leaders have a good opportunity to rehabilitate and strengthen the flagging economy in their state. Why not send a small delegation across the Atlantic to learn more about how Scotland and Ireland have managed to accomplish so much industrialization despite their isolation and decidedly scarce natural resources?

What is your problem? _**North Dakota's economy is not growing and it is**_ _**not benefitting from the high-technology jobs associated with**_ _**today's modern high-technology economies.**_

PROBLEM

④ VISUALIZING A FRUITFUL ANALOGY

Creative individuals learn to see connections between things others fail to see. Visual and verbal analogies lead to particularly powerful solutions. Draw a sketch at the top of the next worksheet that visually illustrates your problem or how you feel about it.

Below that sketch write a description filled with emotional words, images, and symbolic characteristics.

In the middle of the next worksheet, characterize your problem with three or four well-chosen similes and metaphors. Use picturesque, colorful words.

"My problem is like a . . . ."

"My problem reminds me of the time . . . ."

Think about these visual and verbal images. Make notes and balloon diagrams expounding on any novel or interesting solutions they may suggest.

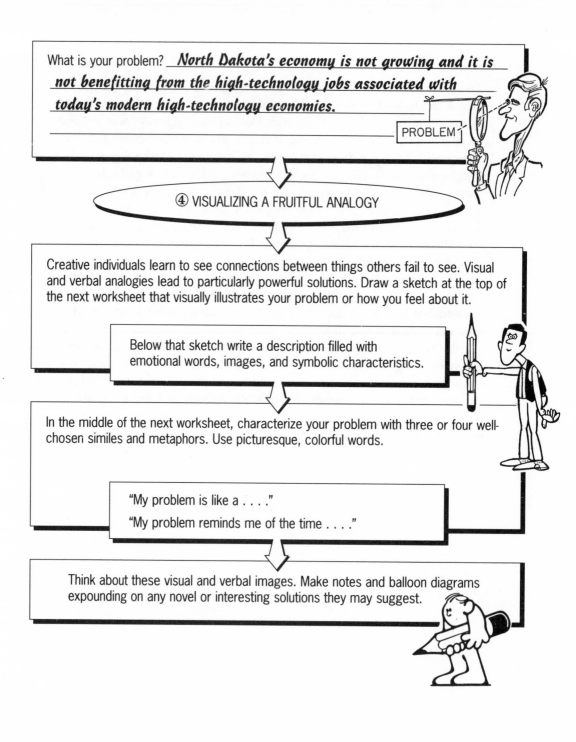

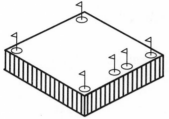

In my fanciful image, North Dakota is like a big, flat sheet of ice (especially in winter). Barren and desolate, the state is beautiful and green, but without people, it would resemble the moors in the movie "Wuthering Heights."

It is cold there and everyone knows it so in commercials touting the state, they should make cold weather seem fun like Vance Packard described in <u>The Hidden Persuaders</u>. This is what marketeers did with prunes. They made eating prunes fun.

North Dakota's problem is much like the problems faced by Ireland and Scotland: Stagnant populations and stagnant economies, young people leaving, agricultural dependence, cruel weather, too.

*Scotland set up the "Scottish Development Agency" much like America's Agricultural Extension programs, but oriented around industry rather than agriculture.

*Ireland encouraged excellence in education. This led to local software production for large, international companies, computer chip production, and film animation.

Both of these "fruitful analogies" could be used to help North Dakota's stagnant economy and discourage out-migration of talented citizens.

Lesson 75
Searching for Useful Order-of-Magnitude Changes

"One man that has a mind and knows it can always beat ten men who haven't and don't."
— British Dramatist, George Bernard Shaw

Leaders in a state such as North Dakota with a sparse population and limited natural resources may be able to make up for any perceived shortcomings by searching for useful order-of-magnitude changes that can be exploited to their own practical benefit. For the foreseeable future, farming will undoubtedly provide a steady, moderately prosperous standard of living for a limited number of families in the state. But any projected change in farming would seem unlikely to pull the region up to a much higher level of economic activity over the long haul.

Help and advice from the federal government will also be of limited benefit to the people of North Dakota who are hoping to find a better way to make their farmland provide a decent standard of living. President Eisenhower lived and worked in Washington, D.C., for many years, so he was keenly aware of the practical limitations of desk-bound bureaucrats. "Farming looks mighty easy when your plow is a pencil, and you're a thousand miles from the corn field," he once remarked in answering a farmer's question in a Midwest farmbelt state. In a similar vein, "the happy warrior," Hubert Humphrey, in reflecting on his own practical education, told a reporter: "I learned more about the economy from one South Dakota dust storm than I did in all my years at college."

On the worksheets at the end of this lesson I have attempted to suggest a few new ways to exploit useful order-of-magnitude changes to help North Dakota become a more prosperous and competitive state. In particular, ideas center around new ways for making various things large or small, fast or slow. Some of the proposed concepts also deal with doing things with varying amounts of human labor.

?

What is your problem? _**The economy of North Dakota is not evolving in**_ _**suitable ways. The population is not growing.**_

⑤ SEARCHING FOR USEFUL ORDER-OF-MAGNITUDE CHANGES

An Alice-in-Wonderland view of the world, in which things change by a factor of 10 or more, often helps us tease out useful solutions. Describe how your problem would be affected if you or some of the objects involved were suddenly 10 times larger. _**If**_ _**each person, each car, each house was 10 times larger, but the**_ _**area of the state stayed the same, the state would seem**_ _**crowded instead of sparsely inhabited.**_

PROBLEM
10 X =

What if you or some of the objects were 10 times smaller? _**If the same objects**_ _**(and people) were 10 times smaller, the state would seem virtually**_ _**uninhabited.**_

Review these observations and make notes on any new solutions they may suggest. ___ _**City dwellers in other states often live on lots that are only 1/5**_ _**of an acre or less. How about setting up retirement**_ _**communities on the abundant land in North Dakota where**_ _**each lot is 1/2 acre? How about smaller retirement**_ _**communities with no cars inside (except emergency**_ _**vehicles)?**_

How would your problem be affected if things were suddenly speeded up 100-fold? _If everything in North Dakota was speeded up 100-fold, the place would seem very crowded and congested._

What if things were slowed down 100-fold? _If everything in North Dakota was slowed down 100-fold, everyone would die of boredom._

Radio waves, video images, and electronic devices such as computers can speed things up or slow them down. Make notes on how electronics might help solve your problem. _With enough videos, fax machines, satellite dishes, and the like, the people of North Dakota could have as many rich interactions as the people living in any city like Boston or London._

Gravity, atmospheric pressure, and viewing areas change dramatically when we move into space. Brainstorm ways in which space technology might help. _With satellite dishes, North Dakota could become a video production center making educational and industrial videos together with advertising videos for cable and local TV stations and regional networks._

People make a big difference. How could you solve your problem if you suddenly had 100 times more people? _If North Dakota had 100 times more people all complaints would switch to congestion, pollution, cost-of-living, and the like._

What would you be forced to do if you suddenly only had one person part time? _One person part time could only catalog and record the solutions proposed by others. This might be a fairly efficient approach. (It gets rid of committees.)_

Review the notes on this page. Make more notes in the margins on any new solutions they may suggest.

Lesson 76
Looking for More Productive Ways to Experience Happy Serendipity

"Creativity: discontent translated into art."
    — American Philosopher, Eric Hoffer

The one-page worksheet at the end of this lesson is based on serendipity's golden rule:

GO SOMEWHERE YOU DON'T USUALLY GO,
TO DO SOMETHING YOU DON'T USUALLY DO.
ALONE.

The specific thing you are planning to do may or may not be directly related to the problem you are attempting to solve, but it should be something you are likely to enjoy.

I first discovered the power of serendipity's golden rule when I drove down to the UCLA Medical Center alone to listen to four short lectures on how to enjoy better food and a more healthful style of living. The UCLA Medical Center is definitely a place I don't usually go, and, until I had open-heart surgery, listening to medical presentations would not have been something I would have been yearning to do.

Since I was alone in that gigantic medical center, engaging in a totally unfamiliar activity, I was practically forced to interact with other people: to find my way to the right auditorium, to locate the best parking lot, and to determine exactly which books the various lecturers had told us to buy. By the time that afternoon was over, I had made two marvelous new friends. And why had that happened? Because I had wandered off the beaten path without my usual cordial layer of friendly insulation.

As the worksheet at the end of this lesson shows, in trying to solve some of North Dakota's pressing problems, I have outlined two border-crossing junkets—one to Canada, the other to a neighboring state, both to be executed alone. During those two preplanned outings, I intend to be as alert as possible and to absorb as much information as I can. No one can say for sure if serendipity will strike during this little exercise, but my chances will undoubtedly be better than they would be if I spent that same amount of time staying home with my family and friends doing the same things I usually do.

What is your problem? _How to make North Dakota more popular? Not enough people stay in North Dakota and not enough come for visits to the state._

⑥ BEING ALERT TO HAPPY SERENDIPITY

Serendipity is most likely to help you solve your problem when you are doing something completely unrelated to your usual occupation. Watch out for happy serendipity. Has serendipity already helped you solve a portion of this or some other problem? If so, explain: _My visits to Scotland and Ireland revealed to me methods that have been used elsewhere to attack somewhat similar problems._

Your chances of experiencing happy serendipity will increase if you go somewhere you don't usually go to do something you don't usually do—alone.

In the spaces below plan two visits that are at least vaguely related to the problem you are trying to solve.

☆ Where are you planning to go?   (two places)
1. _A border crossing station with Canada._
2. _Morehead, a border town in Minnesota._

☆ What are you planning to do?   (two tasks)
1. _Try to see the state from the viewpoint of the visitor._
2. _Evaluate how North Dakota now impresses visitors._

☆ How do you plan to get away alone?   (two plans)
1. _Tell my wife what my plan is._
2. _Agree to take her the next time I do this._

Lesson 77

Harvesting a New Crop of Creative Solutions to Help the State of North Dakota Find a Better Way

"Many people would sooner die than think. In fact they do."
— British Philosopher, Bertrand Russell

Thinking of simple, creative solutions is an enjoyable enterprise, but by itself it is never enough to change anything. We also need to select our best solutions, then formulate practical plans to move toward implementing them in the real world. That is why the last worksheet labeled "Harvesting Your Best Ideas" is filled out at the end of this lesson.

Problem formulation aside, the worksheet is divided into two separate parts. In the first part I have followed the instructions and gone through the worksheets in the previous six lessons to gather up the best available solutions to North Dakota's problems from among the ones previously proposed. In following the instructions in the second part, I have formulated four "action items," which outline the ways in which I plan to conduct additional research so I can further refine and improve the proposed ideas. Among other things, I am planning to contact potentially helpful people in Minnesota, Colorado, Scotland, and Ireland to see how their ideas and actions might help the state of North Dakota.

Of course, the creative problem-solving is usually an *iterative* process. Now that the various worksheets have yielded a number of promising solutions, I can take those specific leads and go back through the worksheets again in hopes of sparking still more useful ideas. That approach, in fact, often produces new ideas and action items in abundance.

Other types of action items might also be appropriate at this point. One strong possibility is the preparation of any relevant one-page summary sheets, written reports, or oral presentations designed to get specific concrete proposals accepted by those who happen to have influence and power. Usually, however, this advanced stage will come only after we have done quite a bit more work on the specific solutions under consideration.

One of the German rocket scientists, Dr. Krafft Ehricke, once told me that "a society can either choose to create wealth, or distribute poverty." Since that day, I have always been proud and happy to be a member of a society that has devoted most of its energy toward the creation of new wealth.

If you feel a need to accelerate that process, learn to focus your attention on simple, creative solutions. How can you manage to accomplish that?

- Listen to Abraham Lincoln's advice: If you have eight hours to chop down a tree, spend six hours sharpening your ax.

- Surround yourself with supportive people who will help nurture your creative ideas during the critical germination phase.

- Use liberal amounts of paper to record, revise, polish, and partition your creative solutions.

- Harness the power of the six winning strategies on the arc of creativity.

If you do these things with sufficient enthusiasm, you, too, may someday make a billion-dollar breakthrough. And, when you do, don't forget to send me 1%!

What is your problem? _**North Dakota has a stagnant population with valuable young people streaming out of the state. The economy, which is largely based on agriculture, is not expanding. How can we help the state?**_

HARVESTING YOUR BEST IDEAS

Review your notes on all the previous worksheets. In the spaces below list a sampling of your best ideas. Reword them as necessary to make them clearer, cleaner, and more self-contained.

A BRIGHT IDEA

**1. Set up an "Expatriots Newsletter" to try to bring young people back to the state.**

**2. Institute a campaign to attract high-tech industries like film animation and software development.**

**3. Put together "Welcome Wagon" travel kits for Canadian tourists.**

**4. Set up and advertise "Winter Wonderland" train rides for the snow season.**

In these spaces list the specific things you intend to do to further research, refine, and improve the ideas in the box above.

**1. Write to the Scottish Development Agency to learn what they do to help Scotland's economy.**

**2. Write to Ireland to find out how they have attracted film animation and computer software.**

**3. Visit Morehead, a border town in Minnesota.**

**4. Write to Colorado to see how they have fared with "Winter Wonderland" train rides.**

The Problem ——————————————————————— **The Solution**

Hint: One way to improve your ideas is to take the best ones and quickly go back through the previous worksheets to make a new set of sketches and notes. Try it. You may be surprised at the results.

Appendix A
Composing New Captions for Old Cartoons

"Success depends in a very large measure upon individual initiative and exertion. It cannot be achieved except by dint of hard work."
— Russian Ballet Dancer, Anna Pavlova

Composing new captions for old or unfamiliar cartoons can be a stimulating way to enhance your natural creative problem-solving skills. Professional gag writers and cartoonists call this process *switching* because, when they do it, they switch one gag into another. Of course, if the results turn out to be useful, they do a new drawing, too.

Whenever you run across a panel cartoon in a newspaper or magazine, try a little switching of your own. Let your imagination range into unfamiliar terrain as you practice this highly productive gag-writing technique. Once you learn how to handle various types of humor confidently, your oral and written presentations will become more effective and, quite possibly, more memorable, too. Peter Ustinov has spent a great deal of time thinking about the many ways humor affects an audience. "Comedy is simply a funny way of being serious," Ustinov told a friend.

The cartoons in Figures A.1 through A.4 focus on the playful antics of a strange, bird-like creature called a Blurble who is constantly making careless mistakes. A boyhood friend of mine and I accidentally ended up drawing the world's first primitive Blurbles when we were trying to construct a row of stars, which some-how ended up with only three "points" each. Once we had added feet and anten-nas, the Blurbles seemed to have personalities of their own, so we began to write Blurble jokes. Years later, when I took a course on cartooning on the Irvine campus of the University of California, I learned how to add facial expressions.

The cartoons in Figure A.1 are the ones from Lesson 6 of the introductory chap-ter. Notice how their original captions from 30 years ago have been restored. A half dozen other captionless cartoons follow those two so, if you like, you can continue to try your hand at switching.

Figure A.1

Figure A.2

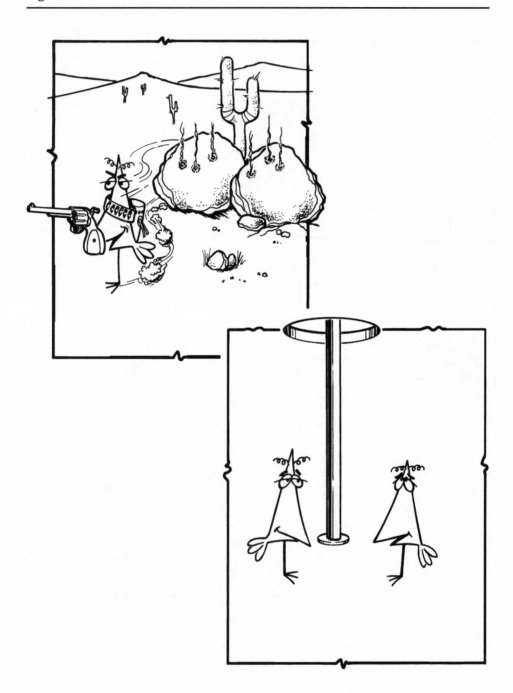

Figure A.3

Figure A.4

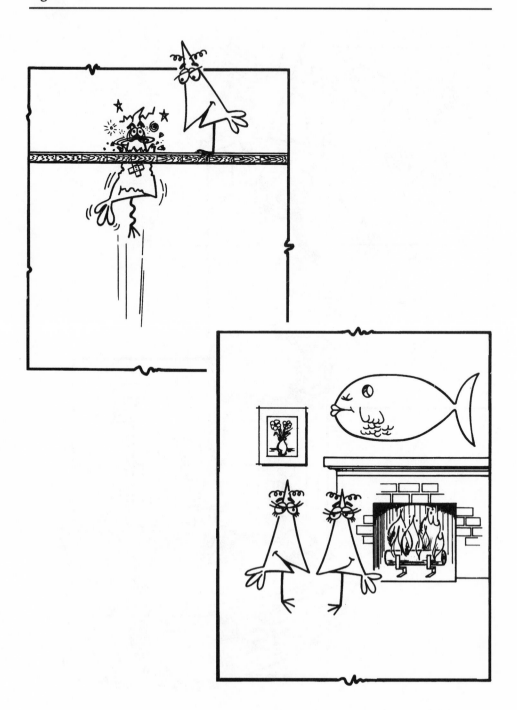

Appendix B
Analyzing Your Target Audience

"Diligence is the mother of good luck."
— American Statesman, Benjamin Franklin

The more you learn about the characteristics of your target audience, the more focused your written or oral presentation can be—and the more likely you are to strike a responsive chord.

One powerful method of audience analysis is to choose a single, specific individual who embodies the key features of the larger audience you are trying to reach. When you are scheduled to do an important presentation, write a two- or three-page analysis describing the hopes and desires, personality traits and attitudes of your stand-in audience. Then, as you are preparing your writeup or your oral presentation, visualize how that particular individual is likely to react to what you have to say and how you are planning to say it. Your presentation will almost always be less technical, more informal, and more persuasive when you write or speak directly to an audience of one. By way of illustration, here is a target-audience analysis I put together before I began writing the manuscript for my book *Striking It Rich in Space*:

> I write my books not for a specific audience but for a specific individual, a symbolic stand-in for the larger audience I hope to reach. Five years ago at sunset in Cocoa Beach, Florida, I met my audience for *Striking It Rich in Space*. His name was Anthony Ralyea, a bright, intense high-school stu-

dent from Titusville—population 7,000. Anthony had just heard me give a talk on manufacturing in space before 250 residents of the Cape Kennedy area. When it was over, he edged his way up to the podium bristling with curiosity and enthusiasm.

For nearly three hours we talked about the High Frontier until fatigue made us nearly incoherent. I never saw him again. I don't know where he is now. But every word of this book was written for Anthony Ralyea.

Are there enough people like Anthony to justify its publication? My travels convince me there are more than enough. A few weeks after I left Anthony, I had dinner with 12 of them, mostly middle-aged couples, at a Lake Arrowhead resort. We dined on succulent trout as I gradually unraveled the story of the industrial facilities we were planning to construct in space. What would it be like to live and work out there high above the earth they wondered? Would there be cigars and vintage wines? Concerts and picnics? Children climbing trees? Like Anthony Ralyea, they smiled when they talked and their eyes were filled with wonder and hope.

Last year I spoke to 50 more of Anthony's kinfolks in a summer seminar at Northridge University in the San Fernando Valley. Every individual there that day had given up three hours of California sunshine to come and learn about the colonization of space. No matter how long we talked, their polite curiosity never seemed to wane. And as their teacher wrote in her thank-you note: "Your talk was terrific! I think those students would have sat there and listened until they just wore out . . . they were learning physics and it didn't even hurt."

The news magazines give us further indications that our population includes a large number of Anthony Ralyeas. Consider these revealing statistics:

- The recent "Star Trek" conventions in Chicago, San Francisco, and Los Angeles were jammed to capacity. Each session drew more than 20,000 enthusiastic participants.

- The Air and Space Museum in Washington, D.C., has quietly become the most popular permanent exhibit in our country. Last year it hosted 12 million visitors.

- The *Star Wars* trilogy has smashed every box office record. According to *Newsweek*, one of the films "grossed $140 million within four months after it was released."

Clearly, Anthony is a part of a much larger group, a group that is enthralled with our future in space. But what else do we know about Anthony Ralyea? He is a curious individual with an itch to know and learn. He loves hopeful television documentaries, especially Charles Kuralt. He understands a little about computers, owns the latest pocket calculator and the latest video games. He loves challenges. He believes the future will be better than the past. He enjoys popularized scientific books: *The Double Helix, The High Frontier, The Andromeda Strain.* How will he react to *Striking It Rich in Space*? He will find it, read it, pass the word on to his friends.

How many Anthony Ralyeas are there? Millions. We all have a little of Anthony's adventurous blood running through our veins.

Appendix C
Blank Worksheets Designed to Lead You through the Arc of Creativity

"The way I see it, if you want a rainbow, you gotta put up with the rain."
— Country Singer, Dolly Parton

The blank worksheets at the end of this appendix are designed to help you enhance your creative problem-solving skills. Once you have copied the forms, jot down a specific problem you are hoping to solve in the blank space at the bottom of the first worksheet. Then follow the other instructions, as you gradually work your way toward simple, creative solutions. When you have finished a complete set of the worksheets and successfully harvested your best ideas, you may want to continue refining only those solutions—or a subset of them—by working your way through a second copy of the worksheets.

The arc of creativity embodies the six most powerful thought processes creative individuals use when they are making billion-dollar breakthroughs. As you complete the various exercises, pause periodically to reflect on a few of the major breakthroughs made by your predecessors. Patterning your thought processes on some of the techniques they perfected may provide new insights and fresh motivation as you uncover and polish your own creative problem-solving skills.

BREAKING THROUGH

Six simple strategies for enhancing your creative problem solving skills

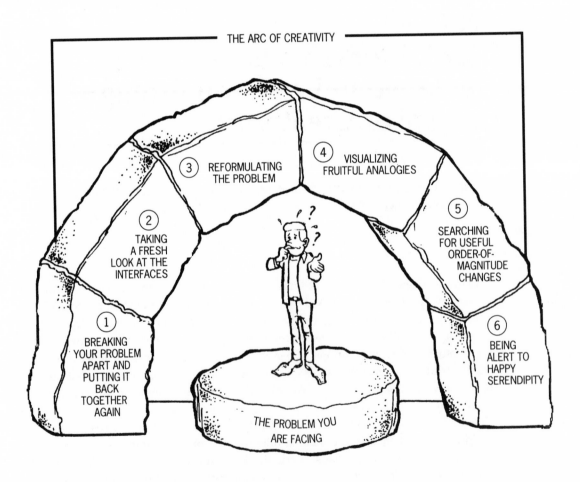

BREAKING THROUGH

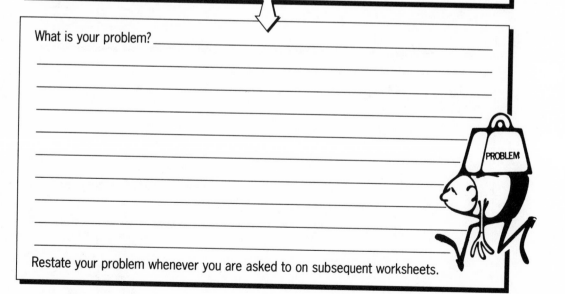

CHOOSING THE PROPER PROBLEM

Simple, well-formulated problems lead to practical, creative solutions. Choose a simple problem that bothers or concerns you. In the box below, state your problem clearly and concisely in ordinary, everyday language. Use action words and personal pronouns in complete sentences like this:

> *Injuries costing $2 billion each year are caused by amateur baseball and softball players sliding into second, third, and home plate. How can we reduce these costly injuries?*

Don't try to solve the problem yet. Just state it clearly and simply.

What is your problem? _____

_____

_____

_____

_____

_____

_____

_____

_____

_____

_____

Restate your problem whenever you are asked to on subsequent worksheets.

What is your problem? _____

_____

_____

_____

① BREAKING YOUR PROBLEM APART AND PUTTING IT
BACK TOGETHER AGAIN IN A DIFFERENT WAY

Balloon diagrams are powerful tools that can help you break your problems apart
and put them back together again in novel and interesting ways. Draw a balloon
diagram that breaks your problem—or some aspect of that problem—into its
component parts. Relax and enjoy this exercise. Leave a little space at the bottom of
the page.

At the bottom of the page list solutions that occurred to you while you were drawing
the balloon diagram.

Is there some way to modify, combine, or eliminate some of
these parts for improved efficiency?

THINKING YOUR WAY TO SUCCESS

What is your problem? _____
_____
_____
_____

② TAKING A FRESH LOOK AT THE INTERFACES

An interface occurs where two dissimilar things come together. One way to focus your attention on the interfaces is to highlight them in your balloon diagrams.

Working with the balloon diagram you drew on the previous worksheet— or a new balloon—add notes between the ovals describing the interfaces that are causing the problems you have encountered.

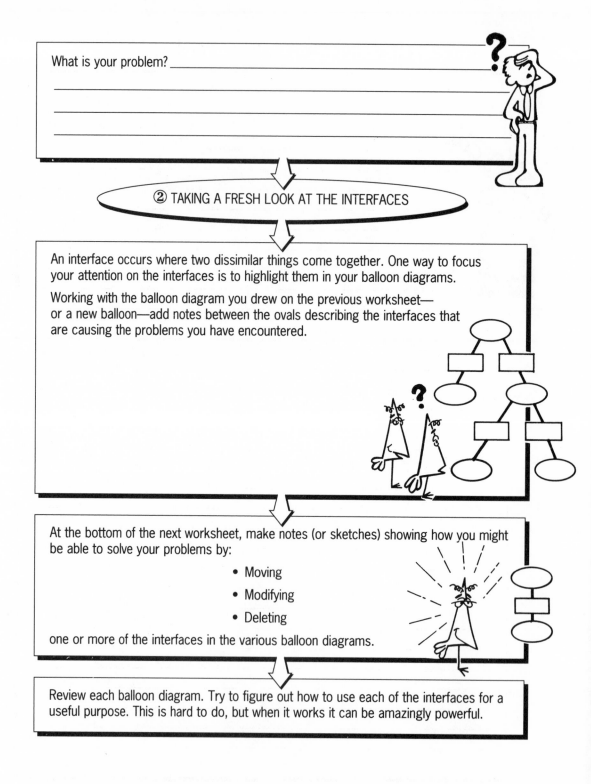

At the bottom of the next worksheet, make notes (or sketches) showing how you might be able to solve your problems by:

- Moving

- Modifying

- Deleting

one or more of the interfaces in the various balloon diagrams.

Review each balloon diagram. Try to figure out how to use each of the interfaces for a useful purpose. This is hard to do, but when it works it can be amazingly powerful.

BREAKING THROUGH

What is your problem? _____

_____

_____

_____

③ REFORMULATING YOUR PROBLEM

The way you state your problem has an important influence on the way you attempt to solve it. Restate your problem three different ways. In each new formulation change the wording and your way of looking at the problem as much as you can.

1. _____

_____

_____

_____

2. _____

_____

_____

_____

3. _____

_____

_____

_____

Review these three new formulations. Put a star (☆) beside your favorite, then make notes on new solutions.

_____

_____

_____

Play the devil's advocate. Reformulate your problem the way a vocal opponent might to make any changes in the *status quo* difficult to justify. Explain how you could quiet or circumvent that opposition. _____

_____

_____

Restate your problem so it sounds like the present situation is highly advantageous to you and your company. Be playful and preposterous in your new formulation. _____

_____

_____

_____

_____

_____

_____

Is there a small grain of truth in this way of formulating the problem? Explain how you might be able to capitalize on that grain of truth. _____

_____

_____

_____

_____

_____

_____

List three other problems that are in some way related to the specific problem you are trying to solve.

1. _____

_____

_____

2. _____

_____

_____

3. _____

_____

_____

PROBLEM NO. 1
PROBLEM NO. 2
PROBLEM NO. 3

Make notes on possible ways you might combine these various problems to make one or more of them go away. _____

_____

_____

_____

_____

What is your problem? _____

_____

_____

_____ PROBLEM

④ VISUALIZING A FRUITFUL ANALOGY

Creative individuals learn to see connections between things others fail to see. Visual and verbal analogies lead to particularly powerful solutions. Draw a sketch at the top of the next worksheet that visually illustrates your problem or how you feel about it.

Below that sketch write a description filled with emotional words, images, and symbolic characteristics.

In the middle of the next worksheet characterize your problem with three or four well-chosen similes and metaphors. Use picturesque, colorful words.

"My problem is like a . . . ."

"My problem reminds me of the time . . . ."

Think about these visual and verbal images. Make notes and balloon diagrams expounding on any novel or interesting solutions they may suggest.

BREAKING THROUGH

What is your problem? _____

_____

_____

_____

⑤ SEARCHING FOR USEFUL ORDER-OF-MAGNITUDE CHANGES

An Alice-in-Wonderland view of the world, in which things change by a factor of 10 or more, often helps us tease out useful solutions. Describe how your problem would be affected if you or some of the objects involved were suddenly 10 times larger. _____

_____

_____

_____

_____

_____

What if you or some of the objects were 10 times smaller? _____

_____

_____

_____

_____

Review these observations and make notes on any new solutions they may suggest. __

_____

_____

_____

_____

_____

_____

How would your problem be affected if things were suddenly speeded up 100-fold? ___
_____
_____
_____
_____

What if things were slowed down 100-fold? _____
_____
_____
_____
_____

Radio waves, video images, and electronic devices such as computers can speed things up or slow them down. Make notes on how electronics might help solve your problem. _____
_____
_____
_____
_____

Gravity, atmospheric pressure, and viewing areas change dramatically when we move upward into space. Brainstorm ways in which space technology might help. _____
_____
_____
_____
_____

People make a big difference. How could you solve your problem if you suddenly had 100 times more people? _____
_____
_____
_____

What would you be forced to do if you suddenly only had one person part time? ___
_____
_____
_____

Review the notes on this page. Make more notes in the margins on any new solutions they may suggest.

What is your problem? _____

_____

_____

_____

⑥ BEING ALERT TO HAPPY SERENDIPITY

Serendipity is most likely to help you solve your problem when you are doing something completely unrelated to your usual occupation. Watch out for happy serendipity. Has serendipity already helped you solve a portion of this or some other problem? If so, explain: _____

_____

_____

_____

_____

Your chances of experiencing happy serendipity will increase if you go somewhere you don't usually go to do something you don't usually do—alone.

In the spaces below plan two visits that are at least vaguely related to the problem you are trying to solve.

☆ Where are you planning to go?   (two places)

1. _____

2. _____

☆ What are you planning to do?   (two tasks)

1. _____

2. _____

☆ How do you plan to get away alone?   (two plans)

1. _____

2. _____

What is your problem? _____

_____

_____

_____

HARVESTING YOUR BEST IDEAS

Review your notes on all the previous worksheets. In the spaces below list a sampling of your best ideas. Reword them as necessary to make them clearer, cleaner, and more self-contained. _____

A BRIGHT IDEA

_____

_____

_____

_____

_____

_____

_____

_____

_____

In these spaces list the specific things you intend to do to further research, refine, and improve the ideas in the box above. _____

_____

_____

_____

_____

_____

The Problem

The Solution

Hint: One way to improve your ideas is to take the best ones and quickly go back through the previous worksheets to make a new set of sketches and notes. Try it. You may be surprised at the results.

Bibliography

General References

Ackoff, Russell L., *The Art of Problem Solving*, John Wiley, New York, 1978.

Adams, James C., *Conceptual Blockbusting*, Addison-Wesley, Reading, Mass., 1974.

Augustine, Norman R., *Augustine's Laws*, American Institute of Aeronautics and Astronautics, New York, 1983.

Bennett, Steven J., and Michael Shell, *Executive Chess*, New American Library, New York, 1987.

Crane, George W., *Psychology Applied*, Hopkins Syndicate, Mellott, Ind., 1970.

de Bono, Edward, *Bono's Thinking Course*, Facts on File Publications, New York, 1982.

de Bono, Edward, *Lateral Thinking*, Harper and Row, New York, 1970.

Fabun, Don, *The Dynamics of Change*, Prentice Hall, Englewood Cliffs, N.J., 1970.

Florman, Samuel, *The Existential Pleasure of Engineering*, St. Martin's Press, New York, 1977.

Gabor, Andrea, *The Man Who Discovered Quality*, Random House, New York, 1990.

Ghiselin, Brewster, *The Creative Process*, New American Library, New York, 1952.

Halpern, Diane F., *Thought and Knowledge: An Introduction to Critical Thinking*, Lawrence Erlbaum Associates, Hilldale, N.J., 1989.

Levine, Marvin, *Effective Problem Solving*, Prentice Hall, Englewood Cliffs, N.J., 1988.

Mayer, Richard E., *Thinking, Problem Solving, Cognition*, W. H. Freeman, New York, 1983.

Osborne, Alex F., *Applied Imagination*, Charles Scribner's, New York, 1953.

Petroski, Henry, *Beyond Engineering*, St. Martin's Press, New York, 1977.

Roberts, Royston M., *Serendipity: Accidental Discoveries in Science*, John Wiley and Sons, New York, 1989.

Thompson, Charles "Chic," *What a Great Idea: Key Steps Creative People Take*, Harper Collins, New York, 1992.

von Oech, Roger, *A Kick in the Seat of the Pants*, Harper and Row, New York, 1986.

von Oech, Roger, *A Whack on the Side of the Head*, Warner Books, New York, 1983.

Introduction: Getting into the Proper Frame of Mind to Devise Simple, Creative Solutions

"A Flow of Technology: Engine of Change," *Science*, May 22, 1987, pp. 21–22.

Allison, John R., "Five Ways to Keep Disputes Out of Court," *Harvard Business Review*, January–February 1990, pp. 166–177.

Buhagiar, Marion, *The Book of Secrets*, Boardroom Classics, New York, 1989.

Chapman, Fern Schumer, "Businesses Push for More Daylight Time," *Fortune*, November 12, 1984, pp. 149–159.

"Do We Live As Well As We Used To?," *Fortune*, September 14, 1987, pp. 32–45.

Galloway, John, "In Search of the Roots of Genius," *New Scientist*, July 17, 1990, p. 55.

Hart, Michael H., *The 100: A Ranking of the Most Influential Persons in History*, Citadel Press, Secaucus, N.J., 1987.

Howe, Michael, "Perspiration Beats Inspiration," *New Scientist*, December 24/31, 1988, p. 35.

Huey, John, "Wal-Mart: Will It Take Over the World?," *Fortune*, January 30, 1989, pp. 52–61.

Iapoce, Michael, *A Funny Thing Happened on the Way to the Boardroom*, John Wiley, New York, 1988.

MacKay, Harvey, *Beware the Naked Man Who Offers You His Shirt*, Ivy Books, New York, 1990.

Main, Jeremy, "A Golden Age for Entrepreneurs," *Fortune*, February 12, 1990, pp. 120–125.

"Malaria Stalemate," *Science*, January 26, 1990, p. 379.

Morris, James A., Jr., *The Art of Conversation*, Simon and Schuster, New York, 1976.

Ramirez, Anthony, "Factories That Shine," *Fortune*, April 24, 1989, pp. 93–105.

Sellers, Patricia, "Getting Your Customers to Love You," *Fortune*, March 13, 1989, pp. 38–49.

Sellers, Patricia, "How to Handle Customers' Gripes," *Fortune*, January 30, 1989, pp. 52–61.

Sellers, Patricia, "How to Remake Your Sales Force," *Fortune*, May 4, 1992, pp. 96–98.

Sobel, Robert, and David B. Sicilia, *The Entrepreneurs: An American Adventure*, Houghton Mifflin, Boston, Mass., 1986.

Waltenberg, Ben J., *The Good New Is the Bad News Is Wrong*, Simon and Schuster, New York, 1985.

Chapter 1: Breaking Your Problem Apart and Putting It Back Together Again

Dorman, Lesley, and Peter Edidin, "Original Spin," *Psychology Today*, July/August 1989, pp. 45–52.

Halpern, Diane F., *Thought and Knowledge: An Introduction to Critical Thinking*, Lawrence Erlbaum Associates, Hilldale, N.J., 1989.

Logsdon, Tom, *An Introduction to Computer Science and Technology*, Franklin Publishing Company, Palisade, N.J., 1974.

Logsdon, Tom, *Computers and Social Controversy*, Computer Science Press, Rockville, Md., 1980.

Logsdon, Tom, *Computers Today and Tomorrow: The Microcomputer Explosion*, Computer Science Press, Rockville, Md., 1985.

Macaulay, David, *The Way Things Work*, Houghton Mifflin, Boston, Mass., 1988.

Mansfield, Howard, "The Razor King," *American Heritage of Invention and Technology*, Spring 1992, pp. 40–46.

Olivero, Magaly, "Get Crazy: How to Have a Breakthrough Idea," *Working Woman*, September 1990, pp. 145+.

"Shuttle Diplomacy," *Air and Space*, April/May 1990, pp. 16–17.

Weber, Eric, *The Indispensable Employee*, Berkeley Books, New York, 1991.

Chapter 2: Taking a Fresh Look at the Interfaces

Bagin, Carolyn Boccella, "Oh, Those Formidable Forms," *Modern Maturity*, February–March 1990, pp. 67–71.

Braham, James, "Eureka!" *Machine Design*, February 6, 1992, pp. 22–36.

Butcher, Lee, *Accidental Millionaire: The Rise and Fall of Steven Jobs at Apple Computer*, Paragon House, New York, 1988.

Gold, Karen, "If All Else Fails, Read the Instructions," *New Scientist*, June 13, 1992, pp. 38–41.

"I Can't Work This Thing!" *Business Week*, April 29, 1991, pp. 58–66.

Koenenn, Connie, "Golden Ideas to Make Life Easier," *Los Angeles Times*, August 9, 1990, p. E-16.

Logsdon, Tom, *The Rush Toward the Stars*, Wm. C. Brown, Dubuque, Ia., 1969.

"The Quest for 'User Friendly'," *U.S. News and World Report*, June 13, 1988, pp. 54–55.

Rice, Faye, "Hotels Fight for Business Guests," *Fortune*, April 23, 1990, pp. 265–274.

Rogers, Michael, "The Right Button: Why Machines Are Getting Harder and Harder to Use," *Newsweek*, January 7, 1991, pp. 46–48.

Sellers, Patricia, "What Customers Really Want," *Fortune*, June 4, 1990, pp. 58–68.

Chapter 3: Reformulating the Problem

Butcher, Lee, *Accidental Millionaire: The Rise and Fall of Steven Jobs at Apple Computer*, Paragon House, New York, 1989.

"Dissolving Golf Balls End Dolphins' Distress," *New Scientist*, April 18, 1992, p. 5.

Dumaine, Brian, "Earning More by Moving Faster," *Fortune*, October 7, 1991, pp. 89–94.

Dumaine, Brian, "How Mangers Can Succeed through Speed," *Fortune*, February 13, 1989, pp. 54–59.

Hackworth, David H., "Last Taps for Fort Ord," *Newsweek*, March 9, 1992, pp. 38–39.

Hammer, Michael, "Reengineering Work: Don't Automate, Obliterate," *Harvard Business Review*, July–August 1990, pp. 104–112.

Heernstein, R. J., "Brains in the Workplace," *Fortune*, June 22, 1987, pp. 183–184.

Henkoff, Ronald, "Make Your Office More Productive," *Fortune*, February 25, 1991, pp. 72–84.

Huey, John, "New Frontiers in Commuting," *Fortune*, January 13, 1992, pp. 56–58.

Labich, Kenneth, "How Airlines Will Look in the 1990's," *Fortune*, January 1, 1990, pp. 50–56.

Linden, Eugene, "Challenges for Earth Patriots: Stalking Dwarf Hamsters in Siberia," *Time*, April 2, 1990, p. 70.

"The Man Who Fired a Dog to Save a Buck," *Time*, October 28, 1991, pp. 18–22.

Naisbett, John, *Megatrends*, Warner Books, New York, 1984.

"Pick of the Crop," *Discover*, July 1990, p. 14.

Samuelson, Robert J., "Technology in Reverse," *Newsweek*, July 20, 1992, p. 45.

Stalk, George, Jr., and Harold Sirkin, "Fix the Process, Not the Problem," *Harvard Business Review*, July–August 1990, pp. 26–33.

Thompson, Charles "Chic," *What a Great Idea: Key Steps Creative People Take*, Harper Collins, New York, 1992.

Walt Disney's American Classics: Brer Rabbit in the Briar Patch, Mallard Press, Greenwich, Conn., 1989.

Worthy, Ford S., "Japan's Smart Secret Weapon," *Fortune*, August 12, 1991, pp. 72–75.

Chapter 4: Visualizing a Fruitful Analogy

"Airship Prototype Rolled Out," *Aviation Week and Space Technology*, November 30, 1981, p. 60.

"Chopper Challenge," *The Houston Post*, May 30, 1980, p. 2B.

Davis, Ruth M., "National Strategic Petroleum Reserve," *Science*, August 7, 1981, pp. 618–627.

Dembart, Lee, "Serendipity: Eurekas Where They Weren't Expected," *Los Angeles Times*, October 5, 1989, p. 6, Part V-A.

Labich, Kenneth, "The Innovators," *Fortune*, June 6, 1988, pp. 51–56.

Logsdon, Tom, *An Introduction to Computer Science and Technology*, Franklin Publishing Company, Palisade, N.J., 1974.

Logsdon, Tom, *Computers Today and Tomorrow: The Microcomputer Explosion*, Computer Science Press, Rockville, Md., 1985.

Perel, David, "Discoveries That Happened by Mistake: Lab Test Flops and Chemist Creates Teflon by Mistake!" *National Inquirer*, June 6, 1989, p. 19.

"A Snowball's Chance," *People*, February 24, 1992, p. 68.

Chapter 5: Searching for Useful Order-of-Magnitude Changes

Augustine, Norman R., *Augustine's Laws*, American Institute of Aeronautics and Astronautics, New York, 1983.

Bridges, William, *Managing Transitions: Making the Most of Change*, Addison-Wesley, Reading, Mass., 1991.

Cross, Michael, "Farewell to Computing's Fifth Generation," *New Scientist*, June 13, 1992, pp. 12–13.

Edwards, L. K., "High-Speed Tube Transportation," *Scientific American*, August 1965, pp. 30–40.

Freedman, David H., "Breaking the Quantum Barrier," *Discover*, February 1992, pp. 72–77.

Huey, John, "Wal-Mart: Will It Take Over the World?" *Fortune*, January 30, 1989, pp. 52–61.

Kirkpatrick, David, "Big Hopes for Machines So Small You Can Hardly See Them," *Fortune*, May 4, 1992, p. 111.

Logsdon, Tom, *An Introduction to Computer Science and Technology*, Franklin Publishing Company, Palisade, N.J., 1974.

Logsdon, Tom, *Computers Today and Tomorrow: The Microcomputer Explosion*, Computer Science Press, Rockville, Md., 1985.

Logsdon, Tom, *Space, Inc., Your Guide to Investing in Space Exploration*, Crown Publishers, New York, 1984.

Logsdon, Tom, *The Robot Revolution*, Simon and Schuster, New York, 1984.

Morrison, Phillip, *Powers of Ten*, W. H. Freeman, San Francisco, Calif., 1982.

Nash, Madeleine, "Adventures in Lilliput," *Time*, December 30, 1991, pp. 75–78.

Nown, Graham, *The World's Worst Predictions*, Arrow Books, London, 1985.

Sassaman, Richard, "Historic Preservation," *Invention and Technology*, Spring 1993, p. 64.

Seideman, Tony, "Bar Codes Sweep the World," *Invention and Technology*, Spring 1993, pp. 56–62.

Tufte, Edward R., *The Visual Display of Quantitative Information*, Graphics Press, Cheshire, Conn., 1983.

Tully, Shawn, "Full Throttle Toward a New Era," *Fortune*, November 20, 1989, pp. 131–135.

von Oech, Roger, *A Whack on the Side of the Head*, Warner Books, New York, 1983.

Chapter 6: Being Alert to Happy Serendipity

Anthony, H. D., *Sir Isaac Newton*, Abelard-Schuman, London, 1960.

Bernstein, Peter W., "Unforgettable Dr. Seuss," *Reader's Digest*, June 1992, pp. 60–62.

Chronicle of the World, Longman Group, U.K., 1989.

Cocks, Jay, "Let's Get Crazy," *Time*, June 11, 1990, pp. 40–41.

Feldman, Anthony, and Peter Ford, *Scientists and Inventors*, Bloomsbury Books, London, 1989.

Hart, Michael, *The 100: A Ranking of the Most Influential Persons in History*, Citadel Press, Seacaucus, N.J., 1987.

Linden, Eugene, "Megacities," *Time*, January 11, 1993, pp. 28–38.

March, Robert H., *Physics for Poets*, Contemporary Books, Chicago, Ill., 1983.

Peirce, B. K., *Trials of an Inventor, Life and Discoveries of Charles Goodyear*, Carlton and Porter, New York, 1966.

Roberts, Royston M., *Serendipity: Accidental Discoveries in Science*, John Wiley and Sons, New York, 1989.

Schwartz, David J., *The Magic of Thinking Big*, Simon and Schuster, New York, 1965.

Sobel, Robert, and David B. Sicilia, *The Entrepreneurs: An American Adventure*, Houghton Mifflin, Boston, Mass., 1986.

Sutton, Caroline, *How Did They Do That?*, Hilltown Books, New York, 1984.

Thompson, Charles "Chic," *What a Great Idea: Key Steps Creative People Take*, Harper Collins, New York, 1992.

Chapter 7: Getting Your Ideas Adopted in a Gangling Bureaucracy

Applebaum, Judith, and Nancy Evans, *How to Get Happily Published: A Complete and Candid Guide*, New American Library, New York, 1982.

Crane, George W., *Psychology Applied*, Hopkins Syndicate, Mellott, Ind., 1970.

"Fruitycake: A Yummy MIL-F-14499F," *Time*, January 6, 1986, p. 48.

Harwood, Charles, and Gerald Pieters, "Review Specs Face to Face," *Electronic Purchasing*, September 1990, p. 12.

Hoff, Ron, *I Can See You Naked: A Fearless Guide to Making Great Presentations*, Andrews and McMeel, Kansas City, Mo., 1988.

Iapoce, Michael, *A Funny Thing Happened on the Way to the Boardroom*, John Wiley, New York, 1988.

Klechel III, Walter, "How to Give a Speech," *Fortune*, June 8, 1987, pp. 179–182.

"Malaria Research—What Next?" *Science*, January 26, 1990, pp. 399–402.

Preacher, Georgiana, *Speak to Win*, Bell Publishing Company, New York, 1985.

"Private Languages," *Air and Space*, April/May 1990, p. 94.

Prochnow, Herbert V., and Herbert V. Prochnow, Jr., *The Successful Toastmaster*, Harper and Row, New York, 1966.

Wallechinsky, David, Irving Wallace, and Amy Wallace, *The Book of Lists*, William Morrow, New York, 1977.

Zitter, Mark, "Bizspeak," *American Way*, March 18, 1986, pp. 16–20.

Chapter 8: Applying What We Have Learned

Packard, Vance, *The Hidden Persuaders*, Dell, New York, 1955.

"Vision 2000 Study," State of North Dakota, Fargo, N.D., 1990.

Index